RUDOLF HESS

THE BRITISH ILLUSION OF PEACE

RUDOLF HESS

THE BRITISH ILLUSION OF PEACE

John Harris

Jema Publications

First published in 2010 by
Jema Publications

© John Harris 2010

ISBN: 13 978-1-871468-44-1
ISBN: 10 1-871468-44-2

Printed and bound in Great Britain by
Impress Print, Corby.

The Jema Publications website is
www.jemapublications.co.uk

This book is also available on
www.rudolfhessbook.com

All photographs provided by the author with the exception of:
Borenius and Dansey - The National Portrait Gallery; Burckhardt and
Hess (front cover) – Getty Images; Battaglia – The Polish Institute and
Sikorski Museum.

Jema Publications
40 Ashley Lane
Moulton
Northampton NN3 7TJ

Contents

Acknowledgements

Introduction

1	The Case of Rudolf Hess: The Evidence To Date	7
2	Working Backwards to the Basic Premise	11
3	Rudolf Hess: Dungavel	23
4	So Where? Any Available Peers?	35
5	So Where? Trains and Airfields	45
6	So Where? Maps, Light and Lighthouses	55
7	The 'Atlantic Air Bridge' and its Significance in The Hess Case	68
8	Rudolf Hess: So Where? The Answer	76
9	The Flight of Rudolf Hess. The British Perspective	86
10	The Flight from Rudolf Hess's Point of View	101
	A Brief Interregnum	111
11	Rudolf Hess: The Big Picture	112
12	Enter Mrs Roberts	118
13	Rudolf Hess and Wartime Communication	128
14	The Letters – September 1940	130

15	The Intrigue Deepens September 1940 To May 1941	147
	The Second Interregnum	158
16	Carl Jacob Burckhardt 1891-1974	159
17	Carl Burckhardt's Unlikely Wartime Visitors	177
18	Douglas Douglas-Hamilton 14th Duke of Hamilton	195
	The Final Interregnum The Big Stumbling Block	206
19	Completing The Circle	209
20	The Aftermath and Some Unexpected Consequences	223
21	The British Illusion of Peace The Conclusions	242
Appendix 1	Some Friends of Carl Burckhardt	249
Appendix 2	The 'Twin Track' Approach	261
Appendix 3	Floreat Etona and the British Governing Class	262
Bibliography		265
Index		268

ACKNOWLEDGEMENTS

My attempt at explaining the flight of Rudolf Hess started in the early 1990's and so over a period of nearly 20 years I have made myself a nuisance to a considerable number of persons and organisations. Consequently, in no particular order, I would like to thank the following for their skill, kindness, perseverance and tolerance.

- The staff of the National Archives, Kew, England and Bundesarchiv, Koblenz, Germany.
- The staff of Cambridge City Library, Cambridge University Library and Cambridge Crematorium, England.
- The Archivist of Gonville and Caius College, Cambridge, England.
- The staff of Northampton Central Library, England.
- The Archivist of 'The Tatler', London, England.
- The staff of East Kilbride Library and in particular, Sheena Taylor of the Carnegie Library, Ayr, Scotland.
- The staff of the Royal Airforce Museum, Hendon, England, in particular Peter Elliott and Gordon Leith.
- The staff of the Indian and Oriental Collection, London, England.
- The staff of the Imperial War Museum, Duxford and London, England.
- The staff of the Camara Municipal de Cascais, Portugal.
- The staff of 'Who's Who', London, England.
- The staff of Trinity House, London, England.
- Neil Flanagan, Archivist, Eton College, England.
- Celia Lee, biographer to Lady Hamilton.
- Andrea Schroder Haushofer, Munich, Germany.

- The late Wolf Rudiger Hess, Munich, Germany.
- The late Stephen Prior, Gullane, Scotland.
- Aurelia Borenius, Wiltshire, England and the Archivist of The Burlington Magazine, London, England.
- The gatehouse men of British Aerospace, Bishopton, Scotland for the information on Dargavel House.
- Mr and Mrs Dougal McIntyre.
- Charles Entwhistle of the Chavril Press, Abernethy, Scotland.
- Edward Iveagh, Lynne Peake and Robin Guinness for their investigative work concerning Loel Guinness.
- The English and Welsh Company House Archive Section for information concerning Scottish Aviation Limited.
- Ruth Richardson and Nick Ullswater, concerning their respective predecessors, John Hales and John Lowther.
- Susan Donaldson, Scottish Borders Heritage Hub.
- Victoria Brown, The National Archives of Scotland.
- Dominic Hunger, University of Basle Library, Switzerland.
- Peter Padfield, as always.
- Wasyl Sydorenko, University of Toronto Library, Canada.
- Gudrun Bauer Seurne, Deutsches Museum, Munich, Germany.
- Chris Tabraham, Edinburgh Castle, Scotland.
- Jacub Forst-Battaglia, Vienna, Austria.
- Dr.A.Suchcitz, The Polish Institute and Sikorski Museum, London, England.
- Emily Oldfield, British Red Cross Museum, London.

- Matthew Hogan Research Services, US National Archives, Virginia, United States.
- Alfred Smith and Robert Tickle for reading the manuscript.
- Robert Anderson, the 100 year old witness to the events at Eaglesham on 10th May 1941.
- The staff of John TG Harris, Chartered Accountants, Chantrey Vellacott DFK and most recently Harris & Clarke, Chartered Accountants for dealing efficiently with some definitely 'non accountancy matters'. Time sheets yet to be verified, Messrs Cara, Liptrott and Coates.
- Tony Noble, my publisher and editor.
- Richard Wilbourn for continued support, common sense and an innate sense of what was practically possible.

And lastly I would like to thank the other members of the Wilbourn and Harris families who have been dragged all around Europe looking at things they would rather not be looking at and listening to people they would rather not be listening to. Thank you all.

INTRODUCTION

To date I have lived all my life on a family farm in a small village in Northamptonshire, England. The rest of the village is virtually all owned by one family who live in 'The Hall'.

Like most children I had not a clue as to what to do for a living, English livestock farming not being particularly profitable, so eventually I qualified as a Chartered Accountant in 1984. Whilst embarked on that particular struggle I did however learn the various disciplines that subsequently have proven invaluable to me in my Hess research.

Although never a 'swot' at school, during the 1980's I became interested in the history of the aristocratic families who lived in and owned villages such as my own. Northamptonshire, being the County of *'Spires and Squires'* was literally full of them. Typically, though not exclusively, in the 1930's such people with many possessions and much to lose saw Hitler as a far better bet than the threat of Communism. Since the turn of the 20th century, Kings had been deposed and thrones lost throughout Europe. The German Nazi regime was seen at worst as a buffer between Stalin and themselves, at best as an economic miracle worker.

This led me to look at the various 'Anglo-German' movements prevalent at that time and the various post 1939 peace initiatives that were then known about. Hess, who was still alive at the time, seemed to me to represent the last manifestation of the various peace feelers, if that is what it really was. I had read James Douglas-Hamilton's

'Motive for a Mission' but that book raised more questions than it answered.

Then, in 1987, Hess suddenly died. This brought a flurry of articles on all the aspects of the case known at the time and I was completely hooked, spurred on by the simple fact that it just didn't make sense to me. There must be more to it.

I started my research by reading about Violet Roberts, who had been described by David Irving as,

"The daughter in law of Lord Roberts of Kandahar".

Mrs Roberts had, somewhat bizarrely, acted as a conduit between Albrecht Haushofer, Hess's unofficial diplomat and the Duke of Hamilton in 1940. She had first 'surfaced' in connection with Hess in 1962. Her name had been published in the James Leasor book *'The Uninvited Envoy.'*

This lady seemed a good place to start and I was not to be disappointed. I quickly found out that Lord Roberts did not have a daughter in law. His only son, Patrick, was killed at Colenso in the December 1899 Boer campaign. He had not married. Was this an honest mistake or was there more to it?

So, the next 2-3 years was spent finding out who precisely Violet Roberts was and effectively creating a Roberts family tree. (In 2008, 18 years later, I found the last piece of the jigsaw). The culmination of this initial research in the early 1990's was the discovery that her nephew Walter Stewart Roberts was an important intelligence officer at Woburn Abbey, part of SO1, until 1948.

I thought (and still think) this to be terribly important and relevant to the Hess affair. In order to preserve and 'bank' these facts I published *Hess: The British Conspiracy* under the name of John McBlain (an old family name) in 1994. It provoked a degree of interest, in particular from Richard Spencer at the Daily Telegraph, but had a secondary benefit of far more value.

I had been friendly with Richard Wilbourn, a farm manager, for a number of years. Richard possesses one of the most logical and analytical minds I have come across and we also like to kid ourselves that given our agricultural backgrounds, we are very practical in our interpretations of events. So, when I was invited to Ober Ramstadt, Germany to address the Anglo German Fellowship in 1995, I, in turn, asked Richard to accompany me on what turned out to be the first of many British and European trips.

Subsequently we have travelled to the Bundesarchiv at Koblenz, Munich, to meet Wolf Hess, Nuremberg, Berlin, Berchtesgaden and many other locations whilst en route debating what we consider likely or plausible. Without such 'chewing the fat' we would not have got very far. On occasion our wives and then young children would be dragged along, sometime literally screaming. They still complain of seeing 'too much German concrete in too many European locations'.

I felt I was making progress in solving the mystery and was delighted when Andrew Lownie, my former agent, introduced me to Mei Trow who helped me to achieve an ambition when in 1999 *Hess: The British Conspiracy* was published at Andre Deutsch.

It is fair to say that the reaction was mixed. MRD Foot rubbished it, though without giving explanation, whilst the Spectator and Peter Padfield thought it 'worthy.' Andrew Roberts thought it 'honest.' All good fun I thought. I continued with the research, but was also not at all content with the story in toto.[1]

I was also frustrated because if official papers are not released anyone writing about a subject must try and interpret the 'gaps' not covered by the documentation. Anyone who tried to fill the gaps was duly labelled a conspiracy theorist, which of course I remain unapologetically (and quite correctly) to this day. After all, the Hess affair is without doubt a conspiracy!

I then leapt fullsquare onto the 'Polish' bandwagon when I found out via the Sikorski Institute in London that Wladsylaw Sikorski had landed at Prestwick, Scotland on the morning of 11th May 1941. Prestwick is no more than 20 miles from the crash site. Pure coincidence? Possibly. Richard and I duly travelled to Poland, visited the Sikorski birthplace and his (eventual) resting place and mentioned this possible revelation in the paperback edition that came out in 2001.

Since then various things have happened; flirtations with TV documentary makers, a slow drip feed of 'official papers' (nothing startling to date), *'Double Standards'* which, whilst flawed in conclusion brings a lot of 'original research' to the table and, if honest, an intermittent loss of interest mingled with acute excitement when a seemingly important fact or linkage is discovered. More foreign travel has been undertaken; more foreign beer has been drunk and still more debate with Richard.

My Mother who lived through the events of 1941 often asks me,
"Why are you bothering? It all happened so long ago. Surely it doesn't matter."
Nothing could be further from the truth. It matters greatly because at present we, the great unwashed, are still led to believe that Hess, out of favour, went crazy and flew into Britain on a solo mission. In my opinion that is quite inaccurate, an insult to the individuals concerned and

4

an affront to history in just the same way as the recent insertion of fake documents into the PRO. We must know what actually happened. Then we can judge properly.

I suppose the Hess case is now a fixture in my life. I didn't think I was capable of being obsessive about anything prior to starting and whether it is still possible to solve the mystery without the official papers (which I am convinced still exist) I am not sure. I do know it will not be through lack of effort.

John Harris
Cottesbrooke

Winter 2009/10

---

[1] *Hess: The British Conspiracy has just been reprinted in 2009.*

Rudolf Hess: The British Conspiracy Published 1994

Hess: The British Conspiracy Published 1999

6

1

THE CASE OF RUDOLF HESS

THE EVIDENCE TO DATE

> *'He who controls the present controls the past'*
>
> *George Orwell - 1984.*

At the time of writing in winter 2009/2010 it is quite correct to state that we still do not know or understand the complete sequence of events which led Rudolf Hess to fly to the United Kingdom in May 1941. It may well be we never will.

Certain facts were made available very early on in the affair. The Duke of Hamilton was given a 'flight plan'[1] in May 1941. It hangs on his son's wall today.[2] A book was published in 1947 describing Hess's mental state during his captivity to date.[3] Hess's Nuremberg appearances were carefully stage managed and recorded.[4] And yet......

And yet we still do not know why he flew. Who was he flying to meet? Where was he hoping to land? What was he precisely hoping to achieve? These vital questions remain firmly unanswered to the satisfaction of historians, who quite rightly seek hard evidence to support the many theories and explanations.

Consequently speculation has abounded. The official line was the 'lone flyer' theory. Hess was acting on his own initiative and without official approval or sanction. No one really believed that to be the case as it would have been the act of a madman, which clearly Hess was not. Hess, eventually being incarcerated in Spandau was not in a position to speak out and explain. There were no further public utterances after Nuremberg.

The 1960's and 70's saw the Leasor[5] and Douglas-Hamilton[6] books, which introduced the student to the role of Albrecht Haushofer and his father Karl. Further details were slowly coming into the public arena. In 1993, six years after Hess's death, Douglas-Hamilton expanded the 1970 *'Motive for a Mission'* into the *'Truth about Rudolf Hess'*.[7] If only it was.

1999 saw my first real attempt at solving the mystery,[8] based on the discovery that Mrs Roberts, rather than living in Portugal and passing messages between the Duke of Hamilton and Haushofers actually was in residence in Cambridge, England. Moreover her nephew was a member of SO1, the Black propaganda unit based at Woburn Abbey. It appeared to me that Hess had been duped into flying. It still does.

From that scant beginning I suspect that I perhaps over egged the case that Hess was duped into flying into the UK, (given the available evidence at that time) a theory first espoused back in 1943[9] and supported by Hess's son Wolf, who I had met back in 1995.

Two years later in 2001 the paper back edition was published, which also disclosed the 'Polish Link', describing how Sikorski had flown into Prestwick on 11th May 1941, the morning after the Eaglesham crash.

Slowly progress was being made. Perhaps.

During the late 1990's I had been interviewed by and had come to know Stephen Prior who was working on what was to be *'Double Standards'*.[10] Whilst wholly impressed with his research of events leading up to the flight, I couldn't really go along with the latter conclusion that Hess was on the Duke of Kent's plane that crashed in 1942. Not impossible, but likely? I think not.

Stephen Prior had however raised the important issue of the Royal connection, an issue that I had earlier alluded to. This, too, I give credence, but unlike Stephen (who has sadly since died) remain wholly unconvinced that Hess was aiming to land at Dungavel; the airstrip just wasn't big enough.

The PRO[11] has slowly been releasing some Hess documents. The 1992 batch proved the case that MI5 were not expecting Hess (No surprise there, they weren't in on the ruse) and the 'establishment historians' were pleased to use this as their definitive proof of the 'lone flyer theory'. More significantly, no MI6 documents have yet seen the light of day and only a selection of the SO1 paperwork.

So that is really where we currently are. Hugh Thomas still remains convinced that it was not Hess that died in Spandau. Peter Padfield's amended *'Flight for the Fuhrer'*[12] remains the best all round work on the subject to date, whilst Martin Allen's *'Hitler Hess deception'* duplicates the *'Double Standards theory'* whilst being totally discredited by reason of the PRO 'document insertion' scandal. The insertion of falsified documents into any archive is a disgraceful act and I do not wholly understand why the PRO has not taken the matter further.

The purpose of this work is therefore to bring the various strands together, to contrast and compare and, if possible, add to the sum of current understanding. Since 1999 Richard Wilbourn and I have continued to travel and research the Hess case and now are pleased to present further information that we believe adds substantially to the understanding of the affair. We remain convinced that we were wholly on the right track back in 1999 and the Hess case was a dramatically successful Intelligence sting, albeit played out with massive stakes at risk.

It may well be the case that a complete explanation will forever provide illusory, but I am clear in my role. It is to present the current best evidence available some 67 years after the fateful flight. You must then be the judge.

---

[1] *Forwarded to the Duke of Hamilton 22nd May 1941 after vetting by the Intelligence Department.*
[2] *Lennoxlove House, Haddington, Scotland.*
[3] *J.R.Rees - The Case of Rudolf Hess - Heinemann - 1947.*
[4] *James Owen - Nuremberg - Headline Review - 2006.*
[5] *James Leasor - Rudolf Hess The Uninvited Envoy - George Allen and Unwin - 1962.*
[6] *James Douglas Hamilton - Motive for a Mission - Macmillan - 1971.*
[7] *James Douglas Hamilton - The Truth about Rudolf Hess - Mainstream 1993.*
[8] *Hess: The British Conspiracy - Andre Deutsch - 1999.*
[9] *The American Mercury, No.233, May 1943.*
[10] *Picknett, Prince and Prior - Double Standards - Little Brown - 2001.*
[11] *Public Records Office, Ruskin Street, Kew, London.*
[12] *Peter Padfield - Hess The Fuhrer's Disciple - Cassell & Co - 2001.*

2

THE CASE OF RUDOLF HESS

WORKING BACKWARDS TO

THE BASIC PREMISE

> *'In politics, nothing happens by accident. If it happened you can bet it was planned that way.'*
>
> FD Roosevelt, 32nd US President

The main criticism of *Hess: The British Conspiracy* when published 10 years ago was that it failed to draw on the paper trail of official documents so beloved by 'proper historians'. Most people who read the book thought that it brought new evidence to the debate, but most felt it was not conclusive enough in its interpretation of the new evidence.[1]

Confirming this view, Richard Wilbourn's daughter, Elizabeth, (who has grown up trying to deal with her father's obsession), graduated from Newcastle University in 2006. Her chosen subject was history and she was perhaps a little too quick to tag us the 'Hillbilly Historians', based on her wholly flawed perception that we didn't have any reliable evidence!

We could only take these 'cheap shots' on the chin because at that time it was indeed partly the case. Richard and I had worked around the known facts, gnawing away at the periphery of the case to achieve the break through concerning Mrs Roberts. We certainly had not concentrated on the same 'official documents' as everyone else. (Had we done so we may well have come to the same flawed conclusion as everyone else). We also have tried to contend with the inevitable problem of 'tempus fugit.' The sad fact is that the main players are all now dead. Hamilton in the 1970's, Hess in the 1980's and even some of the next generation have unfortunately already succumbed, Wolf Hess, for example in 2001. Arithmetically, even the youngest survivors of the Second World War have to be currently at least 64 years old.

MRD Foot, a severe critic of *Hess: The British Conspiracy,* was born in 1919 and is therefore 90 years old. At the outbreak of the war he was 20 years old and joined the Royal Engineers. Hence, even the 'experts' in intelligence matters (and I certainly do not dispute that he is) had little first hand experience of wartime intelligence (Foot was an exception serving later in France), they simply were not old enough to be 'in' on the important issues.

Therefore, I think it wholly wrong to presume that there are modern day 'keepers of the secret' who know far more than the rest of us. I fully acknowledge and am quick to do so, that there are experts in Intelligence who know far more than I. However, I strongly dispute the notion that they have a monopoly of knowledge of the Hess affair. There are too many facets and strands to the affair and I simply find it inconceivable that a current day 'expert' has been quietly taken to one side and told the complete story from beginning to end. In other words, from an evidential standpoint I suspect that we are largely all in the same position. Perhaps an Intelligence Archivist, or a Royal

Archivist have a grasp of that part of the story pertaining to their masters, but I suspect that very few people in the country know the story as a whole. Her Majesty the Queen may well be one, perhaps a senior civil servant another, but precious few others.

I also hope to demonstrate that the nature of the conspiracy, with a very limited number of participants, provides the reason for why we have not had the usual 'death bed' revelations, or junior members of the armed forces coming forward, confessing their part in the Hess affair. Whilst many people were potentially involved, most did not realise it or have any reason to realise it; they were just doing their jobs. That was the clever part. The lighthouse keepers maintaining their lights, the Thomas Cook postal system, the wartime radio navigation beacons, all were working properly, all were playing a part, but all were wholly ignorant of their role in the affair.

However, the principal problem that remains is that there are few important official documents concerning the Hess issue that have seen the light of day, presumably because the flight remains shrouded in necessary secrecy for reasons that I hope will become clear by reason of this book. Whilst certain relatively unimportant facets are plastered in minute detail,[2] any important papers[3] concerning the reasons, precise personnel and rationale behind the flight remain firmly locked away, or may even have been destroyed.

Moreover, in the UK there are two types of official documentation; that pertaining to the security services and that not pertaining to the security services. Whilst the 30-year rule and the Freedom of Information Act cover the latter, the release of the former is a wholly discretionary matter. So far, little such discretion has been exercised in relation to the Hess case.

In fairness, I am quite content that the 30-year rule and the Freedom of Information Act work well. I made an application under the Act with regard to Roman Battaglia, the 1941 Polish Consul in Glasgow and got the information requested. The sticking point is the security services; albeit given the implications of the bigger picture, possibly quite rightly and properly. In 1998 Robin Cook, the then British Foreign Secretary said, *"The Secret Service must remain secret ... their effectiveness and their lives depend on their identities and work remaining out of the public eye."*

In 1992 MI5 released some of their papers on the case, to date MI6 and SO1 have not. The latter are the papers that will reveal the truth. Interestingly enough, whoever placed forged documents into the PRO, sought to forge SO1 documentation, presumably because they too thought an understanding of these to be the key.

Lastly, on the subject of archives, the Royal Archives are probably the most annoying, not being subject to any rules in particular. Superficially their officers always politely return telephone calls, always eventually reply to correspondence, but always fail to answer your questions! As an example the whereabouts of the Duke of Kent and Princess Marina diaries seem a mystery to the officers themselves. The Royal Archives say they do not hold them, the families say the same thing. Both pass the buck to the other. Consequently, I have no official confirmation as to the whereabouts of Prince George on 10th May 1941. (I do have other written evidence) I must say I do believe the diaries to be in existence somewhere, but the Freedom of Information Act does not cover the Royal Archives.

So, I am sorry, but without these papers that would provide the explanation, we have continued to try and think laterally, prowl the periphery; dissect the detail and research the trivia in an attempt to pan a nugget from an ever-expanding stream of information. I believe we have struck lucky again but this time have started by working backwards, by asking ourselves what Hess was hoping to achieve and how he might achieve it.

We hope this now convinces, you, the reader.

The signing ceremonies of International treaties are normally the culmination of months or even years of diplomatic activity conducted between diplomats and assorted, transient politicians.

As a young lad I can just remember the SALT[4] treaties of the 1970's. SALT 1 commenced negotiations in November 1969 and Leonid Breznev and Gerald Ford flew into Vladivostock in November 1974 to sign.

More recently, George Bush signed the 1991 START[5] with Mikhail Gorbachev in Moscow and in 2002 Vladimir Putin met with George W Bush in Moscow to sign the SORT.[6]

Typically they are high profile events, with the leaders flying in too much aplomb, photo opportunities and smiles all around. The leaders rarely are individually involved in the myriad of preceding detail. They are there to conclude the years of detailed, hard work that has come before and preceded the bright lights, shiny pens and flash photography. It is also fair to say that the bright lights, shiny pens and flash photography are an integral part of the overall deal. There is little point in having a treaty that no one is aware of. Otherwise why should anything change? Simplistically, if no one were aware of a peace treaty for example, the armed forces would continue to fight, as they would not know to put their arms down. When World War Two eventually ended General Montgomery revelled in his theatrics on Luneburg Heath. The iconic pictures of the Japanese surrender on board USS Missouri will stay in the memory forever. Just as they were intended to do. The world had to understand and realise that the Japanese were beaten. That way the world had changed.

So, to put the Hess flight into context, if Hess was to achieve his goal, the world would have to know. If a secret treaty[7] were to be negotiated to keep Britain out of the war when Germany attacked Russia then why fly? That could surely be achieved through diplomatic bags and ambassadors.

No, the reason that Hess flew was that he thought he stood a chance of pulling off the 'big one'. The wartime peace of 1941 between Great Britain and Germany. This would appeal on a number of levels; history, ego and necessity being just three contenders. Hess was not stupid, nor was he mad. If he were mad he would not have been able to pilot one of the world's fastest aircraft across Europe. He would have simply crashed and killed himself.

Even the medics at Nuremberg adjudged Hess mentally fit to stand trial. He knew precisely what he was doing and why he was doing it. If he thought the mission folly he would not have undertaken it. He calculated that the chance of success made the risk worthwhile.

As it says on his gravestone in Wunsiedel,

> 'Ich Habs Gewagt'
>
> 'I dared'

The other line of thought that should be addressed is quite how Hess, if successful, was to actually achieve his desperately needed peace?

In May 1941, wartime Britain had Winston Churchill as its leader of its government, a man who had made his name as a longstanding opponent of Germany. Churchill was the man who had spent the First World War fighting Germans; the 1930's warning of the need for rearmament against Germany and had declared in June 1940 that *'We shall fight on the beaches'*. In February 1941 he had pleaded for the tools *'to finish the job'*.

This is a wholly personal opinion, but I cannot conceive of any circumstance that Churchill would have ever been party to a negotiated peace with Nazi Germany. Whilst politicians do change their positions as and when it suits them, (sometimes quite properly), I do not believe in Churchill's case this would ever have occurred. I think in the final analysis, had the need arisen, he really would have 'taken one with him' rather than sue for a peace settlement.

The Halford Mackinder 'Heartland' theory provides a pragmatic reason for my support of Churchillian and British stoicism (see later chapter) but overwhelmingly Churchill had staked all on his opposition to Germany and (as far as I am concerned) that was set in stone. Oran had already demonstrated his resolve.

So, that having been said, how on earth was Hess going to instigate a peace, if the London based government led by Churchill would not countenance any such thing?

Interestingly, David Irving has transcripts of interviews with Hess's staff conducted after the war. In particular he states that Hess had obtained books on the British Constitution in the weeks leading up to the flight.[8] I suspect I now know why.

The Royal Prerogative

Britain has no written constitution. Instead it is based on largely on precedent and conventions, the most important of which is that the Sovereign should act on ministerial advice.[9]

However, the extent of the Sovereigns 'acting on advice' has over the years been very much a moot point. Rodney Brazier lists the following actions where the monarch has acted independently of ministerial advice:

- The 1903 trip to Paris by Edward VII, arranged without telling the government
- The choice of Stanley Baldwin as Prime Minister in 1923
- The implied threat of veto during the Irish Home rule debates of 1912-1914.

In addition there are also the 'reserve powers', which the Sovereign has over the years accumulated. They are rarely used and indeed only ever considered in times of Constitutional Crisis. Again, as Rodney Brazier states,

"Rules and powers which are part of the common law do not merely become extinct merely through lack of use".

So what are these powers that seem to be a throw back to a time before 1688 or even 1649?

Helpfully, the Labour government of 2003 in a moment of reforming zeal, made a list of the Royal prerogatives in 2003, presumably with a view to abolishment. (The Labour MP's were annoyed that Tony Blair had gone to war with Iraq without a vote on the matter. Inconveniently for them, constitutionally he didn't need to). The powers were listed as such:[10]

Domestic
- The appointment and dismissal of ministers;
- The summoning, prorogation and dissolution of Parliament;
- Royal assent to bills;
- The appointment and regulation of the civil service;
- The commissioning of officers in the armed forces;
- Directing the disposition of the armed forces in the UK;
- Appointment of Queen's Counsel;
- Issue and withdrawal of passports;
- Prerogative of mercy. (Used to apply in capital punishment cases. Still used, eg to remedy errors in sentence calculation);
- Granting honours;
- Creation of corporations by Charter.

Foreign Affairs
- The making of treaties;
- Declaration of war;
- Deployment of armed forces overseas;
- Recognition of foreign states and the accreditation and reception of diplomats.

So, what is clear from the above list is that in a time of constitutional crisis, and should the need exist, the King or Queen could in theory act virtually independently of the government of the day.

This is the very reason that Hess was busy obtaining books on the British constitution in April 1941. If successful, he could request the Monarch to invoke the Royal Prerogative, dismiss the Prime Minister and presumably appoint in his place a Prime Minister who would act in accordance with the King's wish (presumably) to make peace with Germany. Exceptionally, it would appear that the King could make peace with Germany without recourse to Parliament at all, but that would be a wholly empty gesture as the government would continue (at least in the short term) to control the armed forces. If the King were to act in this way he would need to be sure of firstly a viable governmental alternative and secondly be persuaded that the British people would back the action.

There had been a precedent; William IV in 1834 had been the last monarch to appoint a Prime Minister against the will of Parliament.

However, if there was either a lack of parliamentary support or general support from the population at large the King would look an absolute fool and in the worst case potentially civil war was possible. The Monarchy would in all probability come to an end and the British war effort be undermined, in all likelihood, terminally.

I now believe this is exactly why Hess flew. He had been led to believe that this would happen on his arrival. His was the gesture to act as the catalyst to the above sequence of events. He was not looking for the Duke of Hamilton. He was looking for King George VI. The Duke was to be a mere chaperone.

I am not alone in my theorising. Lt Col.Gibson Graham the army physician who looked after Hess during most of May 1941 wrote in a memorandum dated 23rd May 1941;

"(Hess was)... seeking the Duke of Hamilton and then the King in order to be on hand with peace proposals when a new government arose in this country. Why a new government should arise he could not say, but he seems convinced of this; nor did he know its composition. The present British Government would try to prevent peace

proposals taking shape; moreover his government would not deal with them only with their successors"

"Hess was seeking the chivalry of the King."[11]

Sir Anthony Eden when instructing John Simon prior to his meeting Hess also commented,
"...the man dreams of a change of government"[12]

Unfortunately for Hess, he was making a massive misjudgement. The people telling him what he desperately wanted to hear before deciding to fly were under the ultimate control of British Intelligence and consequently (albeit not necessarily automatically), Winston Churchill.

Again, Sir Anthony Eden, when instructing Simon commented,
"I will speak to Alex Cadogan (who alone here knows of the project).........."[13]

The use of the word 'project' is self explanatory to me. Surely an Intelligence project, what else? (But I am, after all, a self confessed conspiracy theorist in this case!) And here is the irony. What made the whole thing so plausible to Hess was the fact that many of the people implicated in the Hess affair were indeed sympathetic to the German cause. Allied to that fact was that Hess was receiving precisely the message that he wanted to hear, from people he knew, or knew of, made this an overwhelming opportunity to achieve a major Nazi coup. That is what made the ruse so believable. It may well even be the case that some of those taking part believed they *were* participating in a coup. Make no mistake. Hess was not a 'Messenger of Peace'; he was an unrepentant Nazi who saw the flight as 'his big chance'. He has, had and should have no moral standing whatsoever.

The next chapters give the details of how this goal was to be achieved and what ultimately went wrong.

If you do not agree with this basic premise, then put the book down now and condemn it as another conspiracy theory nonsense. However, it is not. Realistically it is the only way the desired change could have been implemented.

Lastly, no forged documents are utilised, inserted into archives, or relied upon.

---

[1] *Peter Padfield: "The new facts Harris has brought to the table do not prove clandestine British involvement in Hess's flight beyond reasonable doubt but.... are so suggestive as to make the existence of a British deception, in my view, a practical certainty".*
[2] *An example: The Duke of Kent's trip to the USA in the summer of 1941.*
[3] *An example: Papers revealing the Duke of Kent's whereabouts on 10th May 1941.*
[4] *SALT - Strategic Arms Limitation Treaty.*
[5] *START - Strategic Arms Reduction Treaty.*
[6] *SORT - Strategic Offensive Reduction Treaty.*
[7] *Such as the 1939 German/ Russian Treaty.*
[8] *Pintsch - 'In late April (1941). FPP Website.*
[9] *Vernon Bogdanor - The British Constitution - The British Academy - 2003.*
[10] *Commons public administration committee- See The Guardian – 21st October 2003.*
[11] *FO 1093/11 - 23.5.1941.*
[12] *FO 1093/11 - 28.5.1941.*
[13] *FO 1093/11 - 28.5.1941.*

3

RUDOLF HESS

DUNGAVEL?

> *'We're not lost, we're
> locationally challenged.'*
>
> *John M Ford*

If the reader is content with the basic premise of the previous chapter the flight to Scotland begins to make sense.

A flight to an English airfield could not guarantee that Hess would be met by an individual who was 'in on' the plan. Moreover, with the much more concentrated air defences it would be much more likely the aircraft would be intercepted and shot down[1].

A flight to England would actually be a pointless exercise. It would be a wasted effort as far as Hess was concerned and the likely outcome would most likely, be exactly **that as actually happened.** Those who followed their orders would capture Hess, some might recognise him, and most would not. Eventually he would come under the control of those who wielded power and I am quite convinced the eventual outcome would have been broadly similar to the events that unfolded in lowland

Scotland in May 1941. Peter Fleming's book would have been seen to be even more prescient.[2]

No, the reason that Hess flew to Scotland was that he believed that he was flying to people who were a) sympathetic to his cause and b) would help him achieve his goal as outlined in the previous chapter. It would be that much easier to meet people who were likely to help him.

Yet this is where Dungavel does not make sense. Any sense at all.

I am not sure how many of the Hess historians have actually visited Dungavel. Richard and I have now visited on three occasions, on the first of which I was arrested and taken to explain my photography to the Governor of HM Prison Dungavel. I don't think he had met a Hess 'nutter' before and when I explained why I was photographing his playing fields he seemed to be quite pleased to let me go.

No, Dungavel is a bizarre target and that is why I do not think it was any such thing. However, for all those looking to support the 'lone flyer theory' it is ideal. Hess would have to be either mad or suicidal (just as they believe) to attempt a landing. This is why.

The Duke's of Hamilton ancestral home was really Hamilton Palace and not Dungavel at all.[3] It had been the largest non- Royal palace in the United Kingdom though had fallen into disrepair after its World War One use as a hospital. Ironically, due to the coalmining activity, which in part had provided the family with part of their wealth, subsidence had also partly claimed the Palace that eventually was demolished in 1921. From that time the family moved to Dungavel House, near Strathaven, but also had the use of other houses throughout England and Scotland. The Duke of Hamilton involved in the Hess affair was the 14th Duke. However, his father, Alfred, the 13th Duke had only died in 1940.[4] Therefore it was as the

Marquis of Clydesdale that Douglas Douglas-Hamilton
had been previously known and it was as the Marquis of
Clydesdale that he lived at Dungavel House, until March
1940, when he succeeded to the title.

It is also relevant to comment on the fact that Dungavel
House was built as a shooting lodge, not a 'replacement
Palace'. Whilst Dungavel was obviously larger than the
usual shooting lodges, with its turrets and towers, shooting
lodges are built as buildings to shoot from and as such
tend to be in the more remote locations. Without really
wishing to state the obvious I cannot name an urban
shooting lodge, or a shooting lodge near to houses. That
would somewhat defeat the object.

A study of the House's location will show that to be
exactly the case. It is remote.

So, the **first point** is made. What is the attraction or
point of a remote location? If a clandestine location is
required then perhaps, but being in the west of Scotland
meant that a) secrecy was potentially *less* likely as the
plane would have to cover a far greater time in the air over
enemy territory and b) finding the place itself would be
that much more difficult. There is also the obvious
difficulty of flying across lowland Scotland from the east
coast to the west coast. It was never going to be easy,
particularly in 1941 with enemy aircraft to potentially
contend with and rudimentary navigational techniques to
implement in the already growing darkness.

Topographically the east coast of Northern
England/Southern Scotland is obviously at sea level, but
within a few miles the hills rise, for example, to the 2700
feet Cheviot. Thereafter the contours and hills rise and fall
until the west coast is reached. Aeronautically it is difficult
territory, particularly if one wishes to land in the middle of
nowhere. Once far inland, away from the east coast life
becomes even more difficult as events bore out.

Secondly, let us consider the airstrip itself. A visual survey of the strip shows that it approximately 500 yards long in what is essentially a boggy field. It is not flat. It has a mild gradient as it follows the contours of the hill that continue behind the Prison on the other side of the road.[5] From the air there is only one line of approach; Hess would have to flown past the House on his east-west path and then turned to land *going uphill* onto the strip. It would have been impossible to land going downhill and stop without catastrophe. We made our last visit in June 2008 and it is now just a farmer's field quietly grazing sheep. There were clear ruts where the farmer had used his tractor earlier in the year to feed fodder and there were large patches of water reed, a sure agricultural sign of a wet field. On a previous visit we noted that the top of the field had been converted to a football field, but this use had apparently finished and a broken goalpost the only evidence of past use.

The derelict goal posts erected on the former airfield. The water reed in the foreground demonstrates how wet the field has become.

I duly obtained the weather records for Glasgow in 1941. The spring of 1941 was a marginally wetter spring than normal with the following rainfall:

Jan 1941 - .76 inches
Feb 1941 - 3.17 inches
Mar 1941 - 3.46 inches
Apr 1941 - 1.98 inches
May 1941 - 3.28 inches[6]

An inch of rain represents 540 tons of water per acre.

We tried desperately to imagine the picture that *'Double Standards'* had painted; The Duke of Kent and various dignitaries waiting in the Kennels[7] for Hess to land. The airstrip lit up with landing lights and then suddenly switched off.

I am afraid we now do not believe a word of it.

If one actually analyses the third party evidence that Stephen Prior produced, there is precious little save a photograph that he alleges proves Dungavel to be much more than the private airstrip it actually was. He even misquoted me by trying to say that I had seen evidence of a Beaufighter landing on the strip on 25th April 1941.[8] I had actually been referring to the newly opened Satellite Landing Ground at Lennoxlove, Haddington.[9] I now wonder if that was a wholly honest mistake.

The said photograph shows one large hangar surrounded by a ring of small sheds, no bigger than hen houses. They are certainly not hangars. They seem to me to illustrate a typical private airstrip.

The issue of lights are also interesting. Stephen states that the lights were switched on and off from the house following various telephone calls. This is based on the evidence of two ladies who continue to remain anonymous. I have severe doubts that there were any lights at all. (As indeed does Roy Conyers Nesbit and Dougal McIntyre). I also wonder about the two ladies. Stephen's statement that the lights were switched on and off from the house also seem odd. Dungavel House must be at least 400 yards from the 'kennels' and it just seems odd that any electricity would come from the big house itself. I would have thought that were there to have been lights a generator on site would have been the more likely power supply? Please remember that many private houses did not even have 'mains' electric lighting until after the Second World War.

On 'front line' stations the RAF adopted what was known as the 'Drem' lighting system in 1943, following development work by RLR Atcherley (1904-1970). At the time a Wing Commander, he subsequently became an Air Marshal, but his relevance to this story is that he developed the standard runway lighting system whilst station commander at Drem, East Lothian in 1940.

Whilst Dungavel was a completely different animal to a mainstream RAF base, the point is that if the mainstream bases did not have effective lighting systems until 1943, I am quite sure that Dungavel, even if it were to have had any lights, would have had only the most rudimentary. When landing an aircraft it is obviously important that the landing strip is marked out to the extent that its size is demarcated. However during the late 1920's and 1930's lighting systems were also being developed so that the angle of approach could be measured.

Therefore, already I have three main issues with Dungavel. Location, condition of airstrip and lighting.

That is before we even consider the plane itself. A Bf110 could not have landed at Dungavel, it simply wasn't long enough. Roy Conyers Nesbit,[10] who I have never found to be particularly helpful, even states that, *"It was certainly inadequate for a heavy aircraft such as the Bf110."*

I have been trying for a number of years to find out the typical landing distance of the Bf110. This has proven difficult in the extreme. Part of the difficulty is that there were many types of the B110 from the 1935 Bf110V1, through to the Bf110H-4 /U8. Even between 1st January 1945 and the cessation of hostilities there were 45 machines produced.[11] As with most planes with that extended longevity as they became more powerful they also became weightier.

For example, the prototype Bf110 started life with two DB 600 engines developing 900hp. The Bf110 G-0 was fitted with twin DB605B engines that had increased output to 1475hp.[12] The normal loaded weights rose from 15,300 lbs (Bf110C) to 20,700 (Bf110G).[13] What Roy Conyers Nesbit has done brilliantly is to identify the correct type of Bf110 in which Hess flew. His analysis and conclusion of a Bf110E-2/N, works number 3869 is undeniable.[14]

This model sported the new DB601N engine and so I would estimate the normal weight to be somewhere between the 15,300lbs and 20,700lbs previously quoted. Roy Conyers Nesbit specifies the weight at 6750kg loaded, which equates to 14,850lbs.[15] This seems a little light to me by comparison to the other models, but is still some 6.5 tons. However, as I had seen with my own eyes, the farmer's tractor (which would weigh less than half of the above) had made a significant mess on the field in the spring of 2008. I therefore dread to think of the implication of a say, 7-ton plane landing at 90-100mph on a wet Scottish field in the dark.

During the war a Bf110 was captured by the Allies and evaluated. Gordon Leith of the RAF Museum was kind enough to send me a copy of the evaluation.[16]

The evaluation states, *"The ground run (after touchdown) is about the same as a Blenheim."*

Very helpfully Mr Leith also sent details of the Blenheim specification which states that a Blenheim 1V Bomber (weighing c.12,000lbs) would take 850 yards whilst landing. The landing strip, even at its theoretical longest is not anywhere near 850 yards and the Bf110 is almost certainly heavier than the equivalent Blenheim. I understand that the difference between a concrete and grass strip is approximately +/-25% in terms of distance. 25% shorter when landing because of the lack of friction, 25% longer on take off, because of the additional friction. We know the Augsburg-Haunstetten airfield from where Hess took off was 1100 metres long (1202 yards).[17] By contrast however, Capt EM (Winkle) Brown who tested most German aircraft of the period stated (in the case of a MeBf110) *"The landing run was short as the brakes could be applied heavily without any tendency for the tail to rise".*[18] This test was however, probably conducted on the concrete strip at RAF Farnborough,[19] not a wet, undulating Scottish field.

So, I contend that if Hess had attempted to land at Dungavel House on 10th May 1941, he would have crashed, probably been killed and the purpose of the mission would have been prematurely nullified.

When travelling to Scotland in 2008 I had originally arranged a flight with a company based at Prestwick airport to study from the air, certain key areas. The proprietor is also a follower of the Hess affair and he commented that the Duke had crashed at Dungavel in the 1930's whilst flying a Hawker Hart.

A visit to Lennoxlove, the current Dukes' house, duly shows the visitor pictures of the 4 Hamilton brothers[20] in their RAF uniforms and further pictures of the Hawk squadron (Glasgow 602) diving in formation. If a plane like this struggled at Dungavel to land then the much heavier Bf110 would have also correspondingly struggled. The Hart weighed approximately one third of the weight of the Messerschmitt.

The only conclusion I can reach is that Hess would have been extremely lucky to land alive at Dungavel House.

It may well be for the above reasons that the Marquis of Clydesdale applied in 1936 for the construction of a new airstrip at Kilnburnside, a small village between Strathaven and Glasgow. Was this because Dungavel was considered already inadequate at that time?[21]

Public Record Office file AIR40/195 clearly shows that even if Hess had landed, he could not have taken off. The evaluation of the Bf110 shows that there was a 'special loading chart' and weights of 8500-9300kgs would only be permissible from a concrete strip.

Furthermore, in all the works on the subject I have never seen or heard of any record, which notes Hess to have practised parachuting. The lack of practice nearly cost Hess his life when he struggled to jump from the plane. As far as I am aware his descent was actually the first and only time that Hess had parachuted. I therefore contend that had he intended to parachute he would have practised the skill in typically Germanic fashion. One surely does not leave a 'life or death' skill to chance as Hess seemingly did?

Lastly, even if the intent was to parachute then what of the plane? Clearly the crashed remnants of a BF110 would not automatically be taken as a sign that Rudolf Hess had landed, but at the very least the crash would draw attention to the area and instigate the very recovery procedures that actually took place. This just seems to me to be an unnecessary risk to take if Hess were really to succeed.

The actual flight itself would also seem to back up my reservations. As I have said to the point of boredom, we know pretty precisely where Hess actually went, what we do not really have a clue is *where he was intending to go.* I am now absolutely convinced it wasn't Dungavel.

It is accepted, I think, that Hess flew past Dungavel on his East-West flight, before turning back inland when meeting the sea. Had there have been lights on as per *'Double Standards'* then why fly on to the sea? Had the strip been lit and Hess was to have seen it, he could have easily turned his plane around (The Bf110 handled well for a plane of its size[22]) and attempted to land on the uphill slope (all other issues being disregarded for the moment).

The fact is that he had to go to the sea to try and get his bearings. Either he was lost, or there were no lights for him to see and he was collecting his thoughts *or he was actually heading elsewhere.*

And lastly we should return to the old chestnut of fuel and range.

The Bf110 had a normal fuel capacity of two 375-litre tanks and two of 260 litres. When fitted with the auxiliary tanks of 900 litres each, a total capacity of 3070 was available to the pilot. Roy Conyers Nesbit again provides valuable service by analysing the flight in terms of consumption, time taken and distance. This was done to prove that the plane could actually reach Dungavel from Augsburg; having flown the 'plan' that Hess claimed to have flown.[23] This fact had been the subject of previous debate and some authors contended that the plane could not have made the 'target' of Dungavel.

They all miss the point.

Conyers Nesbit calculates that the 1953km that was covered in 5 hours 26 minutes used 2950 litres of fuel.

Very good. The flight was possible. However, if the total capacity was 3070 litres, when the plane crashed it could have had no more than 120 litres on board! (3070-2950).

In other words, when the plane crashed the maximum literage of 120 would have kept it airborne for probably no more than 13 minutes at most. (Average fuel consumption = 2950/326 minutes = 9.04 litres per minute). 120 litres/9.04 litres = c.13 minutes.

However, given that Hess had allegedly been travelling at high speed at certain parts of the flight, I suspect that the reality was that Hess either had run out of fuel just prior to crashing, or was perilously close to doing so. This suspicion is reinforced by the fact that there were no reports of explosions or fire when the Bf110 came to earth and the available photographs do not reveal fire ravaged remains. So that raises the issue of whether a German pilot would set out on such a trip knowing that in all likelihood there was barely enough fuel to reach his destination. As I made the point in *'Hess: The British Conspiracy'* the flight up the North Sea had the advantage of a following wind. Had the converse been true, yet more fuel would have been required.

As a percentage the 120 litres left represents 3.9% of the fuel loaded at Augsburg. I believe this is again an indication that Hess was not headed for Dungavel.

So where was he going?

[1] *The 'Dowding System' gave Britain the most advanced Early warning System in the world in 1939/40.*
[2] *Peter Fleming - The Flying Visit - Johnathan Cape 1940.*
[3] *For full details please see http//www.rcahms.gov.uk /Hamilton.*
[4] *Alfred Douglas-Hamilton, 13th Duke, died 16th March 1940 at Ferne Hill, Dorset.*
[5] *The B743 Muirkirk to Strathaven Road.*
[6] *Courtesy of Graham Bartlett, Library Information Officer, Met Office. June 2008.*

[7] *The Kennels are a single story house at the top of what was the airstrip.*

[8] *See Double Standards page.*

[9] *See http//www.eastlothianatwar/lennoxlove.*

[10] *Conyers Nesbit and Van Acker - Myths and Reality - Sutton 1999.*

[11] *The Messerschmitt Bf110 - Profile Publications - Profile pre 1971.*

[12] *Ibid.*

[13] *Ibid.*

[14] *Page 91 - 'Myths and Reality.'*

[15] *Appendix F - 'Myths and Reality.'*

[16] *Letter to JTGH - 28.9.2007.*

[17] *Roy Conyers Nesbit - Rudolf Hess: Myths and Reality - Sutton p 52.*

[18] *Capt Brown - Wings of the Luftwaffe - Carousel.*

[19] *RAE Farnborough, the oldest Military airfield in the UK was the home of the enemy plane evaluation unit during WW2.*

[20] *The 4 male sons of the 13th Duke of Hamilton.*

[21] *Hamilton records.*

[22] *Capt EM Brown - Wings of the Luftwaffe p 166 - 'manoeuvrability proved surprisingly good for so large a fighter'.*

[23] *Appendix G - Myths and Reality*

4

SO WHERE?

ANY AVAILABLE PEERS?

The alert reader will have noticed that the previous chapter did not reveal where Rudolf Hess was actually intended to target. It reinforced the case (I hope) that it wasn't Dungavel House and that wherever actually heading, logically it was perhaps more likely to have been on the eastern side of Scotland.

If the reader is also still content with the basic premise that Hess was actually planning to meet the King so as to attain his goal then I am afraid that there will have to be a further diversion. This diversion explains *why* Hess was seemingly targeting a Duke (or Dukes). He *had* to make contact with his chaperone as quickly as possible and meanwhile keep out of the control of the British Government.

We have known since *'Motive for a Mission'* days[1] that the primary 'link man' between Hess and the Duke of Hamilton was actually Albrecht Haushofer who knew both men extremely well. There has also been the, 'Did Hamilton meet Hess in 1936' debate for some while.[2] I am not sure it actually matters. Hess did not fly because he believed the Duke of Hamilton could actually force a peace between Britain and Germany. He flew because he desperately needed the Duke of Hamilton, or another member(s) of the peerage, as part of the constitutional process he sought to invoke, not as the process itself. Hence the need for this further diversion.

The peerage of Great Britain is itself a reflection of the history of the nation. Disregarding the Irish peerage completely (because *it is* irrelevant to the Hess affair), the English and Scottish peerage is split into two parts; pre and post the 1707 Act of Union.[3] The earliest English Peer created was in 1387 when Richard II created Baron Kidderminster. In Scotland the title of the Duke of Rothesay was created in 1398 for the heir apparent to the Scottish throne. This was one David Stewart.[4] Typically the creation of the role was in recognition of the recipient's importance either in geographic terms, political terms, or both.

Returning to our story, on April 12th 1643 the title of the Duke of Hamilton was created, whilst Charles I was at Oxford. Quite why is not particularly obvious, as the first Duke seems to have flitted manically in and out of favour with Charles I.[5] He was finally executed in 1649 following his capture by Cromwell at the Battle of Preston in 1648.

A biography of the First Duke is called, *'Captain Luckless..........'*[6] which does seem to characterise the 1st Duke of Hamilton well.[7] Titles are of course part of the control system of the establishment, even more so in the days before 1649. The government of Tudor England has been described as a partnership between the King and the landed classes. However, Britain being Britain, various privileges survived the change to a constitutional monarchy in much the same way as we have already established in the chapter pertaining to the monarch. These rights or privileges are listed as being:

- *Trial by the House of Lords (abolished in 1948),*
- *Freedom from arrest (so as not to prevent the Peers ability to advise the Monarch),*

And, thirdly,

- *Access to the sovereign,*

Access to the sovereign in the first instance was necessary as part of the governmental process of Middle Ages England.

In 1765, William Blackstone the Barrister and Academic wrote, *"it is usually looked upon to be the right of each particular peer of the realm, to demand an audience of the King, and to lay before him, with decency and respect, such matters as he shall judge of importance to the public weal. "*[8]

Amongst the photographs that are routinely published in the Hess books is the one showing the Duke of Hamilton and his brother playing the accordion to the Princesses Elizabeth and Margaret. Clearly the two families were very well acquainted, a not surprising fact given that the various Dukes of Hamilton have been the Keeper of Holyrood Palace since 1646. The Duke of Hamilton is often described as the Premier Peer in Scotland. In June 1953 the Duke of Hamilton played an important part in the Service of Dedication of the newly crowned Queen at St Giles Cathedral, Edinburgh.

Therefore, it is plain that the Duke of Hamilton was constitutionally an ideal target for Hess to meet, notwithstanding the fact that they may or may not have met previously. He knew the King in both formal and informal capacities; he was the Premier Peer in Scotland and as a Peer held a *right* to access to the King. In theory he held all the cards if, for example, Parliament didn't wish him to meet with the King, (Right of access) or if they wished to place him under arrest for whatever reason, (Freedom from arrest). It is also pertinent to note that there are five 'ranks' of peers with Dukes heading the list, followed in order by Viscount, Marquess, Earl, Baronet and Baron. Clearly, the Duke of Hamilton was and is very much in the 'premier league' of Peers, particularly as in addition to the Dukedom he held a multitude of other titles including some English titles so as to ensure his eligibility for the English based House of Lords.[9]

So thereby ends the diversion. However, the Duke of Hamilton was by no means the only Peer that inhabited Lowland Scotland in May 1941. As part of my research I felt I had to try and eliminate other possible candidates, given their powerbase in Lowland Scotland, particularly if they lived near airfields!

Other possible intermediaries? The lowlands of Scotland into which Hess was flying, was literally full of Peers of the Realm and independently minded Scots, some titled, some not. In no particular order and certainly not exclusively:

1. *General Sir Ian Hamilton.*
2. *Alec Douglas Hume (then Lord Dunglass) - The Hirsel, Coldstream.*
3. *The Earl of Rosebery - Dalmeny House, South Queensferry.*
4. *The Duke of Sutherland - Mertoun House, St Boswells.*
5. *The Usher family - Various, see The House of Usher.co.uk.*
6. *The Duke of Bedford - Cairnsmore, Newton Stewart.*
7. *The Duke of Buccleuch - Drumlanrig Castle, Thornhill and Bowhill, Selkirk.*
8. *The Duke of Roxburgh - Floors Castle, Kelso*
9. *The Lord Palmer - Manderston, Duns.*
10. *The Earl of Haddington - Mellerstain House, Gordon and Tyninghame House, North Berwick.*

11. *The Marquis of Lothian - Monteviot House, Jedburgh*
12. *The Marquess of Bute - Dumfries House, Cumnock.*
13. *The Earl of Stair - Castle Kennedy, Stranraer.*
14. *The Earl of Glasgow - Kelburn Castle, Fairlie.*
15. *The Marquesses of Linlithgow - Hopetown House.*
16. *The Earl of Wemyss - Seton House Castle/ Gosford House, Longniddry.*
17. *The Marquess of Tweeddale - Yester House, Gifford.*
18. *Lord Semphill - Craigevar Castle, Alford.*
19. *Captain Ramsay - Kellie Castle, Arbroath (Interned May 1940).*

The above listing is neither exhaustive, nor intended to be a 'Poirouesque' list of suspects, but does illustrate the fact that there were many suitable, well qualified candidates to act as intermediary should the Duke of Hamilton not be available. Using the above numbering I would add the following information:

1. General Sir Ian Hamilton

- General Sir Ian Hamilton (1853-1947) is interesting on a number of counts:
- As we will see, when Hess was contemplating opening peace overtures in September 1940, General Hamilton was mooted as a possible intermediary by Karl Haushofer.[10]
- Somewhat coincidentally, the General and his wife Jean, spent the summers at Lennoxlove, Haddington, from 1934 and were there when war was declared on 3rd September, 1939.[11] The Duke of Hamilton acquired Lennoxlove from the Baird family, after the war, once Dungavel had been sold to the National Coal Board.

- During the 1930's Hamilton had travelled to Germany with the British Legion (1935) and had met Hitler and Hess at Berchtesgaden in 1938. He had subsequently invited Hess to Scotland.
- In 1928 he formed the 'Anglo German Association', but disbanded the same in 1936.
- I understand that Sir Ian was at Blair Drummond in bed with flu on 10th May 1941. (He was 88 at the time).
- I am also interested in the General in connection with Mary Violet Roberts. As has already been explained, Mrs.Roberts was originally described as 'the daughter in law of Lord Roberts of Kandahar'. Whilst this was palpably not possible, (Lord Robert's only child was killed whilst unmarried), it is perhaps interesting to note that Sir Ian was Aide de Camp to Lord Roberts 1882-1893.
- Sir Ian was the military attaché of the Indian Army, serving with the Japanese Army during the Russo/Japanese War. In 1908 Karl Haushofer was sent on behalf of the German Army in a similar role. I am unable to confirm whether the two men met.
- I am also unable to confirm that the General had the opportunity to meet Patrick Maxwell (Mary Violet Robert's father) who spent most of his career in India. (It is more likely that Patrick Maxwell knew Lord Roberts, both men serving at the time of the 1857 Indian Mutiny).

I conclude therefore that whilst General Sir Ian Hamilton was undoubtedly well known by the Nazi hierarchy and it appears also the Haushofer family, I am unsure as to when the associations were forged, other than the high profile 1930's visits, by which time Sir Ian was into his 80's. I suspect that is the limit of his involvement.

2. Alec Douglas Hume

Lord Dunglass (1903-1995) served as Parliamentary Private Secretary to Neville Chamberlain (1937-1939) but thereafter was incapacitated with spinal tuberculosis for 2 years thereafter. He resided at The Hirsel, near Coldstream.

3. The Earl of Rosebery

Albert Primrose, 6th Earl Rosebery (1882-1974) served in the 1945 caretaker government as Secretary of State for Scotland. In February 1941 he was appointed as Regional Commissioner for Civil Defence in Scotland.

4. The Duke of Sutherland

George Sutherland - Levenson Gower, 5th Duke of Sutherland (1888-1963). As the Royal Archives are seemingly reluctant to advise as to the location of the Duke of Kent on 10th May 1941, I took an advertisement in the *Daily Telegraph* asking if anyone knew his whereabouts on 10th May 1941. Almost by return, Elizabeth Sutherland, 24th Countess of Sutherland (b.1921) telephoned my unsuspecting secretary, advising that the Duke spent the weekend at Dunrobin Castle. Elizabeth was a ward of the 5th Duke on account of her parent's early deaths. Apparently she was working at the nearby Inverness Hospital and returned to Donrobin for the weekend. The family still had a part of the castle, the rest being a hospital. We will debate this statement later in the book.

5. The Usher family

The Usher family (who donated £100,000 in the 1890's to build Edinburgh's Usher Hall) had properties throughout Lowland Scotland, financed from the profits of the Victorian Whisky industry. One of its last members, Stuart

Usher, is currently (in 2009) embroiled in a legal battle to reclaim part of the above estates that he claims a leading firm of Scottish lawyers had negligently administered. Consequently there are various websites that deal with the various legal issues. The above litigation is quite well known in Scotland and one of his advisers maintains a 'blog' which discloses the fact that the family knew the Hess family whilst in Egypt. This appears quite plausible as two senior members of the Usher family died in Cairo.

On 23rd September 2009, I spoke with Stuart who refuted the allegations. It was quite true that Stuart's descendants had died whilst in Egypt, but, he says, they were on holiday. It is also quite true that Hess was born and brought up in Alexandria, Egypt, but there the coincidence ends...... I think.

Stuart's Mother was a German, very well connected and, according to Martin Frost caused the family various problems on account of her pro Nazi views. Any more I cannot say as I have no evidence to produce.

6.   The Duke of Bedford

The Duke of Bedford and his part in the peace overtures of 1935-1940 deserves on its own merits to be the subject of a book.[12] Hastings William Sackville Russell was born in 1888 and succeeded to the Dukedom following the death of his father in 1940. Previously he was known as the Marquis of Tavistock. An avowed pacifist he mounted his own peace effort by travelling to Dublin to meet with the German legation in 1940. In *Hess: The British Conspiracy* I speculated that this was actually an act of treason but nevertheless he still avoided detention under Section 18(b). Throughout the war he published pro-peace pamphlets. His Scottish base was at Cairnsmore, Newton Stewart, Wigtownshire and it was here that the Duke spent much of May 1941. Ironically, it should be noted that the Duke's principal residence at Woburn Abbey,

Bedfordshire was the wartime home of SO1, of which much more will be written later in this book.

7.   The Duke of Buccleuch

Walter John Montagu Douglas Scott, the 8th Duke of Buccleuch was born in 1894. The family are one of the largest landowners in Britain and the family still resides at Bowhill near Selkirk and Drumlanrig in Dumfriesshire. He was the Scottish Unionist Party MP for Roxburghshire and Selkirkshire for the period 1923 to 1935, at which time he succeeded to the Dukedom and joined the House of Lords. However, the 8th Duke was known as being enthusiastically pro-German,[13] to the extent that the King took away the honorary title of Lord Steward away from him in May 1940. This significant action will be analysed further in the later chapters. The successor to this post was the Duke of Hamilton and Brandon. According to some sources the Duke was held under virtual house arrest thereafter.

8 to 19. The other Dukes and members of the Peerage are merely listed to illustrate the surfeit of the same in Lowland Scotland during the period under enquiry. However, I do not believe they play a part in our story.

So who and where was Hess targeting?

---

[1] *1971*

[2] *Hamilton had attended a dinner at the 1936 Olympics at which Hess was present. Hamilton denied meeting Hess personally, others, including Chips Channon, stated that the two had in fact met. Hamilton had spent much time in Europe during the 1930's, so it would not be too much of a surprise if such a meeting had taken place, if not then perhaps later.*

[3] *There is a further subdivision, pre and post 1801.*

[4] *Consequently, today, Prince Charles is the Duke of Rothesay.*

---

[5] *Charles I actually imprisoned Hamilton in Pendennis Castle in 1644.*

[6] *Captain Luckless: James Douglas Hamilton (1603-1649)-Hilary L.Rubenstein.*

[7] *The same could be said of 14th Duke of Hamilton?*

[8] *Blackstone, W. (1765) Commentaries on the Laws of England - Oxford: Clarendon Press.*

[9] *The Duke holds 13 subsidiary titles; 10 Scottish, 2 English and 1 British (created post 1707).*

[10] *Letter - Karl Haushofer to Albrecht Haushofer - 3rd September 1940.*

[11] *Celia Lee - A Soldiers Life - Celia Lee - 2001.*

[12] *If the Bedford Estate allow access to the papers. I have already been refused.*

[13] *Richard Griffiths- Fellow Travellers of the Right - Constable 1980. "...Lord Buccleuch who, with Brocket had been among Hitler's' frequent visitors".*

5

SO WHERE?

TRAINS AND AIRFIELDS

I hope that the reader is now able to see the line of questioning that we are applying. It is rather tedious perhaps, but we are looking at all the viable alternatives, examining them and then discounting as appropriate or otherwise. The previous chapters have dealt with why Dungavel has been discounted as a potential landing strip; the possible alternative Peers available to Hess to act as intermediary and so now we must look at the possible alternative landing strips capable of receiving a MeBf110.

It is one thing challenging accepted thought in connection with the Hess case; only a fool would not. However, it is quite a different proposition when attempting to quote historical facts pertaining to British railways and its rolling stock. Why this is so I am not sure, save it allows the middle aged and elderly men of Great Britain the opportunity to relive their youthful aspirations, by allowing them to devour facts, details and statistics, often to an unnerving extent.

So, it is with a respectful degree of trepidation that I impart to the reader the following information.

Since 1846 it has been possible to travel from London to Edinburgh by train, albeit in 1846 by using the track of three companies. In 1923 the same three companies merged into the London and North Eastern Railway Company, which nationally henceforward was known as one of the 'big four'. The route of the line is relatively well known: London, Peterborough, Doncaster, Newcastle, and Edinburgh. Very much a main transport artery, as it remains to this day. In Victorian times railways sprung up connecting places that needed to be connected to some that just did not justify the expenditure. The first 'Railway mania' had arrived. Northumberland was no exception, but being Northerners they were also canny. The branch lines that were built were usually built for a specific purpose. Relevant to this explanation of the Hess affair are two of the branch lines built to transport coal and lime to the Northumberland coast, part of the 'coals from Newcastle' tradition that had been ongoing since the 1500's.[1]

So it was that the North Sunderland Light Railway Company Limited was created by Act of Parliament in 1892. The branch ran for 4 miles from Chathill on the main line to Seahouses on the coast, with stations envisaged enroute at Fleetham and North Sunderland. In 1898 an extension was made to Bamburgh, making use of the 1896 Light Railway Act. In 1898 the line opened, but the proposed station at Fleetham was dropped to save cost. Both freight and cargo were carried for 53 years until the line closed in 1951. In 1952 the Company was wound up and in 1953 the track removed.[2]

A few miles down the coast the same process had already taken place. In 1849 the York, Newcastle and Berwick Railway Company had opened a line from Chevington to Amble a distance of 5.75 miles. By the 1920's some 750,000 tons of coal were being transported to Amble harbour. The line was single track from Chevington to Broomhill and double track from Broomhill to Amble. Passenger numbers were not great and in 1930 the passenger service was withdrawn.[3] The line finally closed on 6th October.

Therefore on the night of 10th May 1941 both of these quiet branch lines were clearly in existence; their eventual fates would be determined after the war. Rudolf Hess, whilst oblivious and uncaring of the underlying economic circumstances of the lines was, however, diligent enough to mark both on the 'Lennoxlove map'. This in itself is not significant as he had also marked woods on the outskirts of Kelso and various lakes and reservoirs across central Scotland, together with many other railway lines. However, more notably perhaps, he does not mark all of the LNER main line. There is a gap between the Amble branch and the North Sunderland spur. In other words he wasn't interested in the main line itself, but he was by inference, interested by the two branch lines. They appear to provide visual boundaries, upper and lower, to the flight plan? Grime marks, where originally folded, on the original map seem to concur with this view. Was he therefore aiming to hit the coast between the two landmarks?

As I have already stated, railway lines are good landmarks for the aviator flying at dusk. If well used, they provide a good visual guideline. These were no exception.

There is also one other fact of consequence; if one follows the line of the Amble branch railway, from the coast, it leads one directly to the site of the former RAF Acklington. On 10th May 1941 RAF Acklington provided realistically, the only landing strip on the North Sea coast, north of Newcastle, capable of safely accepting a Bf110 landing at 95-110 mph. RAF Acklington was very much a modern aerodrome, with three runways and 19 hangars of varying types. It had been built in 1938 and was very much a mainline base. During the Battle of Britain it was the home to 4 fighter squadrons and in May 1941, 72, 315,317 and 406 Squadrons were housed at the base. Indeed the Hess enthusiast will recognise Acklington as being the base that Maurice Pocock was scrambled from in order to intercept the Hess Messerschmitt.

So there we have the first potential candidate; RAF Acklington. A busy aerodrome, on the Hess theoretical flight plan, quite capable of handling a Bf110.

What other alternatives are there?

In May 1941 the United Kingdom was split into 3 in aeronautical terms. Northern England and Scotland was designated as being 13 Group.

When writing *Hess: The British Conspiracy* back in the 1990's I had named Acklington and Lennoxlove as the two potential targets. Both were in 13 Group. As a result of the Harris-Wilbourn 2008 holiday, we had started looking in detail at the other potential airfields in the airspace that Hess entered. Two other East Coast contenders appeared; **Kelso Racecourse** and **Charterhall/ Winfield**. Dealing with each in turn.

Kelso Racecourse. I must confess to a degree of wishful thinking based on some late night, alcohol fuelled, speculation that Hess was possibly aiming for Floors Castle, the largest house in Scotland, located on the outskirts of Kelso. Floors Castle is also the home to the Duke of Roxburghe, so would provide the 'Necessary Peer' if the reader is still happy with the basic premise of this book. The 1941 military map of the Borders marks race courses, presumably as landing grounds of last resort.[4] It is in this capacity that Kelso racecourse was marked, lying no more than half a mile from the house. Fuelling our wishful thinking was the fact that the Lennoxlove map has on it a seeming concentration of markings around the Floors area. There are two arrows; one on the corner of Bowmont forest, the other pointing directly at Floors, parallel to the B6352 going towards Blakelaw. Had we found our target?

Richard and I duly travelled to the area, hoping to find an old disused airfield perhaps. Nothing. We duly verified that the corner of the forest was indeed the corner of the forest, and found there is now a post war quarry nearby. We discovered that the other arrow provided a panoramic view of Kelso, with Floors clearly in view. Surely there would be an old airfield somewhere. I contacted Kelso museum, who again were very helpful. They checked their records and books, but again nothing. There had been rumours of 'balloons on the racecourse', but no airfield. There was also a large, flat, meadow actually in front of Floors itself, but this was getting too fanciful, even for us. We reluctantly desisted.

Having reluctantly discounted Kelso and its racecourse as a landing site, we looked a little further afield and came across mention of RAF Charterhall and its satellite at RAF Winfield. Hess could land there and travel to a nearby mansion? Located approximately 5 miles to the north of Kelso, Charterhall and Winfield were located near the sites of World War One airfields at Eccles Toft and Horndean.[5] Housing 54 Operational Flying Unit from 1st May 1942 to 31st October 1945 the airfield gained the unfortunate nick name of 'slaughterhall' on account of the large number of accidents incurred by the Beaufighters, Blenheims and Beauforts whilst housed there.[6] However, the landowners were only posted their requisitions in March 1941 and pertinent to this story the airstrip was completed in April 1942 after a long period of bad weather. The first aircraft to land was a Boulton Paul Defiant, which emergency landed on the still incomplete airfield on 16th February 1942. The two strips were hard; one being 1600 yards, the other 1100. Winfield opened a little later.

So, again, reluctantly, we had to discount these airfields as targets. They were still fields and not airfields in May 1941.

Lennoxlove is in some ways the same as Floors Castle in that it too is a romantic solution to the problem. The fact that the Duke of Hamilton acquired the house in 1947 would appear to be ironic in the extreme if it were really the case that Hess was actually targeting the same house six years earlier.

Another irony would be that General Sir Ian Hamilton; another on the Haushofers' list of British connections had rented the house during the 1930's. And finally a further potential irony was that the 1941 owners, the Baird family, also were related to the family who owned the farm on which Hess eventually crashed, Floors at Eaglesham, some 50 miles away.

There was certainly an airstrip at the House, an airstrip that was quite capable of receiving a Bf110. Whilst now an arable field, on 25th April 1941 a Blenheim had landed on the strip as part of its use as a SLG (Satellite Landing Ground) to RAF Drem.[7] The website eastlothianatwar.co.uk gives the following information:

'During January 1941 the RAF. authorised work to be carried out to prepare part of the estates of Colstoun and Lennoxlove for use as No 27 Satellite Landing Ground (SLG). The role of RAF Lennoxlove was as a secret place for the storage of replacement aircraft, where the enemy would be unaware of their presence and the aircraft would therefore be safe from attack. The landing ground was to be part of No. 18 Maintenance Unit (MU), which was based at RAF Dumfries. Work extended from January to April, with permission being gained from the 'Chief Constable' at Haddington to close by means of self-shutting gates at each end, a small road running across the landing strip. Finally, on 24th April 1941 a Fairey Battle light bomber made a trial landing at Lennoxlove, which proved successful, and the landing ground was declared acceptable.

On 25th April a Bristol Blenheim was flown in, the first aircraft to be stored at No. 27 SLG. However, despite this achievement it was decided that only smaller aircraft, such as Hurricanes, could be stored at Lennoxlove because the landing strip had not been extended, this being due to delays in getting planning permission to close the road separating the extension from the rest of the landing ground. However, some progress was made, and by the end of May 1941 all flight equipment huts were complete and a telephone line had been installed at the headquarters office. Additionally, an Army guard of one officer, two NCO's and 12 men of the 10th Royal Scots were billeted in Lennoxlove House. Permission to close the road necessary to extend the landing strip was not slow in being given by Haddington Police and once the work was completed, which included lowering the surface level of the road to avoid it sitting proud of the grass runway, many more Blenheims were flown in to Lennoxlove. The Commanding Officer of No. 18 MU visited Lennoxlove in August 1941 and gave some thought to the possibility of landing Westland Whirlwind twin-engine fighters there. The unit's Chief Test Pilot mentioned that the Whirlwind swung badly in crosswinds but was nonetheless prepared to attempt a landing when the wind conditions were considered suitable. This was carried out very successfully and, as a result, many Whirlwinds came to be stored at Lennoxlove. Even larger aircraft were to be flown in to the SLG, with Vickers Wellington bombers making their first appearance in late 1941, and even a Handley-Page Halifax four-engine heavy bomber landing here in the summer of 1942, the SLG being declared ideal for such large aircraft.

By November 1944 No. 27 SLG had 119 aircraft in storage, most of which were Wellingtons. Quite a number of these suffered damage as a result of branches falling from the trees under which they were hidden, and even from trees themselves, uprooted during gales.

In the summer of 1945 Lennoxlove gained a unique distinction. A derivative of the Whirlwind fighter was the Westland Welkin which was designed as a high-altitude day and night fighter, intended for intercepting German bombers flying at great heights. This threat did not materialise and thus the Welkin never saw operational service. However, 67 Welkins were produced (as well as two prototypes), most of these being flown into Lennoxlove for storage at the end of the war, before being scrapped. The end of No. 27 SLG followed not long afterwards, beginning in August 1945 and ending with the closure of the unit the following month.'

In addition to the above information, which demonstrates the plausibility of the location, Lennoxlove is aeronautically viable in terms of visual navigation. Coming in from the sea over Dunbar, there are two large, distinct hills; Trapain Law and North Berwick Law, which provide a visual boundary to the approach to the Lennoxlove strip.

So, it was a plausible target, but as you will have seen there were doubts about its suitability for the larger planes in 1941.

If you are convinced by the lighthouse theory there is also a convenient one at Barns Ness that gave out a white light every 4 seconds to a distance of 10 miles.

However, if Lennoxlove was the location, Hess' actual flight was a long way off, the so called flight plan, an awfully long way off.

Other airfields

This list may not be exclusive, but we believe the following other airfields were possible targets, being in the airspace, or near to the airspace that Hess entered.

- RAF Usworth. This was the Group HQ and in May 1941 home to 55OTU, armed with Hurricane Mk.X.
- RAF Turnhouse. This was home to 64 Squadron in May 1941, armed with Spitfire Mk2a The Duke of Hamilton was based here.
- RAF Drem. A fighter station, but with grass strips. The Duke of Hamilton flew down to Drem on the afternoon of 10th May 1941.
- RAF East Fortune. A satellite station to RAF Drem in May 1941.
- RAF Grangemouth. Home to 58OTU. 'Tactical Exercise Unit'.
- Abbotsinch, Glasgow. An old WW1 airfield that was partially used by 602 Squadron. Was too small for military aircraft and became HMS Sanderling in 1940.
- Renfrew, Glasgow. Renfrew was Scotlands' first municipal airport. Subsequently taken over by Abbotsinch.
- Dundonald. The main runway was not reconstructed until 1943.
- Turnberry. A First World War airfield updated with three concrete strips in 1941.
- Castle Kennedy. A grass strip, housing the Air Gunnery School.
- West Freugh. Opened in 1937 as an armaments training school.
- Wigtown The closest airfield to the Duke of Bedford's house at Newton Stewart.

- Strathaven. Three grass strips, the longest of which is 530 metres.

However, we now believe that we have discovered the actual airfield that Hess was aiming for. It is not listed above.

---

[1] *In 1606, Thomas Heywood in 'If you know not me, you know no bodie: or, the troubles of Queen Elizabeth' wrote: "As common as coals from Newcastle."*
[2] *By the Motherwell Machinery and Scrap Company.*
[3] *7th July 1930.*
[4] *Newmarket racecourse, Suffolk was used as a bomber base, for example.*
[5] *77 Squadron being based their as an ant- Zeppelin measure.*
[6] *JB Thompson - The Charterhall Story-Air Research Publications-2004.*
[7] *It was this fact that Stephen Prior misquoted in 'Double Standards' as relating to Dungavel. Clearly it did not.*

6

SO WHERE?

MAPS, LIGHT AND
LIGHTHOUSES

This is the difficult question. Ever since 1941 Dungavel has been 'held out' to be the target and that Hess had completed a 'miracle flight' etc. This is ideal if you believe the sole flyer theory and that Hess was mad and flying to a location that he couldn't land at to see someone who wasn't there.

Inadvertently and not without irony, the most recent books, *'Double Standards'* and *'The Hitler-Hess'* deception have also played into the hands of the 'sole flyer' theorists. By still concentrating on Dungavel, albeit relying on flawed (and planted!) evidence, the actual, intended target has still been allowed to remain hidden.

The previous chapters I hope have made you at least question the Dungavel proposition.

If asked to arrange a rendezvous between Rudolf Hess and someone who was to take him to meet the King in 1941, I would suggest that you would try to make that rendezvous as easy as you possibly could aeronautically and eliminate any unnecessary risk. You might wish to introduce an element of 'deniability' into your planning (if it all went wrong) but you surely would not require the pilot to pinpoint an airfield in the middle of no-where, which incidentally was too short anyway? You might also suspect that Hess might well have the Luftwaffe check out the proposed landing strip for suitability.[1] There would be little chance of Hess leaving the destination to chance. Germans are not like that. Make no mistake; aeronautical navigation has never been easy. In 1940 the Butt report, commissioned to report on the efficiency of British bombers stated that only one third of all bombers dropped their bombs within 5 miles of the target and only 1% of all bombs actually fell on their target.[2]

By way of reinforcement, my late father in law used to relate tales of cross Atlantic Liberator Ferries due to land at Prestwick, near Glasgow actually landing in southern England having got 'lost' en route.

The list of high profile aeronautical casualties' help to illustrate the difficulties: Amy Johnson, Glenn Miller, Amelia Erheart and the Duchess of Bedford were all solo fliers (except Miller who was a passenger in a 2 seater) and all met their end in part due to navigational difficulties.

So, duly interested by 1940's air navigation I acquired a copy of The EUP-*Teach Yourself Air Navigation, 1942 edition*. The index itself is pretty foreboding as follows:

- Form of the earth
- Map projections
- Elementary magnetism
- Deviation of the compass
- The triangle of velocities
- Maps, scale, relief
- Fixing and reporting position
- Aircraft magnetic compasses
- Elementary meteorology
- Calibration laws
- Ground flight

'SRM' the author, then continues,

> *"It is assumed that the reader has but elementary mathematical knowledge, and whilst trigonometry has been purposely avoided.... for a more advanced reading a knowledge of trigonometry, both plane and spherical....is desirable."[3]*

This is all very well if Hess had nothing else to do. All skills can be learned. However please remember that at this time, most long distance bombers had their own navigators who did nothing else. Please also bear in mind that Hess had the other, far from subsidiary issue, of flying one of the world's fastest planes single-handedly and now we are demanding that he navigates a la 'Teach yourself Air Navigation' too! Global positioning was decades away and trigonometry; with its protractors, logs and slides rules was still very much the vogue.

'SRM' continues,

> *"When flying from one place to another there are two methods of getting to the destination; one is by map-reading pure and simple, paying no attention to compass direction, and the other by navigating.*
> *The first method, of course, can only be done over comparatively short distances, and should cloud be encountered at very low altitudes, obscuring the ground, the user of such a method would very soon be hopelessly lost. ... When navigating, on the other hand, it is not necessary to see the ground until such time as the landing is to be made.*
> *In all probability, one sheet of small scale would be sufficient to enable the navigator to reach position over his destination, but he would require a large-scale map of that area in order to discern the*

whereabouts of the aerodrome or landing ground. It is therefore most appropriate that the scale of the maps be thoroughly appreciated."

Putting the above into the context of the Hess flight. Were Hess really to be aiming at Dungavel it would seem to me that navigation of the detailed type would have to be undertaken. If, however, the actual target was on the east coast of Scotland, not the west, then visual recognition could play a much larger part. This seems to be the case by reference to the map currently at Lennoxlove. The map at Lennoxlove is an enigma as far as I am concerned. The accompanying letter that forwards the map to the Duke of Hamilton on 22nd May 1941(!) makes note of the fact that the intelligence department have seen it.[4] Quite why this comment was necessary I do not know, but I cannot help but have visions of Intelligence boffins with rulers, rubbers and coloured pencils poised over it in Air Intelligence HQ. As such I am not sure it is worth the paper it is printed on as far as our quest for the truth is concerned.

Why did Air Intelligence see fit to release this document only 12 days after the flight? Some relevant documents are still under wraps 67 years later. Consequently, is this map relevant? In any event, what it does **NOT** do is present Dungavel as a target. Dungavel itself is not even marked on the map itself, (though the overlying glass has been marked in red biro later). Instead we have a map of the central lowlands that has been meticulously marked with the physical landmarks that 'SRM' refers to in the *'Teach yourself Air Navigation'* book. Consequently, railways, woods and lakes have all been marked in a fashion of which 'SRM' would no doubt be proud. No target is obviously marked and strangely no intended flight plan has been marked. The actual flight plan appears to have followed the map somewhat to the south of the landmarks mapped and marked out.

I conclude therefore that wherever Hess was intended he failed to reach. I also suspect that for a large part of the time over Scotland Hess was actually lost by reference to his map. I suspect that he went west simply to reach the sea and hope to regain his bearings before he ran out of fuel? He could of course follow a compass bearing and he may well have done so. What he did not do was follow any intended plan intimated by his map. He was actually flying some 10-20 miles south of the flight line suggested by the Lennoxlove map, whatever that may infer, if anything. Without wishing to bore, the map at Lennoxlove is extremely odd. Firstly it is not a single map at all. It appears to be parts of three maps stuck together and mounted. There is nothing sinister in this as such, but in a cramped Bf110 cockpit I can't really envisage Hess trying to jump from one map to another, making the necessary neat folds, in the dark, whilst travelling at 200mph+! The maps are certainly not military in nature. They appear to me to be the type of map that someone setting out on a touring holiday by road might buy. By studying the creases and the grime marks,[5] they appear at one time to have been folded to a smaller size, which concentrates on the corridor across lowland Scotland from the east cost at Bamburgh (in England) across to Ayr on the west coast.

I therefore conclude that the maps at Lennoxlove were probably no more than an indicative route plan, probably marked up in Hess's Munich Harlaching home. It may also be pertinent to record that the majority of the features marked appear on the eastern side of the 'map'. That is not necessarily significant for the simple reason that most of the features; railways, roads etc *are* on the eastern side of the country. Once the terrain changes from lowland to upland there are obviously less distinct features to observe.

So, we have a map of lowland Scotland that may or may not have been altered by Air Intelligence.

Roy Conyers Nesbit makes a useful analysis of the map in his 1999 book, but even he fails to spot (or at least mention) the row of small blue triangles that someone has marked on the map running from the Solway Firth to Bamburgh in a straight line. The marks are the same as those for trigonometric points,[6] which according to Captain Wheatley are the same in use on both English and German maps.[7] These are not easy to spot and we wondered if they might be the mark of radio beams.

There is also a second, possibly more pertinent, map. An early Wilbourn-Harris holiday had seen the families' holiday in North Yorkshire, which gave the male members of the entourage the excuse to have a day out in Durham and visit the somewhat unusual tourist haunt of the County Hall. It appears that Durham Post Office, Providence Row, Durham was the head of the regional Royal Observer Corps and presumably when the organisation was disbanded in 1995 the 'Hess Map' was deposited at the local County Hall.[8]

In some ways this map should be more reliable than the Lennoxlove map. The tracking of the Hess plane by the ROC first came to light in 1976.[9] At that time there perhaps were not the political pressures at play as there had been in wartime Britain, 35 years earlier.

I think that *'Hess: The British Conspiracy'* was the first 'Hess' book to mention it. I only discovered its existence by trawling through the National Register of Archives in Chancery Lane, London whilst on a business trip.[10]

I recall that Richard and I felt rather like Howard Carter when we held the map for the first time. Two points came to our minds; firstly the Hess plane was marked and the well-established flight route was also clearly delineated.

However, there was another plane(s) marked that have never really drawn any attention from the Hess authors. There has always been a degree of confusion concerning the precise tracking of the plane coming in from the sea. Some authors have suggested that more than one plane was involved[11] and that the original raid 42 split into 2, Raid 42 and Raid 42J. This seems to be marked on the map. The real mystery as far as I am concerned is not the so-called Raid 42J (which subsequently seems to have disappeared heading out to sea) but the other plot that is clearly marked on the map. That is the plot that seems to be marked GU and appears to track a plane(s) travelling along the coast from North of Holy Island to below Warkworth on the Northumbrian coast.

I now wonder if this plane actually provides the reason for Hess not 'ending up' where he should have done.

I should state at this point that I have never doubted that the RAF acted exactly as they would normally have done with any other German aircraft. The Hess 'affair' was only privy to an extremely small number of people. So, I have no doubt that Maurice Pocock would have shot the plane down given the chance.[12] Similarly I am quite sure that Flying Officer Cuddie would have shot the Bf110 down had his Defiant been given the chance (and was up to the job).[13]

So, perhaps the plane GU actually made Hess change his flight plan? Clearly we know where he crossed the coast that was well recorded. The Lennoxlove map was not adhered to, (the flight seems to be to the south of the landmarks marked) and we know where Hess crashed. Hess was not shot down by plane GU, we know that too, but perhaps it made Hess veer off course.

And here is the rub. We know that Hess did veer off a straight course. Dramatically.

For those persisting with Dungavel as the true venue may struggle to explain why precisely Hess felt the need to change course, apparently almost due south, so as to almost aim at the Cheviot, the largest hill in the area. Perhaps coincidentally, Dungavel House is on virtually the same line of latitude as Bamburgh and the Farne Islands.[14]

In other words Hess could have reached Dungavel by flying down a compass bearing, after allowing for the compass deviation etc described earlier in the chapter, subject to the problems described in *'Teach yourself Air Navigation'*. For those who think that he was using radio direction techniques, Kalundborg, the Danish station is also on the virtually the same latitude.[15]

But we know he did not fly in a straight line. For some reason he flew virtually southwardly and then changed to a westerly heading. Why?

There were other planes in the sky that night, which again have not had much attention, paid to them. The Polish 317 squadron was based at RAF Ouston and its ORB[16] records,

1941-05-10
Weather: Mild and, cloudy
21.50. 'A' Flight. Three aircraft practice dusk flying. 23.00. One aircraft practices night flying 'B' Flight. R/T used in interception practice[17]

Were these the planes that the ROC plotted as GU?

We shall perhaps never know, but we do know that Hess dramatically changed from his original plan, if the Lennoxlove map has any credibility whatsoever. Did Hess have to avoid the plane(s) GU and in doing so lose his bearings and never regain them?

Roy Conyers Nesbit is quiet on the subject, despite quoting the ORB of Ouston in his bibliography.[18] He seeks to explain the dramatic change of direction as an attempt to avoid anti aircraft fire.[19]

I have researched the location of the World War Two anti aircraft batteries and as far as I can see, there were none in the Bamburgh area. That being the case, why did Hess change course?

Whilst at Nuremberg Hess demonstrated that he was quite capable of lying and deception. As part of his evidence he actually admitted to feigning amnesia [20] and so if he was able to lie in 1946 I suspect he was quite able to lie in 1941. The other authors have slavishly quoted the 1941 Hess letter[21] to his son as gospel, without actually questioning its veracity.

And this is the problem. Whilst much of the Hess affair is still shrouded in mystery, we have been allowed to share the Hess letter to his son (May 1941), the Lennoxlove Map (May 1941) and in 1947 JR Rees in *'The Case of Rudolf Hess'* provides first sight of a flight plan which Hess has actually helpfully annotated by giving precise timings at points of direction change.

Whilst *'Double Standards'* makes the point that the map was actually drawn in 1942, yet again we are privy to the map that illustrates **where Hess went,** with the inference as being **where he was intending to go.**

Therefore I would contend that we actually have no proof or first person evidence that Hess was actually targeting Dungavel House. His planning map does not mark Dungavel, he made no mention of the flight at Nuremberg and the post 1941 maps actually track where he went, rather than where he was intending to go.

I would now like to consider the light conditions.

On 4th May 1941 Britain had adopted Double Summer time as a result of high casualty levels from road traffic accidents arising from poorly lit vehicles. Consequently UK time was GMT+2 hours.

Germany was already GMT+1 hour[22] by reason of longitude and in the summer a further hour was added.[23] Hence on 10th May 1941 German time was the same as UK time. So, when Hess crashed at 23.09 hours in Scotland, it was 23.09 in Germany too.

On 10th May 1941 the sun rose at 0406hrs and set over Bamburgh at 2001 hrs. (GMT). Therefore in local time the sunset at 10.01pm at Bamburgh and 10.14pm at Glasgow, the 13-minute difference again being due to longitude.[24] Hess crossed the coast into Northumberland at 10.23pm. The sun had set 22 minutes previously. There was however a virtual full moon.[25] A 'bombers moon', as central London would discover later that evening.

This all seems very odd to me. By setting off from at Augsburg at 5.45pm it became almost inevitable that Hess would be landing in the dark. That is just a function of time and speed. Indeed, if one believes the 1942/47 Rees map, it appears to be the case that Hess was actually deliberately waiting off the Northumbrian coast for the light to fade. This is fine if the target is close to the coast, but to wait for nightfall before embarking on a cross-country flight over difficult enemy territory is not just mad, it is stupid.

Reverting back to *'Teach yourself Air Navigation'*, it just makes the whole navigational task that much more difficult. Railway tracks and rivers can apparently be seen, particularly in moonlight, but why make it that much more difficult?

If one wished to appear conspiratorial (and I do), a landing in the east of Scotland around 10.30pm would soon be enveloped by the night and its existence hidden at least until the morning. Instead we all know what happened.

Whilst researching the flight I wondered about the lighthouses off the Northumbrian coast. There is a lighthouse at Coquet Island, off Warkworth and a famous lighthouse on the Farne Islands, the Longstone Lighthouse. In September 1838 Grace Darling had helped in the rescue of sailors from the 'Forfarshire' whilst her father served as lighthouse keeper on Longstone.[26] It emits one white light at a 20 second interval[27] It can be seen at a range of 24 Nautical miles.[28] It is situated at 55'36 north. (The alert reader will recall as virtually the same as Dungavel and Kalunborg). The Coquet Island lighthouse (55'20 north) by comparison emits three white and three red flashes every 30 seconds. The white light has a range of 21 Nautical miles, the red light 16. There was also a smaller lighthouse at Bamburgh that has since been decommissioned.

I had been told that during World War Two the lighthouses were switched off and only switched on at the order of the admiralty to aid passing convoys as appropriate. I decided to check this information with Trinity House and found Nigel Jones, the archivist most helpful.[29]

Apparently, whilst the Coquet lights had both been reduced in output, the Farne Island and Longstone lights were maintained at pre war levels. Mr.Jones speculated that the light, being 'out of the way' as far as major towns were concerned were left alone. The logbooks for the lighthouses are usually kept at the relevant location, but these two had coincidentally been recalled to 'HQ'.[30] Therefore, without wishing to state the obvious, from a range of 21 nautical miles Hess could home in on his intended target, safe in the knowledge that he was on the 55'40 latitude. He didn't need the mathematical devices of *'Teach yourself Air Navigation'*, he didn't need radio direction finding equipment, he didn't need maps. A lighthouse was flashing a white light every 20 seconds to guide him in.

After the above research I also reread the early Hess books and was fascinated to learn that James Leasor in 1962 recounted his interview with Karl Pintsch, Hess's adjutant. According to Pintsch, Hess was quite aware of the Farne House lighthouse and the fact that it was not switched off.[31] Pintsch went on to say that once Hess reached the west coast he would look for Troon lighthouse so as to give him another bearing.

I find the second lighthouse a little difficult to believe as this would put Hess directly over RAF Prestwick with the dangers that would bring…. or would it?

---

[1] *The Luftwaffe took aerial photographs in just the same way as the RAF. At the Museum of Flight East Fortune, there is a display of such photographs taken by the Luftwaffe operating from Norway.*
[2] *D.M.Butt - 18th August 1941*
[3] *English University Press - February 1942.*
[4] *Letter to Duke of Hamilton, 22nd May 1941. On display at Lennoxlove House, Haddington.*
[5] *Visit to Lennoxlove House, May 2008. Much subsequent simulation of maps over red wine later that day.*
[6] *Captain.W.Stanley Lewis - Military Map reading - Wheaton and Company - 1942.*
[7] *Ibid - Page 13.*

[8] *Durham was the HQ of the ROC, 30 groups that encompassed Embleton, the first observer base to record the Bf110. It is held at the County Hall, reference D/X1064/1. It is described as 'The actual recording (raid 42) made at the time of the flight at the Durham Operations Room of the Royal Observer Corps'.*

[9] *Derek Wood – Attack Warning Red - Carmichael and Sweet Limited - 1976*

[10] *Quality House, Quality Court, Chancery Lane, London.WC2.*

[11] *This spawning the theory that Heydrich had accompanied Hess.*

[12] *Pocock was scrambled from RAF Acklington at 10.20pm, too late to intercept the Hess plane.*

[13] *Cuddie was scrambled from RAF Ayr at 10.35pm.*

[14] *55' 36''*

[15] *55' 40''*

[16] *Operations Record Book.*

[17] *http//orb.polishaf.pl/317sqn/1941.*

[18] *Air 27/1706 and Air 28/624.*

[19] *Roy Conyers Nesbitt - Hess: Myths and Reality - Sutton*

[20] *30th November 1946 - "I also simulated loss of memory...."*

[21] *FO 1093/1*

[22] *Mitteleuropaische Zeit.*

[23] *Mitteleuropaische Sommerzeit.*

[24] *http//www.aa.usno.navy.mil.*

[25] *Ibid.*

[26] *http//www.britainunlimited.com.*

[27] *Http//www.TrinityHouse.co.uk.*

[28] *Ibid.*

[29] *Telephone conversation June 2008.*

[30] *Trinity House, Tower Hill, London.*

[31] *James Leasor - Hess: The Uninvited Envoy - 1962*

7

THE 'ATLANTIC AIR BRIDGE' AND ITS SIGNIFICANCE IN THE HESS CASE

'Flying to bring us aid, you went

Your oceanic ways until

There hung in the wild firmament

A bridge of air stronger than steel.

Sky Captains, may your flying span

Shine over the far-furrowed seas -

A rainbow of good hope to man,

A storm-born thoroughfare of peace.'

Atlantic Airbridge - HMSO - 1945

I have been slow witted in realising the significance of the Sikorski Atlantic Air crossing of May 1941. Dim almost.

Back in 2001 I learned that General Sikorski had returned from his North American visit by flying into

Prestwick Airfield on the morning of 11th May 1941, the morning after Rudolf Hess had crashed at Eaglesham, 15 miles away[1]. I speculated at the time that perhaps Sikorski was flying in to attend a 'summit' perhaps? I left the matter at that stated the fact in the paperback version of *Hess: The British Conspiracy* and I think it fair to say that all subsequent authors have relied upon and quoted the same fact.

My subsequent research, I believe, now make that possibility virtually a certainty or at least it was designed to create the illusion of just such a summit.

My dim wittedness was based on my quite incorrect preconception that cross Atlantic flights were the norm and that VIP's were jumping in planes all the time and flying off to wherever they chose. (Rather like today). This was based on my schoolboy knowledge of Alcock and Brown's first flight in 1919, Charles Lindbergh's (and subsequently James Stewart's) Spirit of St Louis in 1927 and I suppose, extrapolating from the well publicised Neville Chamberlain's 1938 flight to Germany that VIP air flight was indeed the 'norm'.[2] Nothing could actually be further from the truth. I will now quote verbatim from *'Air Bridge - The Official account of RAF Transport Command's Ocean Ferry'* published in 1945 at the price of nine pence.

"In November, in that dark fall of the year 1940 when the lights of Europe were still guttering out and Britain shook under Luftwaffe bombs, a Canadian military band broke the silences of night in Newfoundland. In the remoteness of that Christmas tree country, already locked in winter and night, the muffled figures of the bandsmen might have seemed a fairy tale incongruity. Their musical honours, however, were historically just and appropriate to time and place, for they were playing on one of the most spectacular acts of flying man in this war. As they started to play *'There'll always be an England'* their music was partially drowned by the motors of the first Hudson bomber to be ferried across the Atlantic. A few moments later six more Hudsons had added their voices and the music was drowned. The following morning the planes landed in Britain. Not at Prestwick, Scotland, but at Aldergrove in Northern Ireland. 11th November 1940."

The simple fact was that there was only the most rudimentary service, between the new world and the old prior to the Second World War. Pan American Airlines had started a regular service between New York and Marseille on 28th June 1939 and New York to Southampton, England on 8th July 1939.[3] Pan Am used the massive (and only recently introduced) Boeing B-314 'Clipper', which could carry up to 74 passengers at a time. Prior to that Zeppelins had made their somewhat stately progress across the Atlantic in the 1920's and 1930's. The commencement of a regular, land based, aircraft service had been oft thought about, but as the weathermen had conceded,

"We were thinking in terms of two or three summers and then a winter of experimental flying before the full development of regular trans-Atlantic traffic by air, when the war broke out".[4]

There had also been the other, far from subsidiary, issues of weather, politics (the provision of landing strips) and technology. Each had to be conquered or dealt with before a safe, reliable service could be contemplated. Moreover, it was only the most recent aircraft that had sufficient range to even contemplate making such a journey. The Ju 52 German transport plane, (1932-1945) had a range of only 540 miles and it was only the 'cutting edge' aircraft, such as the FW 200 Condor (1860 miles), the Boeing 307 Stratoliner (1750 miles) that could actually even geographically contemplate such a trip. So, consequently, as far as I can make out, the six Hudsons (1960 miles range) cited above in November 1940 were the first west - east crossing of war materiel by air: they had flown from their Californian factory to Winnipeg (Canada) then to Gander (Newfoundland) and finally to Aldergrove (Northern Ireland). The aircrews duly sailed back to America. The lend lease agreement was still some 4 months away.

Massive new communities were subsequently built in the remote, Canadian, locations of Gander and Goose, so as to allow the different aircraft ranges to be accommodated.[5]

On 29th November 1940 a further seven Hudsons took off from Gander, with an outside temperature of 16 degrees Fahrenheit. Six landed at Aldergrove and the official history states that the seventh landed 'in England the next day'. This seventh plane is a bit of a mystery in that it didn't land in England at all. It landed at Prestwick! We know this because 'Prestwick's Pioneer' relates how 'a Hudson aircraft, having lost its way en-route to Aldergrove in Northern Ireland, made an accidental but fortuitous landing at Prestwick aerodrome in November 1940.'[6]

We can be even more precise. On 29th November each year from 1942 to 1951, Scottish Aviation held a commemorative dinner to celebrate the event, as according to Dougal McIntyre, *'the virtues of Prestwick aerodrome for this operation became evident and it was quickly designated the principle terminal for all military aircraft flying from North America'*.

Whether the incorrect location of the 29th November flight was mere propaganda, The HMSO account makes no mention of the plane getting lost or an attempt to hide the fact that Prestwick was already perfectly capable of handling large aircraft such as a Hudson, we shall never know.[7] However, on 22nd December a further seven Hudsons took off from the factory, but only four of the planes landed in Britain on 29th December. In January 1941 a solitary Catalina flew into Milford Haven via Bermuda.

These were very much the formative days. As a result of the failure of 3 out of the 7, 22nd December flight to make the journey the concept of 'flights' were dropped in favour of individual aircraft movements. It would also appear that during January 1941, the eventual destination was changed from Aldergrove to Prestwick. The change has been attributed to good weather conditions (Prestwick is famously fog free) and secondly on account of Luftwaffe attention being given to the 'northern English' transit airfield following landings at Aldergrove.

In March 1941, one Liberator and five Hudsons were sent to Prestwick.[8] Interestingly, the runway at this time was still a grass strip.[9]

At that time, VIP air transport was very much 'short haul', as indeed was all air transport. Edward VIII had established the King's Flight in 1936, but this consisted of much smaller planes such as De Havilland Dragon Rapides. (Range 573 miles). So the Sikorski flight is worthy of further consideration.

General Sikorski, leader of the Polish Government in exile had fled Poland for France in 1939 and had set up government in Angers. Following the May 1940 invasion he had decamped to London, (The Rubens Hotel in London became his base) and Scotland, where the majority of his fellow countrymen were based.

In the early days of the war the Poles were certainly in demand. They were the physical incarnation both of resistance to Germany and one of the few allies of Great Britain. Sikorski was also mindful of the bigger picture and was nurturing various ideas as to how Poland might be reincarnated after the war. His main aim for the trip, however, was to recruit exiled Poles and raise money. Churchill had not wished him to go, fearing that he might meddle in European politics.[10]

Anyway, despite the misgivings, Sikorski travelled to Canada, not by air, but instead by the tried and trusted British destroyer. This time HMS Revenge (launched in 1915) was used.

The Sikorski Canadian/American trip was considered a success. Sumner Welles, the Undersecretary of State, recorded, *"Sikorski I found, was one of the most stalwart and attractive statesmen of the war years".*[11]

After the diplomacy was concluded[12], the fundraising began and April 1941 was spent travelling around the States, convening meetings in New York, Atlanta, New Orleans, Fort Worth and Palm Beach.

Towards the end of the trip various anxieties were surfacing as to the need to get back to Europe and this is the bit I don't understand. Victor Cazalet, the British liaison officer states, *"7th May 1941 – General S. not gone yet. He is getting very irritable, poor man"*[13]

Wladyslaw Sikorski was in many ways, at that moment, the most important ally of the British. In many ways he symbolised Poland and the Polish resistance and I find it most odd that the decision was taken to fly back to Prestwick, Scotland. I cite the following reasons:

1) As I hope I have demonstrated the military transatlantic service was very much in its formative stages. I suspect that no more than 40 aircraft it total had attempted the crossing at that stage and certainly not all had arrived safely. Was the decision sensible given the risks? As it turned out it must quite easily have been the longest VIP flight in history at that time.[14]

2) The Liberator aircraft used was amongst the first 30 of over 18,000 produced. It was unproven and proving difficult to fly, partly on account of its new 'Davis wing'. Sadly Sikorski met his end in a Liberator crash two years later.

3) Why Prestwick? Obviously it was the nearest to the Scottish Polish units, but Prestwick had only started to receive planes in February 1941. There was no blind landing system until late 1941.[15] Other bases, such as Lyneham and Aldergrove were, at that time, better equipped.

4) Prestwick was a grass strip with the attendant problems in a wet spring. The obvious attractions of Aldergrove were the 2 concrete runways. Ayr also had concrete runways.

5) Why did Sikorski travel out by ship? Simply because there was no air return system in operation at that time. There was really no other option. Why not return on the same basis? Relatively low risk, slower admittedly, but we are dealing with a very VIP.

One is tempted to surmise that the reason Sikorski took the decision to fly was that he *had* to be back by 10th May/11th May? Would a possible restoration of Poland justify such a risk? Was his choice of Prestwick significant?

---

[1] *Via the services of the Sikorski Institute, London.*
[2] *The historic flight was actually only Chamberlain's second ever flight. David Faber - Munich - Pocket Books - 2008.*
[3] *www.Century of Flight.net. Passengers paid $375 for a one-way trip.*

---

[4] *Atlantic Bridge - HMSO - 1945*

[5] *$4,000,000 was spent on Gander between 1938 and 1940.*

[6] *Page 94 - Prestwick's Pioneer - Dougal McIntyre - Woodfield Publishing - 2004*

[7] *The Lockheed Hudson was a twin-engined bomber, with a maximum take off weight of 18500 lbs.*

[8] *722 aircraft in total were sent in 1941. HMSO - 1945.*

[9] *The 2200-yard tarmac strip was brought into use in September 1941 on account of the grass becoming a 'quagmire' when it rained.*

[10] *"It is a great help to me to know that you, as leader of the largest allied force in this country...are available to give help and guidance at a time when we may at any moment be faced with a heavy attack..." PREM 3 358/73*

[11] *Agreement in Principle - LJ Waszak - Peter Klang Publishing - 1996.*

[12] *Sikorski met Roosevelt on 8th April 1941.*

[13] *Victor Cazalet A portrait - Robert Rhodes James - Hamish Hamilton - 1976.*

[14] *Whilst there had been previous VIP Atlantic crossings by air, these were made in stages, none of which approached the 2000+ miles single stretch that was necessary over the North Atlantic. Germany, in the 1930's used the Gambia to Brazil route over the Southern Atlantic.*

[15] *Air 2 /8131 - PRO.*

8

RUDOLF HESS

SO WHERE?

THE ANSWER!

'We'll keep the home fires burning, but put out the ones Hitler starts.'

'Have you got a Stirrup pump?'

J.W.Robertson - Chief Air Raid Warden, Prestwick, 1941.

We (Richard and I) now firmly believe that the Prestwick/Ayr aerodrome is where Hess was intending to land on 10th May 1941. We have looked at, (and eliminated) the various airstrips in Lowland Scotland and Northern England in previous chapters, but Prestwick does appear to have all the necessary characteristics to enable Hess to land; favourable length of airstrip, conditions and above all else, effective control.

I will try to convince you as follows:

Geographically, Prestwick is 20 miles from Dungavel House and 21 miles from Eaglesham. It is on the Ayrshire coast and is located between Troon and Wallacetown. It is 32 miles south west of Glasgow. When travelling at 2-300 mph in a Me Bf110 clearly these distances can be covered in minutes. At 300mph an aircraft will cover a mile in 12 seconds, at 200mph, 18 seconds. Its location is 55'30 north (Remember - important) and 4'37 west.

Today Prestwick is well known as an international airport, the only place that Elvis Presley has put foot on British soil (allegedly) and for its proximity to the famous golfing resorts of Ayrshire. However, seventy-five years ago in 1934, one David McIntyre was simply looking for a site to build an aerodrome.

David McIntyre was born in Glasgow in 1905 from a Clyde shipbuilding family.[1] Like many boys and young men at that time he was drawn to aviation and in 1927 joined the 602 Squadron of the RAF, at that time, based at Renfrew, just south of Glasgow. Importantly in the context of this story, chronologically, the next pilot to join the squadron was Douglas Douglas-Hamilton, the then Marquis of Clydesdale.[2] The two men were to become life long friends. As McIntyre's son Dougal writes, *'They were men from widely differing backgrounds[3] whose mutual love of flying brought them together at a formative time both for aviation and the Auxiliary Squadron movement.'*[4]

They both reciprocated to be best men at each other's wedding.[5]

The period from 1927 to 1933 appears to have seen the two men having a lot of fun flying various types of planes, from Gypsy Moths to Hawker Harts.[6] A flight to Australia was even mooted. However, in 1933 the two men took part in the Houston Mount Everest Flight,[7] becoming two of the first men to fly over the world's tallest mountain. The impact of this achievement should not be understated, combining aviation, very much the zeitgeist of the age, with the allure and imagery of the world's tallest mountain. On their return they were feted throughout the length and breath of Britain, wrote a book together,[8] and their consequent fame made many demands on their time. McIntyre was also working on plans for a round the world flight.[9]

On a wider stage *The Conference for the Reduction and Limitation of Armaments of 1932-34* was an effort by member states of the League of Nations to prevent a post 1919 escalation of armaments. It essentially failed when Hitler withdrew Germany from both the conference and the League of Nations in October 1933.

The above failure is the reason that Dougal McIntyre cites for his father's decision to try and make money from what he saw as the national need to rearm. He anticipated trouble ahead and consequently came up with the idea of a pilots' training school. Somewhere where the RAF could send their pilots. Hence the need to acquire an aerodrome.

David McIntyre approached his friend, the then Marquis of Clydesdale and his brother 'Geordie' Douglas Hamilton. Apparently on account of a previous Duke of Hamilton having over mortgaged the estate the remaining equity had been placed into a Trust. So it was that the Trustees of the Hamilton Estates became the owner and landlord of the 348 acres located adjacent to Orangefield House, Prestwick, Ayrshire.

A Limited Liability Company was duly incorporated on 9th August 1935 called *'The Scottish College of Aviation Limited'*.[10] Subsequently it changed its name to *'Scottish Aviation Limited'*, once the ownership of the original name had been acquired.[11]

The original share capital of the Company was:

Marquis of Clydesdale	43,545
Geordie Douglas Hamilton	30,045
David McIntyre	25,910
Company lawyer	500[12]

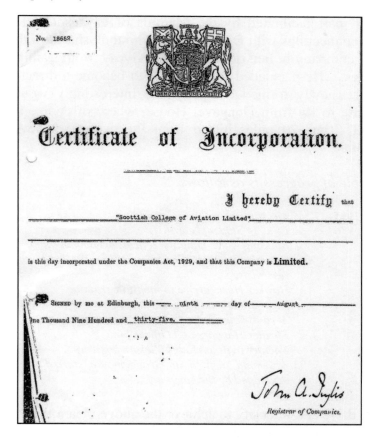

No. 18652.

Certificate of Incorporation.

I hereby Certify that

"Scottish College of Aviation Limited"

is this day incorporated under the Companies Act, 1929, and that this Company is **Limited**.

SIGNED by me at Edinburgh, this ninth day of August One Thousand Nine Hundred and thirty-five.

John A. Inglis

Registrar of Companies.

On account of the Marquis of Clydesdale being a serving MP, his brother Geordie assumed control of the shares, as well as being a director of the Company. Clydesdale, quite properly, was not allowed to be a serving director of a Company whilst engaged in Government contracts. The private nature of the shareholdings was to cause various issues to arise when the airfield was expanded using government funding during the course of the Second World War.

Nevertheless, the period from 1936-1939 was one of rapid expansion for what was formerly the 348 acres of Scottish pastureland. The expansion was by no means in small part facilitated by the Marquis of Clydesdale. He had connections with De Havilland who took shares in the new company in lieu of payment for Gypsy Moth training planes.[13] He persuaded R.L.Angus[14] to become a director of the newly formed company and interestingly would choose to fly from Dungavel House, where of course he lived, (just 20 miles inland from Prestwick) whenever possible.[15]

A table of progress is as follows:

Dec 1935	*Aircraft arrive.*
Feb 1936	*First 34 Students enrol.*
1936	*Building work, hangars, offices, accommodation.*
1937	*School expands to take on training of RAF volunteer reservists.*
	Hawker Harts arrive to facilitate training.
1938	*Navigation training commences*
	Avro Ansons arrive to facilitate training.
	Further Hangars and Offices built.
1939	*Factory built to modify Vickers bombers.*
	A second airfield at Grangemouth started to be developed by the company.

The drive and intensity to achieve the above meant that by 1939 neither Clydesdale nor McIntyre were in command of the 602 Squadron. They simply did not have the time. David McIntyre was appointed CEO of *Scottish Aviation Limited.* Effectively he was in day to day control of Prestwick Airfield. The Marquis was also by this time a serving MP.

I think it incorrect to underestimate the Marquis of Clydesdale's standing in the pre-war aeronautical circles.

He was internationally famous due to his Everest flight, he was a serving RAF officer, he had privately owned a number of aircraft, owned his landing strip and now his family had gained control of what was to become the foremost aviation company in Scotland. Similarly, David McIntyre, whilst never as famous as the Hamiltons, was also a very impressive figure. RAF officer, Everest flight member and now CEO of a fast expanding aviation company.

When Clydesdale and McIntyre took part in the Everest attempt in 1933 they chose to fly the planes to Nepal and back again. The Pilots book of Everest gives the details. Consequently, throughout the later thirties they both flew their relatively small and unrefined De Havillands all around Europe in much the same way as we might today use Ryanair or some other budget airline.

Trips to Switzerland, Austria, Germany[16] and France are well documented and some authors have speculated that Clydesdale (and McIntyre?) were being used as semi-official intelligence agents. Moreover, Clydesdale was not the only member of the family being used in this way; Geordie Douglas- Hamilton was to become the Chief of Air Intelligence - Fighter Command and his brother David, also a serving RAF officer, was fluent in German. Dougal McIntyre's book on his father also shows pictures of his father in various European locations throughout the 1930's and really we should not be surprised by this at all, given both men's standing at that time and what seems to me to be almost an international 'air order' based on a mutual fascination of all things aeronautical. It was also potentially lucrative from a business perspective.

Geordie Douglas Hamilton resided at Eldo House, adjacent to the Orangefield House, a lovely mansion dating back to 1723[17] which somewhat bizarrely had become the control tower of the airfield by the simple expedient of taking off its ancient roof and replacing it with the traditional aerodrome glass canopy.

When World War Two came the usefulness of the airfield became immediately apparent and the Spitfires of 603 Squadron moved in December 1939.[18] Thereafter squadrons 600, 615, 610, 253, 141 and No1 RCAF all occupied the base before 602 Squadron (The old City of Glasgow to which both Clydesdale and McIntyre belonged) vacated on 15th April 1941. The 602 Squadron literally moved to RAF Ayr at the other end of the airfield!

As has already been alluded to the base was then transferred to the Atlantic Ferry Organisation (ATFERO),[19] in early 1941.

Therefore it appears to me that on 10th May 1941, a Saturday evening, Prestwick airfield had no serving RAF Squadron. I also doubt the training school would be at its busiest at that time of the week, its students more likely to be studying women and wine in local hostelries than aerial navigation.[20] Indeed, an indication of the level of activity may be taken by the fact that on 11th December 1940 a Court Martial was held to deal with Messrs. Aircraftsmen Thomas and Nathan who were charged with 'sleeping on post whilst on active service'. The ORB goes on to record the fact that on 10th and 11th May the airfield merely dealt with its 'normal routine'.[21]

We know that Sikorski touched down on the following morning and that a further contingent of planes came in on 15th May, but the airbase, which I hope I have demonstrated was expanding rapidly, was as near as possible empty. It had been busy upto the departure of the last RAF Squadron in April 1941[22] and was to become incredibly busy from mid 1941 onwards, but 10th May

1941 would have seen it at an uniquely quiet state. Was this to enable another visitor to arrive?

I also find it odd, to say the least, that James Douglas-Hamilton makes absolutely no mention of his father's, uncle's, family's and trustee's role in the formative years of Prestwick airfield. Absolutely none whatsoever. Why might that be? His book is quite understandably full of the many other aeronautical achievements of his family. I should also record that for whatever reason he has also sought to distance himself from this book.

There has also been some confusion over the years (at least in my mind) as to the relationship with RAF Ayr. We know from the 'Hess archive' that on 10th May 1941 a Defiant was sent up at 10.35pm to intercept the Bf110, piloted by Pilot Officer Cuddie and crewed by a Sergeant Hodge.[23]

In May 1941 RAF Ayr hosted 141 Squadron, which boasted the Defiant 1 night fighter and 602 Squadron, armed with Spitfires. The Base Commander was Squadron leader Loel Guinness, who commanded the airfield from nearby Rosemount House, a large house that overlooked the airfield. Rosemount House also 'doubled up' as the command base for Prestwick aerodrome.[24]

Somewhat confusingly perhaps, RAF Ayr and Prestwick were literally adjacent to each other, RAF Ayr locally being known as Heathfield. After the war part of RAF Ayr was built upon (the district of Monkton), whilst another part was taken over by the RNAS (Royal Naval Air Service) and became HMS Wagtail.

However, on 10th May there was actually no distinction in terms of command structure, both being controlled from a single command and commander. The single commander took his instruction directly from 13 Group, which in practice meant RAF Turnhouse.

Of further significance perhaps, RAF Ayr had only become operational on 7th April 1941 with three long concrete runways, 4100ft, 4500ft and 4700ft. Being adjacent to Prestwick, which as we have seen had only just started to receive the larger types of American bomber, a combined circuit was arranged for landing traffic. Therefore the two airfields in name were essentially one operationally, next door to each other, with a joint commander, who, in turn took his instructions from RAF Turnhouse. In terms of personnel, the senior operational staff were all well known to each other and when discussing its composition, Richard and I likened it more to an 'Old Boy's Club' rather than a 'front line' airbase.

In fairness, this perception may well be due to the fact that the expansion of the Royal Air Force was only made possible by drawing on pre-war auxiliary squadrons, but I will list the members for you to decide:

Sector Commander: *Wing Commander Loel Guinness. Friendly with the Duke of Kent and Duke of Hamilton. Came to Ayr via 601 County of London Squadron.*
Chief Executive Officer: David McIntyre. Known to all.
Senior Controller: *Sir Archibald Hope. (Ex 601 Squadron).*
Controller: *Huseph Riddle. (Ex 601 Squadron).*
Controller: *Hector Maclean. Recruited to 602 Squadron by Marquis of Clydesdale. Taught to fly by David McIntyre. Maclean's father taught JO Andrews how to fly during the First World War.*

Convenient perhaps?

So Where? The Answer

---

[1] *Prestwick Pioneer - Dougal McIntyre.*

[2] *2nd May 1927.*

[3] *McIntyre came from a family of Glaswegian shipbuilders.*

[4] *602 City of Glasgow was such a squadron.*

[5] *Clydesdale married in 1937, McIntyre in 1935. Clydesdale lent McIntyre his Leopard Moth to travel on honeymoon.*

[6] *It should be remembered that there are stories of Clydesdale crashing a Hart at Dungavel.*

[7] *Dougal McIntyre cites his father's secondment to RAF No 12 squadron in 1932 the means by which his reputation as an exceptional pilot was assured.*

[8] *The Pilot's Book of Everest.*

[9] *This failed to materialise through lack of funding.*

[10] *Company House number: 18652.*

[11] *There had been 2 pre 1920 Companies called Scottish Aviation Limited.*

[12] *Prestwick in the 40's - Kyle and Carrick District Leisure Services - Ayr 1992*

[13] *WE Nixon of De Havilland was appointed Chairman of the Company.*

[14] *Director of William Baird Limited. A mining company. He also lived in Prestwick.*

[15] *Dougal McIntyre mentions monthly flights from June to November 1935.*

[16] *Clydesdale and his brother flew to Berlin in 1933.*

[17] *RCAHMS website.*

[18] *RAF Fighter Airfields of World War 2 - Jonathan Falconer - Ian Allan Ltd 1993.*

[19] *ATFERO became Ferry Command in July 1941.*

[20] *Air 28/653 - On 9th May 1941 a decision was taken to billet the personnel of NO.3 Radio School Training Squadron in Prestwick Town. Only senior NCO's moved into 'hutments' on the aerodrome.*

[21] *Air 28/653.*

[22] *Air 28/653 - 600 squadron moved to Box on 25th April 1941.*

[23] *Air 28 / 40. I do not think that this is contentious and most authors rely upon the statement. The ability and intention of the plane I will discuss later. William Cuddie was unfortunately killed in 1943 whilst serving with 46 Squadron. (See Commonwealth War Graves Commission).*

[24] *Interview Dougal McIntyre. 3.5.2009*

9

THE FLIGHT OF RUDOLF HESS

THE BRITISH PERSPECTIVE

I am now firmly convinced that Hess was not knowingly assisted in anyway to travel through British airspace in his attempt to allow him to land at Prestwick/Ayr. This is for the simple reason that he did not need to be, conspiracy or not. What I am not so sure about is whether the certain individuals who undoubtedly played a part in the lure were actually taking part, hoping for a change in government and negotiated peace rather than being just content to take place in an intelligence sting. Their motives will be debated in later chapters. I do not believe that many people were actually involved. Probably no more than 10 people knew what was going on. I will name them later.

John Costello, way back in 1991[1] made the allegation that the RAF effectively lent a 'blind eye' to the Hess plane and allowed him to travel through British airspace unhindered. John, who I had met prior to his untimely death,[2] was a professional historian who depended on his writing to earn his living. Hence, there was always perhaps the temptation to chase the headline and unfortunately, whilst his conclusion was incorrect, John's research did at least make an attempt to describe the air defence structure that was in place.

Consequently, James Douglas-Hamilton was able to wheel out Roy Conyers Nesbit in his 1993 work[3] that, to a degree, rubbished John's conclusion. Mr Conyers Nesbit quite properly corrected some of the Costello detail, but equally overlooked some important information himself. The main issues revolved around the control of the airspace; so to 'wade in' to the debate, I now give my interpretation.

RAF fighter command was based at Bentley Priory, Stanmore near Harrow. This non-flying station controlled the air defence of Great Britain from 1936, when the former mansion was acquired as the centre of operations for both Fighter Command and The Royal Observer Corps. Hugh 'Stuffy' Dowding had developed the self styled 'Dowding system' in the immediate years before the Second World War, which comprised 4 parts:

1. Radar observation until the coast
2. ROC observation once over land
3. Plotting
4. Radio Telegraphy to vector fighters onto their target.

The 1941 Hess flight came in under this system and I am quite content that at least sections 1 to 3 were carried out 100% in accordance with Dowding's system, which at that time was the most comprehensive in the world.

Roy Conyers Nesbit covers the radar observation part of the flight very well and indeed has interviewed the WAAF on duty at Bentley Priory on the night of 10th May 1941. It was her job to track the incoming aircraft from the radar reports being received by way of plots and relay or 'tell' them to the operations room via telephone.

Felicity Ashbee,[4] I have no doubt, did her job as instructed and noted the incoming plane from the reported plots. The Chain Home system at that time could stretch out 120 miles or so out into the North Sea and so with the Hess plane travelling at say, 240-280 mph, Felicity would have approximately 20-30 minutes to 'tell' the plane, before it passed into the responsibility of the ROC.

Indeed, in *'Aeroplane Monthly' in 1987*, Felicity writes, *"It appeared 90 miles east of Amble, flying west, is how raid 42 was logged onto the main plot at 22.08 according to the 10th May 1941 Fighter Command Headquarters War Diary."*

It appears to me that the system worked perfectly. Felicity recounted to John Costello[5] that she waited for 10 minutes to 'tell' the operations room because the original report had come from Ottercops Moss Chain Home Station who didn't have a good reliability reputation at that time.[6] Once cross-confirmed by Bamburgh it was 'told' as Raid 42. Therefore during the 10 minutes that Felicity waited for confirmation, the plane would have travelled 40-50 miles. At 22.18 Hess would be 40-50 miles out at sea, travelling at 4-5 miles a minute.

Bentley Priory must have then decided to act for at 22.20 hours (a mere 2 minutes later) Maurice Pocock was scrambled from RAF Acklington in a Spitfire of 72 Squadron. I also have no doubt that Mr.Pocock would have shot down the Bf110, if able. The scrambling of the plane seems wholly consistent with the Dowding system as far as I can see. Pocock was in the air as were the RAF Ouston planes of 317 Squadron. There were now 4 planes in the sky capable of attacking the Bf110. The Dowding system was working effectively - so far.

I am afraid that I now am doubtful that Part 4 was carried out as efficiently as the preceding three parts. If one chooses to believe John Costello who interviewed

Cecil Bryant DFM, a then 20-year-old Radio Telephone Operator, an order was given **not to attack the plane, or use ack-ack fire against it**.[7] This does directly contradict the 'Pocock evidence'.

Clearly, if no vectoring instructions were given, the planes in the air would be searching for a needle in a haystack, moreover in the near dark.

If one chooses to disregard the Costello evidence as the mere wishful thinking of a conspiracy theorist, then, at the other extreme, the laws of probability prevail. Roy Conyers Nesbit quotes the statistic that in May 1941, '3,280 sorties were carried out by RAF night fighters, with a success rate of approximately 3%, given that 96 enemy aircraft were destroyed.' Therefore, statistically, Hess stood a 97:3 chance of avoiding being shot down. However, the reality of the situation must surely even widen those odds. With or without vector radio, which in the early days could be indistinct to the point of being nicknamed 'huff/puff'.[8] I would have thought that Bentley Priory had done their job and put Pocock in a position to intercept, or perhaps at least see the Bf110. However, Pocock, according to Conyers Nesbit, climbed to 15,000 feet, which would have taken between 4-5 minutes.[9] So at 10.25pm he was 15,000 feet above the Northumbrian coast. Conyers Nesbit quotes Maurice Pocock as having been vectored on to the flight path and that may well be the case, but he was far, far too high. Hess according to the ROC was at virtual sea level, nearly 3 miles beneath him!

Hess was reported by the ROC at Embleton as having already crossed the coast at 10.23pm. Therefore I suspect that unless Pocock was lucky enough to spot the Bf110 whilst climbing, it was then too late once at his cruising height. Hess was already away to the west, travelling at a similar speed to the Spitfire, trying to find the Cheviot.

There were also the 317 Squadron planes already in the sky. According to Conyers Nesbit these were not instructed to intercept as 'they were not considered capable of operating at night and were not in a good position to make an interception'.[10] This I do find odd.

Conyers Nesbit provides no source for what seems to me to be an important statement. Obvious questions:

- If they were 'not capable of operating at night' what were they doing in the sky at 10.20pm on a Saturday night?
- Why were they not in a good position? If they were indeed the plot on the ROC Durham map they were actually patrolling down the Northumbrian coast!

13 Group, based at Usworth, just outside Newcastle, controlled the North of England and Scotland. The subsidiary sector stations were at Acklington, Turnhouse, Dyce and Wick.

So, all the information collected from the ROC and radar stations went to Usworth in the first instance and then was collated and passed to the various sector stations. In turn, where appropriate, the sector stations would instruct the individual airfields under their command.

Relevant to our story the whole of the Hess flight was covered by just two sector stations; Acklington and Turnhouse. Presumably because of the fact that Ayr had only been operational for less than a month it came under the direct control of Turnhouse (as did RAF Drem). Therefore Douglas Douglas-Hamilton, 14th Duke of Hamilton *was* very much in control of events once Hess had passed into western Scottish airspace.

As for the eastern part of the journey then from February 1941 RAF Acklington had a new boss. His name was John Oliver Andrews and prima facie his appointment perhaps seemed an odd choice.

Air Vice Marshal JO Andrews was the son of a Manchester brewer, born in 1896 and had entered the RFC in 1914 after initially enlisting as an Officer in The Royal Scots, Lothian Regiment. He was decorated as a fighter pilot and at the end of the First World War had received the MC, the MC bar and the DSO. During the 1920's Andrews was obviously being groomed for high office, spending time at Cambridge University and in Germany as a member of the Aeronautical Committee of Guarantee. In the early 1930's Andrews was in charge of Seaplanes and from 1932 to 1934 was in charge at RAF Mount Batten in Plymouth. However, the rest of the decade saw him essentially training for the higher ranks. I list his postings as follows:

- *Dec 1932: Officer Commanding, RAF Mount Batten.*
- *Apr 1934: Staff, Directorate of Operations and Intelligence.*
- ***Nov 1936: Re-qualified as German Interpreter, 1st Class.***
- *Jan 1937: Attended Imperial Defence College.*
- *Dec 1937: Supernumerary, No 1 RAF Depot.*
- *Feb 1938: Senior Air Staff Officer, HQ RAF Far East. Feb/Mar 1940: Director of Armament Development.*
- *Nov 1940: Assistant Chief of the Air Staff (Operational Requirements and Tactics*

It will come as no surprise I am sure that I have emboldened the November 1936 appointment. In January 1941 he was made a Temporary Air Vice Marshal an appointment that was confirmed in April 1942.

I presume the appointment was made prior to his posting to 13 Group in the February of 1941, as it appears that it is traditional that Group Commanders hold the rank of Air Vice Marshal.

What I find a bit odd is that JO Andrews seems to be a bit over qualified? He had a brilliant service record, but seems to me to be rather cerebral. For instance, in 1932 he had won the Royal United Service Institute essay award. The 1930's appointments appear to me to preparing him for high command, not essentially an operational posting?

I just wonder if his appointment was more to do with his proficiency in German and intelligence matters, should an unexpected visitor turn up? By way of comparison I looked at Trafford Leigh Mallory who was placed in charge of 12 Group in 1937. His operational fighting record was much shorter than Andrews' yet he took the more prestigious appointment. Somewhat ironically perhaps, Andrews took over at 12 Group in late 1942, following his 13 Group stint. Richard Wilbourn also discovered that JO Andrews learned to fly under Hector Maclean's father during the First World War. (Maclean was of course at Prestwick on 10th May 1941).

I wholly accept that the above interpretation can be seen as stretching facts to fit circumstances and for this I apologise, were it not for a meeting Richard and I held on 3rd May 2009 with Dougal McIntyre and his wife at their Prestwick home. It could just simply be that Andrews was passed over in favour of the more ambitious Leigh Mallory, Park and Dowding? However, Dougal, it will be remembered is the son of David F McIntyre, the joint founder of Prestwick aerodrome and Scottish Aviation Limited. On the night of 10th May 1941 we know he was at Prestwick aerodrome (more later).

For once in my life I went properly prepared to a meeting with a list of questions, one of which was a list of names of individuals that I wanted to know if his father knew. The name of JO Andrews[11] drew the somewhat odd response of, "I can't add anything other than the name".

I took that to mean that his father did know JO Andrews, which should not come as too much of a surprise given that McIntyre was in charge of an aerodrome in 13 Group airspace. Otherwise a simple yes/no would have sufficed. Presumably they must also have known each other reasonably well if his infant son 68 years later knew that the two men knew each other. However, given some of the other answers that were also given that day and will surface later in the book, I would just ask the reader to 'park' that piece of information for the time being.

Consequently, all I think we can say for certainty in respect of the RAF command in Scotland that evening is that the 13 Group Commander was a German expert, the Duke of Hamilton in the Turnhouse sector had 'some significant linkage' with Germany and that the Base Commander at Prestwick/Ayr was an extremely close friend of the Duke of Hamilton and the King's brother, the Duke of Kent. Many of the senior officers at Prestwick/Ayr were also close personal friends of Hamilton and McIntyre.

For the present I think it best left at that.

Once the plane had avoided trouble on the East Coast, realistically it was unlikely to encounter any further problems, given that it would be flying at dark over a very sparsely populated area, until it reached the West Coast of Scotland. This is exactly what happened.

A Defiant was sent up from Ayr, but unfortunately the pilot did not survive the war, being killed in October 1943. Hence, we do not have his testimony in the same way as we do that of Maurice Pocock. We also do not have a record of what instructions were given to Pilot Cuddie in terms of vectoring.

I do not wish to give the impression that I believe Cuddie was told anything other than to shoot down any planes he encountered, because I do not, and doubt we will ever know for sure. What I suspect is more likely is that the same conditions of the earlier east coast crossing would have prevailed.

When crossing the east coast Hess went low, Pocock went high. When passing over the east coast, the same thing happened. Hess was low, because he was coming into land, Cuddie would have taken off and gone to operational height. In other words it would (in my opinion, given what we know) be unlikely that an aerial interception would be easily achieved.

We should also consider why the 141 Squadron Defiant was scrambled in preference to the much faster Spitfires of the 602 Squadron. I think this answer much easier; the Spitfire had an indifferent record as a night fighter being particularly difficult to take off and land with restricted night time visibility. Moreover its exhaust manifold tended to overheat and would obscure the pilot's sight line over the nose of the plane. Furthermore, 141 Squadron had recorded a recent nighttime success against a Junkers 88 on 6th May 1941 and therefore I can wholly understand the decision to prefer the Boulton Paul Defiant to the Spitfire.

Lastly, I believe we should consider the role and actions of the Royal Observer Corps and the Royal Signals Corps on the night in question.

As we have already seen the Royal Observer Corps was an integral part of the Dowding system. Once enemy aircraft crossed the British coast their progress was marked and recorded by members of the Royal Observers

Corps. These were the thousands of men who literally spent their time on the top of hills (typically) armed with little more than tin hats, theodolites,[12] maps and binoculars.

The first such post that recorded Hess's plane was at Embleton,[13] just to the south of Bamburgh.

Each such post was a member of a Group and each Group had a central HQ. Each central HQ had the means of communication to its neighbouring groups, Fighter Command, RAF Sector Command and the local anti aircraft batteries and searchlights. Typically each centre was responsible for 30-40 listening posts. By 1945 the system had expanded to 40 such centres and more than 1500 observation posts. The country was literally covered by a blanket of these posts.

The relevant command centres on 10th May 1941 were:

30 Group - Durham (covering Northumberland)
31 Group - Galashiels (covering Lowland Scotland)
33 Group - Ayr
34 Group - Glasgow

Therefore, the Hess Bf110 would have been tracked across England and Scotland by the relevant observation posts, the information passed onto the above centres and then disseminated to the RAF and relevant anti aircraft batteries.

Consequently, whilst the Bf110 was being tracked under the Dowding system rules, there were in effect, 2 wholly independent tracking systems operating as part of the whole. Firstly, the relatively new 'Chain Home' radar system and secondly the more established Royal Observer Corps system.

I conclude that whilst Maurice Pocock was scrambled by reason of the 'Chain Home' plot, (as has been described) the Ayr Defiant must have been scrambled by reason of the ROC reporting system. This is simply because the plane was not visually observed (by human eyes) until it crossed the coast. Therefore, so as to allow Pocock the necessary time to take off prior to Hess crossing the coast, he must have been alerted via the Radar system. This I think we already knew.

Conversely, the Ayr Defiant must have been alerted by the ROC system, as once the plane crossed the Northumbrian coast the radar didn't work. The masts faced the sea, not inland.

We know that posts from all four Groups had plotted the plane[14] and indeed it was Major Graham Donald at 34 Group who has been recorded as struggling to persuade the RAF that it was indeed a Bf110. (He was so intrigued that eventually he went and identified Hess for himself as he realised that a Bf110 could not carry enough fuel to return to Germany).

The records for 33 Group (Ayr) are apparently missing, so we will never know the instructions received or given that night.

What is quite feasible and likely is that the Ayr Defiant was scrambled without the prior knowledge or approval of the Duke of Hamilton, located at Turnhouse, 60 miles away. He would not be, or need to be, part of that decision making process, albeit in overall structural terms he was responsible for the actions of RAF Ayr. The ROC command centre at either Glasgow, Ayr or Galashiels would have telephoned the RAF Sector Command (at Usworth) who would then telephone the RAF

Ayr/Prestwick airbase direct, (at Rosemount House) which would then react as appropriate.

At the same time the ROC Command Centre would have telephoned Eaglesham House, (also known as Eaglesham Castle) which at that time housed the Royal Signals Corps. It had been requisitioned by the War Office in 1939. Their responsibility was to inform and co ordinate the local Anti Aircraft Batteries in and around Glasgow. I believe it no more than coincidence that Hess crashed so close to this establishment. He was lost and out of fuel.

Therefore, the reports that Eaglesham House had been tracking the Hess plane across Scotland are inaccurate. It was never the Signals job to do so and neither did it have the means to do so. However, it would have known that a Bf110 was in the area for two reasons; firstly the ROC Command Centre would have reported its movements and secondly, and more pertinently, had any member of its staff simply turned their ear to the sky that evening, they would have heard the droan of the twin Daimler Benz engines as the plane approached and then silence before it crashed at nearby Floors Farm, only a matter of a few hundred yards away.

That is why the Signals men were so quickly on the scene. They knew a plane was in the area. I also wonder if that explains the conspiratorial claims that the guns were told to stand down? The controller at Eaglesham House would have known the plane had come down as it had crashed nearly outside the front door! There was consequently no need to try and shoot it down.

Amazingly, there is still a key witness alive that was party to the 'goings on'. Robert Anderson who lives in Burnside, Glasgow has recently turned 100 years of age. On 10th May 1941 he was stationed at Eaglesham House as part of the Signals Corps and when he heard the plane crash was given a rifle and told to 'Go and Defend your Country'.

He saw Hess descend by parachute and was later offered a cigarette by the Deputy Fuhrer.[15]

So what does all this tell us?

As I have already stated I believe the Hess 'lure' was fermented and carried out by a very small number of personnel. Given the large number of potential participants, there was absolutely no way that the ROC, the Royal Signals Corps, various Airbase crew and the Anti Aircraft Batteries would all be pre-warned that Rudolf Hess was 'flying in tonight.' Imagine the implications if he 'didn't show' or if some well-meaning patriot didn't wish to participate.

Consequently, I believe the sequence of events were those to be expected, conspiracy or not. Clearly the Dowding system was implemented and worked as expected. Pocock was sent up, Cuddie was sent up. Pocock via Radar, Cuddie via ROC.

What we do not know and probably never will, is precisely *what* Cuddie and Pocock were told. Maurice Pocock states that he would have shot the Bf110 down and I have no reason to disbelieve him, but what if he and Cuddie were told to fly in an opposite direction. Who knows? Equally, there is no reason to disbelieve the evidence of the two Czech pilots who were on patrol from RAF Aldergrove when told to turn back and disengage. Who knows what they were told and why?

What I do know is that Hess would have smelt a rat had the whole Northern Aeronautical Defence system be stood down by a Government that had no intention of making peace with Germany. The Duke of Hamilton was certainly NOT (nominally anyway) in charge of the whole of 13 Group.

Moreover, there is absolutely no evidence whatsoever that the Duke of Hamilton influenced events in the slightest that evening. Simply because he did not have to! (However, I do not believe that his version of events later that evening, once Hess had crashed, wholly stand scrutiny).

I am also very conscious that the evening's events that I have just described can be interpreted (and have been interpreted) as completely normal and routine and therefore Hess must have gone mad and flown to the enemy. Whilst I accept 100% that the reporting and interception systems were indeed acting normally, I do not believe this rules out a high level conspiracy at all.

We should also not lose sight of the fact that the British would not have been too concerned had Pocock or Cuddie shot the Bf110 down in flames. Realistically, once Hess had passed the point of no return and he no longer had enough fuel to return to German occupied Europe, the British had triumphed. In many ways a dead Hess would be better than a live Hess! Much easier to deal with as later events proved.

The $64,000 question remains what would have happened if a Bf110 had appeared over Prestwick/Ayr at around 11.00pm on May 10th 1941. (As it very nearly did?) I strongly suspect it would have been allowed to land on the lit, concrete runways, because the 3/4 Officers in charge had been told to expect the unexpected.

Clearly, the lower ranks had also been told something 'was up'. Why did Robert Anderson receive the somewhat melodramatic instructions to 'Go and Defend your

Country'? Had they been told that an invasion attempt was likely so as to explain the presence of German planes in the sky? Who knows?

What we do know is that Hess, in all sorts of trouble aeronautically, put on height and baled out. Baled out of his plane and baled out of World War Two.

---

[1] *Ten Days that saved the West - Bantam Press.*

[2] *John Costello died in 1995 aged 52. He was found dead on a flight to Miami Florida after having eaten shellfish 36 hours earlier. From him we learned the important lesson never to assume evidence - go and see it for yourself.*

[3] *The Truth about Rudolf Hess - James Douglas Hamilton - Mainstream 1993.*

[4] *Felicity died in 2008 aged 96.*

[5] *Ten days that Saved the West - Bantam Press 1991.*

[6] *There is a PRO file, which demonstrates the fact that Ottercops was struggling to ascertain the height of incoming aircraft.*

[7] *Ten Days that Saved the West - Bantam Press 1991. Page 6.*

[8] *Huff Puff on account of its acronym of HF - High Frequency.*

[9] *!941 Boscombe Down reports - see www.spitfireperformance.com*

[10] *The Truth about Rudolf Hess - James Douglas Hamilton - Mainstream 1993 - Page 16.*

[11] *Andrews retired from the RAF in April 1945 and died in 1989. Prior to his death he lived in Cookham, Berkshire.*

[12] *Such as the 'Micklethwaite Post Instrument'.*

[13] *Reference A/3.*

[14] *See 'Attack Warning Red' for a very good description of the night's events.*

[15] *Telephone conversation with Karin Fair, Mr Anderson's daughter, 25th February 2010.*

10

THE FLIGHT FROM RUDOLF HESS'S POINT OF VIEW

'The path to our destination is not always a straight one. We go down the wrong road, we get lost, we turn back. Maybe it doesn't matter which road we embark on. Maybe what matters is that we embark.'

Northern Exposure, Barbara Hall, Rosebud, 1993

The Rudolf Hess flight is easy to understand, once one is able to accept that Prestwick/RAF Ayr was actually the target and not Dungavel House as has been previously taken as a given.

If one also can accept the above assumption then the 'Lennoxlove map' and the 'Durham map' also can be taken at face value. It all begins to make sense.

As the man from air intelligence quite rightly said,[1] *"Markings are not in accordance with current German navigational practice, but with those of the last war. Therefore Hess marked it himself."*

This seems to me to be the key. We have already seen how difficult and theoretical air navigation had become, so I now believe that Hess relied on what he knew from his early days; visual recognition and a simple compass.

We know where he crossed the east coast of England; just to the south of the Farne islands and between the gap in the east coast mainline railway as discussed in the earlier chapter. That, I think, is agreed by all and verified by the ROC. What has always intrigued me is why he then flew almost due south immediately afterwards. Earlier I had speculated it was perhaps to avoid the RAF patrol from RAF Ouston that had been plotted on the Durham map. Now I believe it was nothing more difficult than he had to find the Cheviot. Visually find the Cheviot. At 2700 feet it was a visible landmark on the east coast of England and the success of the rest of his flight depended upon its correct identification.

Why? The Cheviot is located at 55 degrees 28 north. RAF Ayr/Prestwick is 55 degrees 30 north. According to a 'Google Earth' trial, the distance between 55 degrees 28 north and 55 degrees 30 north is just over two miles.

Broadlaw, one of the other landmarks highlighted on the Lennoxlove map is located at 55 degrees 29 north, roughly halfway between the two other landmarks.

So, put crudely, all Hess had to do was to find the Cheviot and then fly due west. He would then cross the coast virtually over Prestwick/RAF Ayr. To give him some reassurance en route he would fly over Broadlaw to make sure all was well. Richard and I compared this to the agricultural practice of ploughing a field whereby the ploughman is constantly taking visual references (trees, telegraph poles, hedging etc) and adjusting accordingly, to make sure that the furrow stays true. As Len Deighton states in David Stafford's book,[2] the use of the German radio guidance beams would be unlikely. Deighton states that they would not work that far away. I agree but think it much simpler; Hess did not need them, or at least he believed that he could do without them. Moreover the use of German beam system equipment, if discovered, would straightway infer Luftwaffe involvement and a degree of Nazi approval and connivance that Hess could not deny if things went wrong. (Which is of course precisely what happened)?

The map of the flight that Hess is supposed to have drawn on 8th August 1941 also shows exactly the above route. Drop down to the Cheviot and then fly west.[3] Simple. Much has also been made of the Radio Kalunborg transmitter and how Hess had been tuning into the station in the weeks leading up to the flight. Kalunborg is on 55 degrees 40 north. Hess came in over the Farne islands, also 55 degrees 40 north. As Pintsch relates in the James Leasor book, there was also a lighthouse on Longstones[4] to use as a visual 'back up'.

Therefore I now believe that Hess flew up the North Sea and, when ready, came in at 55 degrees 40, by using the Kalunborg radio station just as a sign as to when to turn left, together with the Longstones lighthouse as the secondary 'back up'.[5] As we have seen earlier in the book it was left on during the war.

Having done so, the next objective was to find the Cheviot, as that was on the same heading as his eventual target. This was absolutely vital. By simply flying west he would then find Prestwick/Ayr. It was on the same heading.

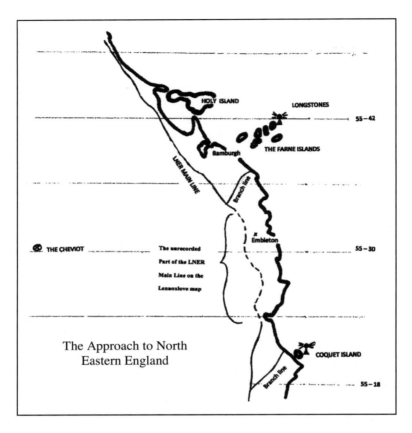

The Approach to North
Eastern England

The Cheviot is a high spot on its own, 2 degrees 08 west. Even in the dusk that Hess was now flying into it would have been discernible, albeit even only in silhouette. Get this part right and the rest should be easy. We know Hess eventually got it right and there are the later dramatic descriptions of flying up the side of the hill etc. All he had to do now was fly west.

The act of flying west was also aided by an unusual astrological event in that on the 10th May 1941, six planets in the sign of Taurus coincided with the full moon. Consequently, this too made flying west that much easier, should, for whatever reason the traditional compass fail Hess.

Richard Deacon in *'British Secret Service'*[6] devotes a whole chapter to this coincidence and attributes to it all sorts of occult influences. I dismiss them, but do believe that Hess would have been quite capable of making use of stars for navigation. Nothing more sinister or occult, than that.

The next visual check was St Mary's Loch, also on 55 degrees 30. Now it was getting more difficult. It was getting dark and the cloud base as detailed at Ayr[7] was 3/10 at both 3,000 and 5,000 feet.

Given that the Tinto hills over which Hess was now heading towards are 2500-2800 feet high (and Hess knew that having marked some heights on his map), one can only presume that his actual altitude would be 4,000-5,000 feet, so as to stay well above danger.[8]

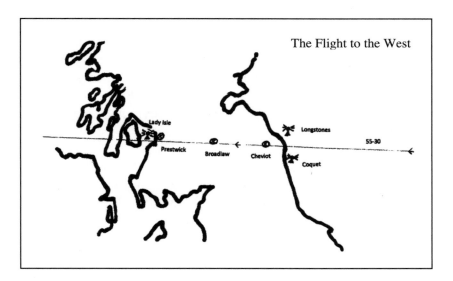

The Flight to the West

This, we believe, is where it all went wrong. On the morning of 4th May 2009, Richard and I set out to try and find Broadlaw which Hess had marked on his map as the highest peak in that range of hills, just to the east of

Tweedsmuir. We were armed with satellite navigation and OS maps. I think it fair to say that we found it extremely difficult to find what we were looking for, even with the 21st century weaponry at our disposal.

The clue is in the name. Broadlaw is broad at its summit. It does not have a peak as such, but is rather a broad plateau, part of which admittedly is 80 feet or so higher than its near neighbours Dollar Law and Dun Law.[9] There is now some radio equipment and generating equipment planted near its highest point.

Approaching from the east in the dusk in a plane travelling at 4 miles a minute, or a mile every 15 seconds I believe that Hess would also have had problems identifying Broadlaw. It would be very difficult indeed to pick out that particular summit, largely because it doesn't actually have one in the usual 'mountainy' way one would expect.

By contrast, the slightly lower, but more 'pointy' Dollar Law and Black Law are more 'pointy' or triangular in profile, but significantly are further north than the marginally higher but rather anonymous mass of Broadlaw.

Hence, we now suspect that Hess, approaching the Tinto Hills from the east, saw the 'pointy' shapes of Dollar and Black Law and took these to be Broadlaw. Richard and I did the same thing in broad daylight. However, in the half dark of May 1941 in so doing Hess had moved his plane further north. Not much at that stage, perhaps only half a mile or so, but the rules of triangulation would mean that when he hit the Ayrshire coast (as he was always intending to do), he would actually be 10-15 miles north of where he was intending to be. Only 2-3 minutes out in flying time but absolutely critical in terms of geography and navigation.

So, once past Broadlaw, we now believe that Hess was actually in the process of getting lost, but had not yet recognised the fact, only heading marginally further to the north than he intended. Again, when the agricultural ploughman loses 'his mark' every other visible marker will not be where expected and the eventual, compounded, results will prove terrible. Hess also had another, potentially far more fatal problem. The fuel gauges on the Bf110 must have been showing that there was virtually no fuel left whatsoever.

When I get close to empty in my Corsa van a light starts flashing and whilst prior experience tells me that I should hopefully have enough fuel left to get to a garage, an increasing sense of unease and anxiety pervades until the uncertainty is doused by the sight of an open garage. Hess had no such luxury. It is easy to imagine the sense of firstly doubt, then unease and ultimately panic that must have started around this time. All he could do was to head to the coast, control both his machine and himself and try to get a sight he recognised.

Purely by coincidence I am quite able to believe that en route he flew over or in the area of Dungavel. That is because he was flying too far north. Certainly not because he was going to land there. If that were his intent and Mr Prior's[10] landing lights were being switched on and off then he would have at least attempted to land. Why go somewhere else?

No, he was heading desperately out of control of the situation and heading recklessly towards his fate.

Lady Isle is a small-uninhabited island in the Firth of Clyde just off Troon and Prestwick. It is 55 degrees 31 minutes north. Apart from a ruined chapel the only other building is the Lady Isle lighthouse, built in 1903, which emits a white flashing light once every two seconds.

I believe that the original intention was to fly to the coast, fly around the Lady Isle lighthouse and then land on the east – west runway at Prestwick. It was all on the same latitude. Again, referring back to the 1962 Leasor book, Pintsch makes specific reference to his master's use of lighthouses as visual recognition aids.

Unfortunately for Rudolf Hess he was too far north. When he hit the coast it was over West Kilbride, not Prestwick or Troon, and spotted by ROC station G3.[11] This station, (it is still there) at the top of West Kilbride cemetery is 55degrees 42 north, some 13 miles to the north of Prestwick and the Lady Isle lighthouse. The gentlemen presiding at the ROC base saw the Bf110 turn left down the Firth of Clyde and noted that they could see the plane flying beneath them. This odd statement, we physically verified, was absolutely possible as the ROC station is atop a hill, at one of West Kilbride's highest points. The plane, at that time was virtually at sea level, as it would have to be. Hess was expecting to turn southwards and then eastwards so as to land. Prestwick airfield is also at sea level.

If one still believes that he was to land at Dungavel, he would not have dipped down to sea level, there was no need, he still had to get back the 20 miles or so inland.

As it was his mission was about to unravel totally. After turning south he turned left, but instead of finding a welcoming airstrip with attendant lighthouse just off shore, he found himself over Ardrossan where there certainly was no landing strip. To insert a note of irony the coastline at this point actually duplicates itself; Ardrossan has a prominent harbour jutting into the Clyde as does

Troon/Prestwick. In the dark it may well be that Hess also mistook Ardrossan for Prestwick thus adding to his difficulties.

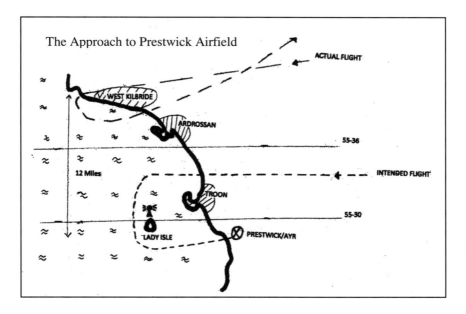

It was at this point that the panic must have really taken hold. The plane was at sea level; Hess could not parachute; it was too low. He was lost. He knew he was virtually out of fuel. I believe he then took the only decision he could. He must put on as much height as he could and bale out. Anywhere over land. Outside the cockpit it was pitch dark and a crash landing was out of the question. Self-preservation was becoming the overwhelming sensation. No. He would head inland, put on the necessary height and try to bale out. That at least was the logical thing to do.

As we know, at least in the latter respect he succeeded and was apocryphally introduced to the end of David Mclean's pitchfork.

---

[1] *Air 19/564 - Melville to Duke of Hamilton - 21st May 1941*
[2] *Flight from Reality*
[3] *Double Standards, between pages 232 and 233.*
[4] *Part of the Farne Islands.*
[5] *Light conditions. On 3rd May 2009 Richard and I travelled to the Prestwick/Ayr area and spent the evening drinking beer whilst waiting for the light conditions to manifest themselves as they would have done 68 years earlier, given double summer time and given that we were a week early. At 10.24 it was dusky, though outlines could still be ascertained by silhouette. At 11.09 it was just plain dark. Admittedly on our trial night there was a degree of cloud and no moonlight, but it was plainly dark to an extent that navigation, visual, radio or otherwise would prove very difficult indeed. Hence the stories of a jovial Hess hedgehopping and waving to people in fields are just nonsense. Lights or signals would have to play a part in any safe landing. If suspicious, the stories of clear visibility may well have come about as a camouflage to the fact that British lights and signals would have been absolutely necessary.*
[6] *Grafton 1991.*
[7] *Air 28/40.*
[8] *Roy Conyers Nesbit in The Truth about Rudolf Hess states that 'Hess climbed to 5,000 feet after crossing the Scottish border' (page 17).*
[9] *Broadlaw 2734 feet, Dollar Law 2680 feet, White Coombe 2695 feet. Ordnance Survey 1946 - The Border.*
[10] *Author of Double Standards.*
[11] *Attack Warning Red - Derek Wood - Macdonald and James 1976*

A BRIEF INTERREGNUM

The last chapters have, I hope, provided the reader with an explanation of:

-   where Hess was hoping to land,
-   why Hess chose Prestwick,
-   what went wrong.

The following chapters now attempt to explain why Rudolf Hess saw fit to fly from Augsburg Haunstetten Airfield at 5.45pm, 10th May 1941.

11

RUDOLF HESS

THE BIG PICTURE

The reason for the flight is well known; the details less clear; Hess was attempting to neutralise Britain in preparation for Nazi Germany to embark on its largest ever military enterprise.

As has been repeated to the point of monotony 'Mein Kampf' way back in 1923/24 had made it quite clear that a '2 front war' was out of the question as that was deemed to be a major factor in the defeat of 1918 Imperial Germany. Yet, 23 years later Nazi Germany was facing exactly that same prospect.

All the relevant buttons had been pressed, the German invasion of Russia was on, and Churchill, even with his 'golden goose' at Bletchley Park was struggling to convince Stalin that Russia was under such a threat. As far as he was concerned, such information was an example of typical British perfidy.

Hitler, throughout his career, I believe, was no more than an opportunist, who stumbled into events[1] and it was a direct result of that opportunism that he found himself in the mess that he was then in (though I very much doubt he would have seen his 1941 position in those terms). His accession to power, Alsace in 1936, Czechoslovakia in 1938 and indeed the whole German militarisation were largely as a result of the weakness of others that he had ruthlessly exploited. Continued, cumulative success had fuelled further, misplaced, confidence.

However, things actually began to go wrong in 1939. Poland was the 'line in the sand' as far as the British were concerned[2] and the Polish invasion saw the first time that Hitler, the chancer, had guessed wrong.[3] However, a Polish invasion was also a pre requisite of a German attack on Russia.

By their unanticipated declaration of war, Britain and France had put Hitler under severe pressure. Particularly if Russia really was to be the eventual target. However, in 1939 there was scant external evidence to support the premise of a Russian invasion. Indeed, the Molotov/Ribbentrop accord would seem to have indicated the opposite and the British and French had previously failed to entice Stalin into a Treaty.

If it is possible to become a genius through deception and lying, then perhaps Hitler really was a genius?[4] Consequently, in Hitler's eyes, the eventual invasion of France and the Low Countries was actually a defensive measure. The French army (which in 1939 was numerically the world largest and egged on by Britain) was perilously close to Hitler's industrial heartland, the Ruhr. If the Ruhr fell so would Hitler. Britain was also increasing the economic pressure by the reimposition of the naval blockade, which had previously brought Germany to her knees in 1918.

Hence, by undertaking the May 1940 invasion (which originally had been intended for October 1939). Hitler had merely safeguarded his frontiers. The construction of the Atlantic wall would reinforce them still further. France was no longer a threat, but Britain was still technically unbowed.

AND YET

And yet Britain, despite being pounded night after night by the Luftwaffe, despite defeat and humiliation in Europe and Africa and despite having no real way of realistically taking the war to Germany, was appearing to be wholly unprepared to either cede or consider surrender. In fact, her future prospects were perhaps not all dire. In March 1941 the US/UK Lend lease deal had been signed which, whilst possibly more important in terms of intent than content, had made it quite clear that (even the pre election) US government would actively support the British war effort. Perhaps Britain and its few Allies would not be alone forever. The longer that Britain could pretend to 'jaw jaw' might mean that actual 'war war' could be that much further away. Consequently there had been a flurry of German peace proposals throughout the spring, summer and autumn of 1940. They simply had to prevent a two front war.

That is why Hess flew. It is of course quite true to say that Hitler's' Germany had yet to be defeated militarily and confidence was naturally running high, but did Hess realise that Russia would be quite a different matter? Did he share his masters' confidence? Was it a risk that he thought didn't have to be taken? Even Hitler knew that Germany was vulnerable in a long war. They didn't have the resources.

However, the interesting question is really what would have happened had Hess succeeded? There were many people in the British Empire that in principle were not against a peace treaty with Germany. That is what eventually made the Hess deception so plausible, so believable. Had the terms Hess brought with him been accepted and implemented then I suspect in the short term, France and the Low Countries would have been restored, the General Government in central Poland be ceded to the

Poles and various African territories perhaps be restored to the Reich. But what would have happened then?

Russia would be the more likely to be defeated and Hitler would have gained the geopolitical 'heartland' as defined by Halford Mackinder.[5] Once the Heartland had been gained then British naval supremacy became irrelevant.

Once British naval supremacy was irrelevant, Britain was a sitting duck. With the 'heartland' under his belt, Hitler was virtually impregnable and I suspect it unlikely that the USA would have backed Britain,[6] or anyone else, against an enemy with virtually unlimited natural resources. The Far Eastern British Empire would come under pressure from Japan and Britain would struggle to supply reinforcements.

The history of the past 60 years would have become very different. Instead of a cold war USA versus USSR, I suspect that a similar impasse would have quickly developed between the USA and Hitler's Germany, assuming the nuclear secret was eventually shared between the two great powers.[7]

Germany, in many ways, would then be geopolitically able to expand throughout the Middle East, firstly by attacking the British Empire, thus further weakening Britain's European position, mutually assured nuclear destruction notwithstanding. Given man's hoped for three score years and ten Hitler would have died in around 1959/1960 the leader of the most powerful nation on earth. That prospect was not the subject of a Robert Harris novel in 1941; it was a very real and scary reality.

It is perhaps therefore, not too great a leap of imagination to see Germany as the world dominant power perhaps, by 1960. That, bluntly, and brutally is why the Hess flight assumes such importance. It was little to do with peace, far more to do with future world domination.

Hess was certainly no 'peace martyr'. That nonsense developed from the family's (quite understandable) post war attempts to release the head of their family.[8]

---

[1] *AJP Taylor - Origins of the Second World War - Penguin 1991 "He got as far as he did because others did not know what to do with him"*
[2] *Perhaps less so the French.*
[3] *FO 800/316, the private papers of Lord Halifax seem to demonstrate that the British, almost upto the last minute, expected Hitler to climb down. Every man and his dog were sending Halifax advice as to what to do, including Kurt Hahn, Lord Londonderry, Neville Henderson, Lord Kemsley, The Duke of Bedford, Charles Roden Buxton, Lord Trenchard and even the Secretary of the Anglo German Fellowship – Conwell Evans (!) John Lowther, PPS to HRH The Duke of Kent, by contrast, wrote to Halifax on 6th July 1939 asking for permission for HRH to go on holiday, starting on 24th/25th July for 3/4 weeks. He hoped to visit his sister in law in Munich, and then go onto Yugoslavia and Italy. I can only surmise that he was not anticipating the inconvenience of the outbreak of World War 2 to disrupt his holidays.*
[4] *AJP Taylor also makes the point that Hitler hoped that the Russian adventure might not develop into a major war. Many felt that Bolshevism would collapse once put under pressure.*
[5] *Halford Mackinder (1861-1947) was an English geographer who is credited with the Heartland Theory of 1904. The idea was that Eastern Europe, Western Russia and the Ukraine if conquered, contained so many natural elements so as to be able to make it impregnable to attack. Karl Haushofer developed the idea in Germany and there has been debate as to the influence of the theory on Nazi Foreign policy. Lebensraum is mentioned in only 7 of Mein Kampf's 700+ pages.*
It was certainly taken seriously enough by the Western powers so as to play a part in the creation of 'buffer states' of the 1919 Treaty of Versailles. 20th Century bombers and missiles eventually condemned the theory as being obsolete.
[6] *The isolationists were still a very powerful body. As Senator Bradley of Michigan told Lord Halifax in early 1941:*
- *England is extremely selfish*
- *She will use anyone to help herself and having gained her ends will dump them overboard*

- *Their statesmen are very smart and have too much experience in power politics for our statesmen to deal with for our best interests*
- *England looks out for herself, first, last and all the time*
- *England has no intention of repayment of any past, present or future war debts*
- *England would like us to help police the world – she to establish the policies – we to pay the bills.*
- *More than ever I am convinced we should stay out of this war.........*

[7] *The extent of the German nuclear program is still a subject for debate. There is some evidence of a low level nuclear explosion in and around Thuringia in March 1945. Richard and I fear that Germany was far more advanced than has been acknowledged to date. Study the two types of nuclear weapons used by the Americans. – Why?*

[8] *See Ilse Hess- Prisoner of Peace. 1954*

12

ENTER

MRS ROBERTS

After describing the world situation in May 1941, the prospect of world domination and the immense stakes that the major players were playing for, it may seem somewhat odd to then take a chapter to describe a lady who in 1941 was already 77 years of age and particularly enjoyed walking her Scottie dog and bottling gooseberries.[1]

However, the more I consider the role that Mrs Roberts played, the more convinced I become that she is, in fact, the key to understanding the Hess affair, simply because her involvement was perceived by the Germans as being wholly non-governmental (indeed it is hard to conceive anybody more non-governmental!).

Hess and Haushofer used Mrs Roberts precisely because she was so non governmental. It was an attempt to negotiate a peace *outside* the usual government channels. Had Hess and Haushofer wanted to negotiate with the British Government directly, there certainly would not be need for the drama of letters and flights to Scotland etc. That is why God created diplomats, albeit diplomats that had seemingly failed in this instance.

No, I now believe that the existence of the correspondence involving Mrs Roberts is the certain evidence that Hess and Haushofer were trying to reach persons **outside** the government (or dissenters within it), persons who, nonetheless, they believed, were apparently quite capable of instigating the changes that Hess desperately sought. The German Government had spent much of 1939 and 1940 trying to forge a settlement with the British Government. Without success.

So, let's now discover precisely who Mrs Roberts was[2] and why she became embroiled in the Hess affair. In many ways she was an ideal, but very unlikely intermediary. As I mentioned in the introduction to this book, Mrs Roberts was responsible for my initial interest in the Hess affair. David Irving had stated that Mrs Roberts as being the daughter in law of Field Marshal Lord Roberts.[3] Quickly, I had found out this to be impossible. Lord Roberts's unmarried son, Frederick, was killed at Colenso in 1899. So who was Mrs Roberts?

Mary Violet Roberts was born 5th September 1864 in Ferozepore, India and baptised on 25th of the same month.[4] Her father was Patrick Maxwell, at that time a Captain in the Bengal Staff Corps. Patrick had joined the Bengal Army as a cadet on 31st January 1845[5] and had progressed to the rank of Captain, late of the 37th Native Infantry and Deputy Commissioner in the Punjab at Googaira. Mary's mother was Louisa Sarah Maxwell, nee Bell originating from Tasmania. They had married in 1853. When looking at Patrick Maxwell's cadet papers I could not help but notice that Patrick's father had to give his consent to his son following a career in the army. His father, William, was described as, *'William Maxwell, Merchant of Dargavel, Glasgow.'* Dargavel is no more than 20 miles from where Hess crashed and has an obvious similarity to Dungavel, the so-called 'Hess target'. Looking backwards further still, I discovered that William Maxwell had married Mary Campbell of Possil Park, which in 1834 was described thus,

'It (Possil House) was then far away from the noise and smoke of the city, and stood among fine old trees. With its beautiful gardens, its grassy slopes, and its clear lake, Possil formed as delightful and retired a country residence as any in the county.[6]

Clearly, here was a family of substance. Next I looked at Dargavel House, the ancestral home of Mary Violet Roberts.

Dargavel House, in Bishopton,[7] is again of a similar standing. Dating from c.1580 the house is still standing, though currently entombed in the 2500-acre estate of the former Bishopton Royal Ordnance factory. Once the largest in Europe and so secret that it did not appear on OS maps, the site has now been decommissioned and is awaiting planning permission so that it can be re-developed as houses.

The house is described thus,

'John Maxwell of Dargavel was the second son of Sir Patrick Maxwell of Newark and his wife Helen, a daughter of Sir Neil Montgomery of Lainshaw. In 1516 John obtained grant for the lands of Dargavel from the Earl of Lennox. Dargavel Castle is a 'Z' plan tower house, it consisted of a rectangular central block of three floors and a garret with two large round towers on opposite corners. The Maxwell armorial stone with a stag's head crest on the east gable is dated 1584 but this is likely to represent some additional building work on the structure as it was greatly extended since its original construction. The whole house was reconstructed and extended in 1849 in the Scottish Baronial style by the architect David Bryce. This

rebuild obscure much of the original features of the early building including the original entrance. Patrick Maxwell of Dargavel, grandson of John, is reputed to have been one of the Earl of Morton's personal supporters and was killed with him at the battle of Dryfe Sands in 1593, although most of the Strathclyde Maxwell families claim the Patrick Maxwell who lost his life there. What is certain however is that the Maxwells of Dargavel were involved in the feud between the Montgomery's and the Cunningham family that embroiled this part of the lower Clyde estuary. The principle line of the Maxwells failed in the early part of the nineteenth century and the heiress married John Hall of Fulbar who took the additional name of Maxwell. The Hall-Maxwells of Dargavel were a prolific family and many of the sons became notable military men. The First World War however claimed three of the last lairds sons and two of his grandsons. The barony was sold between the two world wars and the house and its gardens and parkland were taken over by the Government for the Bishopton Royal Ordnance Factory. The old house is now deep inside this secret area, apparently again much altered.[8]

Again, clear evidence of wealth and status. Further 'googling' revealed that the Maxwells seem to originate back to Caervalerock Castle,[9] in Dumfriesshire in around 1270.

Clearly the Maxwells were well connected and indeed appeared to be an even older family than the Hamiltons. We should not therefore be too surprised to learn that in 1638, Elizabeth, the daughter of James Maxwell married William, 2nd Duke of Hamilton.[10] I have no idea if this family link was carried through to the 1930's. Quite honestly I doubt it, but, at times, in the Hess case it seems anything is possible.

However, returning to 1864, India, the Maxwell family were actually only 8 years away from returning to England and in 1872 Patrick retired to Bath, Wiltshire, England, with the rank of Major General. They lived in a large house at 19 Pultney Road.[11] Mary therefore spent her formative years in the west of England. She also had a brother, Louis. In the late 1880's Mary began her courtship of the senior Maths teacher at the nearby Bath College.[12] Herbert Ainslie Roberts was only marginally older than Mary, being born in the February of 1864. Academically gifted, Herbert had attended Gonville and Caius College, Cambridge, graduating in 1887. Herbert's elder brother, Ernest was also exceptionally academically gifted, becoming the Master of Gonville and Caius from 1903 to 1912.[13]

Mary and Herbert married in 1894 and moved to Cambridge in 1898, Herbert initially becoming a Mathematical coach. The couple were not poor, Mary being the principal beneficiary of her father's will when he died in July 1906. In addition to a specific bequest, Patrick also gave his daughter the proceeds of a marriage settlement that had been settled back in 1853, when he married Louisa.

By the time of his father in law's death in 1906, Herbert had become secretary to the recently formed (1899) Cambridge Appointments Board. It was this position that was to earn Herbert his reputation,[14] so much so, that on his demise in 1932 was summarised as,

'It is hardly too much to say that Roberts achieved the greatest bit of constructive work of a not strictly academic character done in Cambridge by a single individual in the last 25 years'.[15]

The Roberts were becoming comfortable and in 1912/13 they commissioned the then fashionable Mackay

Baillie Scott to design and build a *'Sussex style farmhouse of Mock Tudor design'*. Baillie Scott had also studied earlier in his career in Bath and it is fair to say that it is a lovely house and still stands to this day. Originally designated 33 Storey's Way it is now renumbered 48.

However, of far more relevance to this story is that around this time the Robert's family became acquainted with the Haushofer family, a friendship that certainly lasted for the next 40 years at least. How the two families met I am still not sure (even after 20 years of trying to find out) but we do know that:

- HA Roberts was secretary to the Cambridge Appointments Board, the Indian Civil Service Studies Board and the Foreign Service Students Committee. They may therefore have met through his work.
- ES Roberts may have introduced them through his important position at Gonville and Caius.
- In 1899[16] Karl Haushofer travelled to England and met with Joseph Chamberlain. This appears to coincide with the visit of Kaiser Wilhelm to England in a British inspired attempt to improve relations.
- On 14th August 1925 Mary and Herbert met Albrecht Haushofer. The diary entry says, 'Die Bekanntschaft mit der Familie R. datierte aus der Vorkriegszeit.'[17]
- What is not helpful is Martin Allen's unsourced assertion that the two families met when Karl Haushofer addressed the Cambridge 'Foreign Science Students Committee' in 1898. Firstly, I do not think there has ever been such a committee (I have seen no reference to it) and secondly, even if he meant the 'Foreign Service Students

Committee', that particular body was not formed until 1905.[18]

However, Martin Allen not withstanding, my assertion remains that the friendship was certainly longstanding and durable. It also transcended the generations.

Karl and Martha Haushofer had two boys; Albrecht and Heinz, Herbert and Mary had one son, Patrick. Albrecht was born in 1903, Patrick Roberts in 1895.

Not surprisingly, given the family backgrounds, both sets of children were also extremely, extremely, academic. Patrick went to Eton aged 13, then Trinity College Cambridge before joining the Foreign Service in 1919. His naturally proud Aunt, Mrs Ernest Stewart Roberts, describes his progress as,

"(Patrick) went to Eton as a scholar, and was a most brilliant one, winning almost every possible distinction, including the Newcastle and finishing with one of the best Scholarships at Trinity, Cambridge."[19]

Similarly, Albrecht spent his formative years in Munich and graduated in history and geography from the University in 1924, aged 21. Heinz studied as an agronomist. The Haushofer archives in Koblenz also detail various meetings between the younger Roberts who was rapidly progressing through the diplomatic ranks. In chronological order:

11.6.1925 - Patrick Roberts zum Mittagessen, tee u.abend essen.
14.8.1925 - Mr & Mrs Roberts viel bei mir.Roberts mit Albrecht um ½ I fort.

The Haushofer Family: A photograph taken 1914-18 showing Karl Haushofer in military uniform, wife Martha and children Albrecht and Heinz at his side. It is quite probable that this family were already friends with the Roberts family of Cambridge, England at the time of the photograph.

125

Patrick obviously met up with his parents and their German friends prior to his leaving the Berlin Embassy for Warsaw. (He started there on 15th August 1925).

Later on the family's meetings are less documented and I was very grateful to Andrea Schroder Haushofer who provided me with a copy of the visitor's book at the family estate, Hartschimmelhof. The Roberts visits are recorded, but, to be honest, the copy of the book appeared to me to have been written up in hindsight. All the entries are in the same neat handwriting; the same colour ink and it just seem to be to have been done after the event. Nevertheless, the Roberts are recorded as having visited the Haushofers in 1925 and 1926. In 1932 Herbert Ainslie Roberts died and in 1934 the Haushofers visited London, Cambridge and Oxford. In 1936 Albrecht visited the UK alone.[20]

So, by 1936, when the main events of the story start to unfold, the two families' friendship had essentially passed down from Herbert and Mary, Karl and Martha to the two sons. By 1936, Karl Haushofer was 67. Mary Roberts was already 72 and was living with her high achieving son, Patrick in Athens, Greece, whilst he was working at the British Embassy. Patrick was, by that time, Charge d'Affairs.

However, in 1937 Mary Robert's world was completely shattered. Five years after the death of her husband, Patrick was involved in a car crash at Ikali, some 20km north of Athens and died shortly afterwards. Mary came back to England and was living in London with her nephew, Walter Roberts[21] at 36 Queen's Gate, Kensington when her son's probate was granted in 1938. Eventually, she returned broken-hearted to Wilberforce Road in Cambridge. I suspect none of the family members anticipated the roles they were about to play in World

History, particularly Mary Violet Roberts, who was then more worried as to how she might keep her Cambridge lawn cut and tidy.

----

[1] *Letters to Author.*

[2] *Until 1994 that was certainly not the case!*

[3] *Hess:The Missing Years - David Irving*

[4] *Bengal Baptisms Vol 109 - Folio 59.*

[5] *British Library l/Mil/9/209 - Oriental and India Office Collection*

[6] *The Old Country Houses of the Glasgow Gentry - Strathclyde University*

[7] *www.maxwellsociety.com*

[8] *ibid*

[9] *The only triangular castle in Scotland.*

[10] *www.maxwellsociety.com*

[11] *It now forms part of a hotel.*

[12] *Bath College was founded in what is now the Bath Spa Hotel. It existed as a school from 1879 to 1909. The headmaster was TW Dunn who was a close friend of the Roberts family whilst at Swineshead, Lincolnshire.*

[13] *See Sherbourne, Oxford and Cambridge - Mrs.E.S.Roberts - Martin Hopkinson Limited - 1934.*

[14] *Apparently, before its formation, students were very much left to their own devices, when pursuing their particular careers.*

[15] *Quoted from Vice Chancellor of Cambridge University - 1932.*

[16] *Between 21st September and 6th November.*

[17] *Haushofer correspondence, volume 2, page 453.*

[18] *www.venn.csi.cam.ac.uk/acad/lists*

[19] *Mrs.E.S.Roberts - Sherbourne, Oxford and Cambridge - Martin Hopkinson Limited - London.*

[20] *Haushofer archives, Koblenz Bundesarchiv.*

[21] *Walter Roberts was the son of Mr and Mrs.E.S.Roberts. E.S.Roberts had been Master of Gonville and Caius from 1903 - 1912. After a career in the Egyptian Civil Service, he became a Stockbroker, working for Silverston & Co in the City of London.*

13

RUDOLF HESS

AND

WARTIME COMMUNICATION

Prior to continuing to explain the sequence of events leading up to the Hess Flight it is important to at least consider the topic of wartime communication and the constraints placed upon it.

In the first decade of the 21st Century it is too easy to take the ability of instant communication for granted. Oral communication, Emails, texts, letters, mobile telephones, landline telephones, facsimiles, television, radio and satellites are amongst some of the more obvious contemporary tools.

However, ponder the situation in 1941. Britain is at war with Germany and individuals within those Countries perhaps wish to communicate with a view to reaching a peace accord. Technology was nowhere near as advanced in terms of the available options. To make matters even worse, potentially the British individuals concerned cannot make use of the normal channels as they are under the control of the government, which patently does not wish to make peace. The stakes are high if found out. Such actions could quite easily be construed as being treasonable.

To look at the possible options:

-   Letter: Would fail, or take too much time. The Censor would see to that.
-   Telephone/cable: Disconnected, or subject to eavesdropping.
-   Personal visit: Extremely unlikely in wartime.
-   Diplomatic bag - Again a governmental route.
-   Radio: The British or Germans would have intercepted.

We should also bear in mind that the Germans would realise the predicament that a prospective intermediary was in and would surely 'smell a rat' if communication came via any route where they would realise there was a risk of exposure.

Needless to say, British Intelligence, who I believe were about to become engaged in the 'game', also had exactly the same problem, how to engage without appearing too obvious. However, the solution adopted was very obvious and has been known and written about for at least 61 years.

14

THE LETTERS

SEPTEMBER 1940

I would ask you to now consider the position of the German Government in the late summer of 1940, after the Air Battle for Britain. I think Richard Overy summarises current (2009) opinion well as follows:[1]

> 'The Battle matters because it prevented German invasion and conquest and kept Britain in the war. This achievement was worthwhile enough. Nine European states (ten, counting Danzig) had failed to prevent German occupation by the summer of 1940, with the grimmest of consequences. Nevertheless, some historians have raised serious doubts about the traditional story of the battle, which gave birth to the myth of a united nation-repelling invasion and gave iconographic status to the Spitfires and the 'few' who flew them. There is another history to be discovered behind the popular narrative. The effort to uncover it has already challenged some of the most cherished illusions of the battle story. Take, for example, the generally accepted view that the battle prevented German invasion of southern Britain. Documents on the German side have been used to suggest that this was not so. Invasion, it can be argued, was a bluff designed to force Britain to beg for peace; in the summer of 1940 Hitler's eyes were already gazing eastwards, where there lay real 'living-space'. The

Royal Air Force did not repel invasion for the apparently simple reason that the Germans were never coming. This interpretation has prompted some historians to suggest that Britain should have taken the chance of peace with Hitler and let the two totalitarian states bleed each other to death in Eastern Europe.'

Behind this argument lies still more revision. The picture of a firmly united and determined people standing shoulder to should against fascism has been slowly eroded by the weight of historical evidence. The British were less united in 1940 that was once universally believed. Defeatism could be found, side by side with heroic powerful defiance. Churchill's government, so it is argued, had powerful voices urging a search for peace in the summer of 1940, just like the appeasers of the 1930s."

Peter Fleming, in *Invasion 1940*[2] speculates as to the precise date that Hitler called off the invasion. He concluded,

'It suggests that the between 8 and 14 September Hitler dismissed from his mind the idea of an opposed landing on the English coast. (He may conceivably have dismissed it earlier; the deliberate compromising of his objectives in clandestine broadcasts at the end of August suggests this.....)'

I therefore suspect that Hess also knew this and hence explains why at the end of August 1940 he put into motion the sequence of events that eventually led to the May 1941 flight. Somewhat obviously, had the invasion taken place, the necessity for further action would have been negated. As it was he knew that the invasion was not going to happen so started to take alternative action. Very logical. Very German.

I believe these letters are therefore important in that they demonstrate the thought processes and sequence of events that started the affair. So, I unapologetically reprint them here, together with my inserted notes, Please be aware that this sequence of events only started once the military option had been effectively ruled out:

C109/C002185-87
Dr Karl Haushofer to Dr Albrecht Haushofer
Munich, September 3, 1940

Dearest Albrecht: Cordial thanks for your letter of the 29th from the Hotel Imperial in Vienna. I had almost a vague premonition that you might be there.

If you composed your birthday letter to me in the air raid cellar, I could have reciprocated this kind service on the night of the 1st and 2nd because I promised your mother when I left the mountain cabin to go down when the alarm sounded and consequently spent 1½ hours in exercise and gymnastics.

For, as with you, everything has changed with us too. Through Lisa's sudden departure, which you witnessed, mother's trip to the Hart became unnecessary. Because her stomach and knee both took a turn for the worse, she remained at the Alpine cabin and, only because everything was so arranged, let me go down to the valley alone from the 31st to the 3rd. But I was rewarded, for it brought me a meeting with Tomo[3] from 5.00 o'clock in the afternoon until 2.00 o'clock in the morning, which included a 3-hour walk in the Grunwalder Forest[4], at which we conversed a good deal about serious matters. I have really got to tell you about a part of it now.

As you know, everything is so prepared for a very hard and severe attack on the island in question[5] that the highest-ranking person[6] only has to press a button to set it off. But before this decision, which is perhaps inevitable, the thought once more occurs as to whether there is really no way of stopping something which would have such infinitely momentous consequences. There is a line of reasoning in connection with this, which I must absolutely pass on to you because it was obviously communicated to me with this intention. Do you, too, see no way in which such possibilities could be discussed at a third place[7] with a middle man, possibly the old Ian Hamilton[8] or the other Hamilton.[9]

I replied to these suggestions that there would perhaps have been an excellent opportunity for this in Lisbon at the Centennial,[10] if, instead of harmless figureheads, [11]it had been possible to send well-disguised political persons there. In this connection, it seems to me a stroke of fate that our old friends, Missis (sic) V.R., evidently, though after long delay, finally found a way of sending a note with cordial and gracious words of good wishes not only for your mother, but also for Heinz and me and added the address.

Address your reply to: Miss V Roberts, c/o Postbox 506, Lisbon, Portugal. I have the feeling that no good possibility should be overlooked; at least is should be well considered.

In my opinion, this letter is astonishing. Absolutely astonishing. Karl and Albrecht Haushofer are discussing the European situation and the necessity for a German peace, when, lo an behold, father Haushofer tells his son of 'a stroke of fate' in that Mrs Roberts, their 76 year old English friend has 'finally found a way of sending a note'!

In May 1940 the Treachery Act had made it a capital offence in certain circumstances for helping the enemy and so, be under no illusion as to the potential consequences of this 'stroke of fate'. Was Mrs Roberts was one step away from treachery?

It also appears to me that this letter seems to be a *fait accompli*. Karl is effectively telling his son to go ahead and make the contact. There doesn't seem too much debate, but at this stage the objective seems to be a meeting in a neutral country, 'to discuss possibilities'. There certainly isn't much more alluded to it than that. Certainly not a flight to Scotland.

The next letter in the sequence then becomes:

C109/C002188-89
Rudolf Hess to Dr Karl Haushofer at present at Gallspach[12]

Dear Friend: Albrecht brought me your letter, which at the beginning, besides containing official information, alluded to our walk together on the last day of August, which I, too, recall with so much pleasure.

Albrecht will have told you about our conversation, which beside volksdeutch[13] matters, above all touched upon the other matter, which is so close to the hearts of us both. I reconsidered the latter carefully once more and I have arrived at the following conclusion:
Under no condition must we disregard the contact or allow it to die aborning. I consider it best that you or Albrecht write to the old lady, who is a friend of your family, suggesting that she try to ask Albrecht's friend whether he would be prepared if necessary to come to the neutral territory in which she resides,[14] or at any rate has an address through which she can be reached,[15] just to talk with Albrecht.
If he could not do this just now, he might, in any case, send word through her where he expected to be in the near future. Possibly a neutral acquaintance, who had some business to attend to over there anyway, might look him up and make some communication to him, using you or Albrecht as reference.[16]
This person[17] probably would not care to have to inquire as to his whereabouts only after he got there or to make futile trips. You thought that knowing about his whereabouts had no military significance at all; if necessary, you would also pledge yourselves not to make use of it with regard to any quarter which might profit from it. What the neutral would have to transmit would be of such great importance that his having made known his whereabouts would be by comparison insignificant.
The prerequisite naturally was that the inquiry in question and the reply would not go through official channels,[18] for you would not in any case want to cause your friends over there any trouble.
It would be best to have the letter to the old lady with whom you are acquired delivered through a confidential agent of the AO[19] to the address that is known to you. For this purpose Albrecht would have to speak either with Bohle or my brother. At the same time the lady would have to be given the address of this agent in L.-or if the latter does not live there permanently, of another agent of the AO who does live there permanently, to which the reply can in turn be delivered.[20]

As for the neutral, I have in mind, I would like to speak to you orally about it for some time. There is no hurry about this since, in any case, there would first have to be a reply receiving here from over there. [21]
Meanwhile let's both keep our finger crossed. Should success be the fate of the enterprise, the oracle given to you with regard to the month of August would yet be fulfilled,[22] since the name of the young friend and the old lady friend of your family occurred to you during our quiet walk on the last day of that month.
With best regards to you and to Martha.

Yours, as ever,

R(UDOLF) H(ESS)

Can be reached by telephone through: Linz-Gallspach A.

This second letter I too believe important as it introduces a second option:

- The first option is very much the letter to Mrs Roberts
- Then we have the concept of a neutral intermediary. Unnamed as yet.

Thereafter the letter essentially becomes a 'to do' list.

C109/C002190-04
Memorandum by Dr Albrecht Haushofer
Berlin, September 15, 1940

TOP SECRET
ARE THERE STILL POSSIBILITIES OF A GERMAN-ENGLISH PEACE?

On September 8, I was summoned to Bad G[23] to report to the Deputy of the Fuhrer on the subject discussed in this memorandum.[24] The conversation, which the two of us had alone lasted 2 hours. I had the opportunity to speak in all frankness.
I was immediately asked about the possibilities of making known to persons of importance in England Hitler's serious desire for peace. It

was quite clear that the continuance of the war was suicidal for the white race[25]. Even with complete success in Europe, Germany was not in a position to take over inheritance of the Empire. The Fuhrer had not wanted to see the Empire destroyed and did not want it even today. Was there not somebody in England who was ready for peace?[26]

First I asked for permission to discuss fundamental things. It was necessary to realize that not only Jews and Freemasons, but practically all Englishmen who mattered, regarded a treat signed by the Fuhrer as a worthless scrap of paper.[27] To the question as to why this was so, I referred to the 10-year term of our Polish Treaty to the Non-Aggression Pact with Denmark signed only a year ago to the 'final' frontier demarcation of Munich. What guarantee did England have that a new treaty would not be broken again at once if it suited us? It must be realized that, even in the Anglo-Saxon world, the Fuhrer was regarded as Satan's representative on earth and had to be fought.

If the worse came to the worst, the English would rather transfer their whole Empire bit by it to the Americans than sign a peace that left to National Socialist Germany the mastery of Europe. The present was, I am convinced, shows that Europe has become too small for its previous anarchic form of existence; it is only through close German-English co-operation that it can achieve a true federative order (based by no means merely on the police rule of a single power), while maintaining a part of its world position and having security against Soviet Russian Eurasia. France was smashed, probably for a long time to come, and we have opportunity currently to observe what Italy is capable of accomplishing. As long, however, as German-English rivalry existed, and in so far as both sides thought in terms of security, the lessons of this war was this: Every German had to tell himself: we have no security as long as provision is not made that the Atlantic gateways of Europe from Gibraltar to Narvik are free of any possible blockade.[28] That is: there must be no English fleet. Every Englishman, must, however, under the same conditions, argue: we have no security as long as anywhere within a radius of 2,000 kilometres from London there is a plane that we do not control. That is: there must be no German air force.

There is only one way out of this dilemma: friendship intensified to fusion, with a joint fleet, a joint air force, and joint defence of possessions in the world – just what the English are now about to conclude with the United States.[29]

Here I was interrupted and asked why, indeed, the English were prepared to seek such a relationship with America and not with us.

My reply was: because Roosevelt is a man, and represents a Weltanschauung[30] and a way of life, that the Englishman thinks he understands, to which he can become accustomed, even where it does not seem to be to his liking. Perhaps he fools himself – but, at any rate that is what he believes.

A man like Churchill – himself half American – is convinced of it. Hitler however seems to the Englishman the incarnation of what he hates, that he has fought against for centuries – this feeling grips the workers no less than the plutocrats.[31]

In fact, I am of the opinion that those Englishmen who have property to lose, that is, precisely the portions of the so-called plutocracy that count, are those who would be readiest to talk peace.[32]

But even they regard a peace only as an armistice. I was compelled to express these things so strongly because I ought not – precisely because of my long experience in attempting to effect a settlement with England in the past and my numerous English friendships – to make it appear that I seriously believe in the possibility of a settlement between Adolf Hitler and England in the present stage of development. I was thereupon asked whether I was not of the opinion that feelers had perhaps not been successful because the right language had not been used. I replied that, to be sure, if certain persons, whom we both knew well, were meant by this statement-then certainly the wrong language had been used.[33] But at the present stage this had little significance. I was then asked directly why all Englishmen were so opposed to Herr v. R(ibbentrop). I conceded, that, in the eyes of the English, Herr v. R., like some other personages, played, to be sure, the same role as did Duff Cooper, Eden and Churchill in the eyes of the Germans. In the case of Herr v. R., there was also the conviction, precisely in the view of Englishmen who were formerly friendly to Germany that – from completely biased motives – he had informed the Fuhrer wrongly about England and that he personally bore an unusually large share of the responsibility for the outbreak of war.

But I again stressed the fact that the rejection of peace feelers by England was today due not so much to persons as to the fundamental outlook mentioned above.[34]

Nevertheless, I was asked to name those whom I thought might be reached as possible contacts.[35]

I mentioned among diplomats, Minister O'Malley in Budapest, the former head of the South Eastern Department of the Foreign Office, a clever person in the higher echelons of officialdom, but perhaps without influence precisely because of his former friendliness toward Germany; Sir Samuel Hoare, who is half-shelved and half on the watch in Madrid, whom I do not know well personally, but to whom I can at any time open a personal path; as the most promising, the Washington Ambassador Lothian, with whom I have had close personal connections for years, who as a member of the highest aristocracy and at the same time as person of very independent mind, is perhaps best in a position to undertake a bold step-provided[36] that he could be convinced that even a bad and uncertain peace would be better than the continuance of the war – a conviction at which he will only arrive if he convinces himself in Washington that English hopes of America are not realizable.

Whether or not this is so could only be judged in Washington itself; from Germany not at all. As the final possibility I then mentioned that of a personal meeting on neutral soil with the closet of my English friends: the young Duke of Hamilton, who has access at all times to all important persons in London, even to Churchill and the King.[37] I stressed in this case the inevitable difficulty of making a contact and again repeated my conviction of the improbability of its succeeding – whatever approach we took.

The upshot of the conversation was H's statement that he would consider the whole matter thoroughly once more and send me word in case I was to take steps. For this extremely ticklish case, and in the event that I might possibly have to make a trip alone – I asked for very precise directives from the highest authority.[38] From the whole conversation I had the strong impression that it was not conducted without the prior knowledge of the Fuhrer, and that I probably would not hear any more about the matter unless a new understanding had been reached between him and his Deputy.[39]

On the personal side of the conversation I must say that - despite the fact that I felt bound to say usually hard things – it ended in great friendliness, even cordiality. I spent the night in Bad G, and the next morning still had the opportunity, on a walk together in the presence of the Chief Adjutant, to bring up all the volksdeutsch questions from the resettlement in all parts of Europe to the difficulties as to personnel in the central offices in Berlin – which resulted in H's direct intervention.

A(LBRECHT H(AUSHOFER)

This comprehensive memorandum is, in my view, an excellent resume of the actual thought processes prevalent in September 1940. What it does not do however, is to present the mechanics as to how a peace is to be achieved.

I suspect Albrecht already realises it is an unattainable goal.

C109/C002179-202
Dr Albrecht Haushofer to his Parents
Berlin, September 19, 1940

Dear Parents: I am sending you enclosed herewith some important documents:
First, T's. Letter to Father,
Secondly, my answer to T., which has already been sent and, I hope, has your subsequent approval.
Thirdly, the draft of a letter to D^{40}, which I will keep to myself and not show to anyone else. I request that you examine it to see whether it might involve any danger for the woman who may transmit it.[41] I really believe that it sounds harmless enough. I have inserted the reference to the 'authorities' over there purposely as a safeguard for the transmitter and recipient. So I should like to have your honest opinion and any corrections. Fourthly a report of what I said on the 8th in G., as an accounting before history (save till the last).[42]
The whole thing is a fool's errand, but we cannot do anything about that[43]. According to our latest reports the treaties of union between the Empire and the United States are about to be signed.[44]

Best Wishes,

Enclosure 1
TOP SECRET
My Dear Herr Hess: Your letter of the 10th reached me yesterday after a delay caused by the antiquated postal service of Partnach-Alm. I again gave a thorough study to the possibilities discussed therein and request – before taking the steps proposed – that you yourself examine once more the thoughts set forth below.
I have in the meantime been thinking of the technical route by which a message from me must travel before it can reach the Duke of H(amilton). With your help, delivery to Lisbon can of course be assured without difficulty. About the rest of the route we do not know. Foreign control must be taken into account; the letter must therefore in no case be composed in such a way that it will simply be seized and destroyed or that it will directly endanger the woman transmitting it or the ultimate recipient.

In view of my close personal relations and intimate acquaintance with Douglas H(amilton) I can write a few lines to him (which should be enclosed with the letter to Mrs R., without any indication of place and without a full name-an A. would suffice for signature)[45] in such a way that he alone will recognize that behind my wish[46] to see him in Lisbon there is something more serious than a personal whim. All the rest, however, seems to be extremely hazardous and detrimental to the success of the letter.

Let us suppose that the case were reversed: an old lady in Germany receives a letter from an unknown source abroad, with a request to forward a message whose recipient is asked to disclose to an unknown foreigner where he will be staying for a certain period – and this recipient were a high officer in the air force (of course I do not know exactly what position H. holds at the moment; judging from his past I can conceive of only three things; he is an active air force general, or he directs the air defence of an important part of Scotland, or he has a responsible position in the Air Ministry.)

I do not think that you need much imagination to picture to yourself the faces that Canaris or Heydrich would make and the smirk with which they would consider any offer of 'security' or 'confidence' in such a letter if a subordinate should submit such a case to them. They would not merely make faces, you may be certain! The measures would come quite automatically-and neither the old lady nor the air force officer would have an easy time of it! In England it is no different.

Now another thing. Here too I would ask you to picture the situation in reserve. Let us assume that I received such a letter from one of my English friends. I would quite naturally report the matter to the highest German authorities I could contact, as soon as I had realized the import it might have, and would ask for instructions on what I should do myself (at that, I am a civilian and H. is an officer).

If it should be decided that I was to comply with the wish for a meeting with my friend, I would then be most anxious to get my instructions if not from the Fuhrer himself, at least from a person who receives them directly and at the same time has the gift of transmitting the finest and lightest nuances – an art which has been mastered by you yourself but not by all Reich Ministers. In addition, I should very urgently request that my action be fully covered –vis-a-vis other high authorities of my own country-uninformed or unfavourable.[47]

It is not any different with H. He cannot fly to Lisbon-any more than I can!-unless he is given leave, that is unless at least Air Minister Sinclair and Foreign Minister Halifax know about it.[48] If, however, he receives permission to reply or to go, there is no need of indicating

any place in England; if he does not receive it, then any attempt through a neutral mediator would also have little success.[49]
In this case the technical problem of contacting H. is the least of the difficulties. A neutral who knows England and can move about in England – presumably there would be little sense in entrusting anyone else with such a mission- will be able to find the first peer of Scotland very quickly as long as conditions in the Isle are still halfway in order. (At the time of a successful invasion all the possibilities we are discussing here would be pointless anyway).

My proposal is therefore as follows:

Through the old friend I will write a letter to H. – in a form that will incriminate no one but will be understandable to the recipient-with the proposal for a meeting in Lisbon. If nothing comes of that, it will be possible (if the military situation leaves enough time for it), assuming that a suitable intermediary is available, to make a second attempt through a neutral going to England, who might be given a personal message to take along. With respect to this possibility, I must add, however, that H. is extremely reserved-as many English are toward anyone they do not know personally. Since the entire Anglo-German problem after all springs from a most profound crisis in mutual confidence, this would not be immaterial.[50]

Please excuse the length of this letter; I merely wished to explain the situation to you fully.
I already tried to explain to you not long ago that, for reasons I gave, the possibilities of successful efforts at a settlement between the Fuhrer and the British upper class seem to me-to my extreme regret- infinitesimally small.[51]
Nevertheless I should not want to close this letter without pointing out once more that I still think there would be a somewhat greater chance of success in going through Ambassador Lothian in Washington or Sir Samuel Hoare in Madrid rather than through my friend H.[52] *To be sure, they are-politically speaking – more inaccessible.*
Would you send me a line or give me a telephone call with final instructions? If necessary, will you also inform your brother in advance? Presumably I will then have to discuss with him the forwarding of the letter to Lisbon and the arrangement for a cover address for the reply in L(isbon).
With cordial greetings and best wishes for your health.[53]
Yours, etc
A(LBRECHT) H(AUSHOFER)

Enclosure 2
Draft Letter to D.H.[54]

Mr dear D... Even if this letter has only a slight chance of reaching you – there is a chance and I want to make use of it.
First of all to give you a sign of unaltered and unalterable personal attachment. I do hope you have been spared in all this ordeal, and I hope the same is true of your brothers. I heard of your father's deliverance from long suffering; and I heard that your brother-in-law Northumberland lost his life near Dunkerque. I need hardly tell you, how I feel about all that....

Now there is one thing more. If you remember some of my last communications before the war started you will realize that there is a certain significance in the fact that I am, at present, able to ask you whether there is the slightest chance of our meeting and having a talk somewhere on the outskirts of Europe, perhaps in Portugal. There are some things I could tell you, that might make it worth while for you to try a short trip to Lisbon – if you could make your authorities understand so much that they would give you leave. As to myself – I could reach Lisbon any time (without any kind of difficulty) within a few days after receiving news from you. If there is an answer to this letter, please address it to...[55]

C109/C002203
Dr Albrecht Haushofer to Rudolph Hess

My dear Herr Hess: In accordance with your last telephone call I got in touch with your brother immediately. Everything went off well, and I can now report that the mission has been accomplished to the extent that the letter you desired was written and dispatched this morning. It is to be hoped that it will be more efficacious than sober judgement would indicate.

Yours, Etc
H(AUSHOFER)

C109/C002204-05
Dr Albrecht Haushofer to Dr Karl Haushofer
Berlin, September 23, 1940

Dear Father: I am enclosing the copy of a short letter of serious contents, which perhaps had better be kept by you than by me. I have now made it clear enough that in the action involved I did not take the initiative...

Now to the English matters. I am convinced, as before, that there is not the slightest prospect of peace; and so I don't have the least faith in the possibility about which you know. However, I also believe that I could not have refused my services any longer. You know that for myself I do not see any possibility of any satisfying activity in the future...

Best regards to both of you.

That appears to be the end of the letters. A few things emerge:

- Hess and Hitler had been discussing the continuing need for peace following the failure to gain air supremacy over Britain in summer 1940.
- Hess then spoke with Karl Haushofer about the same issue. Haushofer mentioned Mrs.Roberts and her recent contact.
- Albrecht Haushofer is also consulted, and whilst not convinced of success, for whatever reason goes along with his master's idea of a letter. He makes it clear to Hess and his father that he feels it unlikely to succeed.
- A secondary idea of an intermediary to meet with Hamilton is also mooted.
- The letter is sent.

Please also consider the fact that these letters were taken by the United States at the end of the war and microfilmed in Alexandria, Virginia in 1949.

Copies were also distributed to the other major Archives and the original papers returned to Germany in 1958. So they have been in the public domain for a long period of time. I am just surprised that they do not appear to have been analysed in detail previously. Surely James Leasor in 1962 must have wondered who Mrs Roberts was? James Douglas-Hamilton does not specifically mention Mrs Roberts or whether his family knew of her. It may also be pertinent to record that even if Hamilton didn't directly know the Maxwell family, some of his senior staff at Prestwick on 10th May 1941 lived no more than 10 miles away from Dargavel House, their ancestral home. Hector Maclean, for instance lived at Kilmacolm, home to Newark Castle, another ancestral home of the Maxwell family.

It is these letters that started the Hess affair and provided its impetus.

---

[1] *The Battle - Richard Overy - Penguin 2000.*

[2] *Invasion 1940 - Peter Fleming - Rupert Hart Davis 1957*

[3] *The Haushofer code/ nickname for Rudolf Hess. Tomodaichi is Japanese for 'friend'.*

[4] *Grunwalder Forest, between Munich and Salzberg.*

[5] *Presumably Britain.*

[6] *Presumably Hitler, but had Hitler already already made the decision to postpone the invasion?*

[7] *A neutral location.*

[8] *General Sir Ian Hamilton.*

[9] *Presumably, The Duke of Hamilton, though alternatively one of his brothers?*

[10] *In 1940 Lisbon celebrated 400 years of Independence from Spain.*

[11] *The Duke of Kent attended on behalf of Britain. Please note the dismissive description of the Duke.*

[12] *Gallspach is an area of Upper Austria.*

[13] *The affairs of ethnic Germans abroad.*

[14] *I believe this is important. This sentence seems to imply that the Haushofers and Hess believe that Mrs.Roberts resides away from the United Kingdom.*

[15] *This is presumably the Lisbon address given the previous letter.*

[16] *This too appears to underline the supposition that Mrs.Roberts is in Lisbon.*

[17] *I think this now introduces a second option, that of the neutral intermediary, not Mrs.Roberts, but someone who is seen to be neutral to both sides and 'who has some business over there'.*

[18] *Mrs.Roberts is certainly not an 'official channel'.*

[19] *Auslands Organisation (AO). One of Hess's duties was to head up the AO. By 1940 Hess had turned the organisation into a quasi intelligence service.*

[20] *Essentially postal details.*

[21] *I am not surprised that the name of the 'neutral intermediary' is not given at this stage. I think the identity will become clearer as the story unfolds.*

[22] *Apparent evidence of the Haushofer interest in astronomy.*

[23] *Bad Godesberg, on the Rhine, south of Koblenz.*

[24] *This is a record of the start of Albrecht's involvement in the affair, directly with Rudolf Hess.*

[25] *Apparently an observation made by Haushofer to Hess.*

[26] *I am absolutely the answer to this question is yes. The more relevant is 'how?'*

[27] *The introduction of the 'Hitler issue'. Many German peace proposals had floundered as a result of Hitler having to remain in situ as leader.*

[28] *The fear of the Blockade is a theme. It was this that brought Germany to her knees in 1918.*

[29] *On 3rd September 1940 the British and US governments concluded an agreement for 50 destroyers in exchange for the US acquisition of bases in the Caribbean. The British also agreed not to scuttle the fleet in the event of invasion.*

[30] *World View.*

[31] *Absolutely 'spot on' in my estimation.*

[32] *Ditto.*

[33] *This is a reflection of the criticism of the German Foreign Office and von Ribbentrop in particular.*

[34] *In other words, no peace possible whilst Hitler is the leader.*

[35] *I am not sure about this, yes of course there were some pro German Politicians, but how was peace to be effected, especially given the above issues?*

[36] *What 'bold step'? See Chapter 1.*

[37] *This statement has often been quoted as evidence of Haushofers' naivity. On the contrary, in my view it is actually wholly correct.*

[38] *Ironically, so as not to be accused of treachery later on. Haushofer was executed in April 1945.*

[39] *Clearly Hess and Hitler had been debating the issue. The official line is that Hess was acting alone.*

[40] *Douglas Douglas -Hamilton.*

[41] *Mrs.Roberts*

[42] *The memorandum already analysed.*

[43] *A summary of the reservations already expressed to Rudolf Hess, albeit in more stringent terms.*

[44] *Evidence exists to support this view.*

[45] *Evidence of the closeness of the Haushofer/Hamilton relationship.*

[46] *I think this is the first time a Haushofer/Hamilton meeting to be mooted.*

[47] *Effectively an assurance of safety.*

[48] *This obviously assumes that Hamilton would have to ask for permission to travel to Portugal. This action would also implicate his superiors.*

[49] *A realistic assessment. If the letter route doesn't work then chances are neither will the neutral intermediary.*

[50] *This reiterates the 'neutral intermediary' route, which is now developing into a 3rd party, who may not even know the Duke of Hamilton.*

[51] *A fairly blunt assessment.*

[52] *A return to the 'official channels' again?*

[53] *A request for the final approval.*

[54] *The Duke Of Hamilton*

[55] *A simple letter requesting a meeting.*

15

THE INTRIGUE DEEPENS

SEPTEMBER 1940
TO
MAY 1941

> *'Mein Vater war noch blind*
> *vom Traum der Macht,*
> *Ich hab' die ganze Not*
> *vorausempfunden.'*
>
> Albrecht Haushofer – Moabit Sonnets
> (24) – Acheron.

The previous chapter has seen Hitler and Hess beginning to put themselves under immense pressure.

Operation Sealion had been called off/postponed/delayed in early September 1940, the planning for the May 1941 Operation Barbarossa had already been instigated in July 1940[1] and the clock was ticking....

Britain had still to be neutralised, yet despite the setbacks, the defeats and apparent hopelessness of their position, there was no settlement, or to be honest, little real hope of settlement. America was still neutral, but for how much longer? Time was perhaps beginning to run out.........

Rudolf Hess had at least some ideas, unconventional certainly, but at least some ideas, (The German Foreign Office had failed to date in much the same way as the Luftwaffe) and on 23rd September 1940 Albrecht Haushofer had sent the first letter to the Duke of Hamilton. Albrecht Haushofer was not the only contact Hess had with the British. *The Times* of 13th January 2010 details the activities of Kurt Jahnke who was apparently also reporting to Hess from pre-war Britain. The article speculated that Jahnke may have been a double agent, having been 'turned' by the British.

I believe the idea of growing time pressure is certainly pertinent to Hitler and Hess during this period. It appears to me that when under time pressure, or under the perception of being under time pressure, one often takes decisions that otherwise and in less stressful times would perhaps be more thought through. Furthermore, it is my experience that when under pressure, one often likes to be told what it is one wants to hear, rather than perhaps some more inconvenient truths. Choices that require yet more time to consider and deliberate are not usually welcome.

The 'amateur psychological' part of this analysis finishes with the rather obvious statement that if Britain would not come to the peace table voluntarily, through threat of invasion then they would have to be blasted into attendance. The Blitz of Britain was about to commence.[2]

As we have seen in the previous chapter, the sequence of letters started after Karl Haushofer's walk in the wood with Rudolf Hess at the end of August 1940. He apparently mentioned the fact that after a 'long delay' a letter had been received from their old family friend.

Whilst researching my earlier work, I met with family members of the Roberts family who stated that Mrs Roberts definitely did not leave England during World War Two. This is not particularly surprising, given that she was 76 in 1940, but it does raise the question (amongst others) of why she gave her address as being PO Box 516, Lisbon. It appears to me that Hess too [3]thought that she was in residence there,[4] but this, we know is certainly not the case.

In this connection I can only highly recommend the reader to Chavril Press's *'Undercover Addresses of WW2.'* First published in 1992 by the very helpful Entwhistles of Abernethy, Scotland, it details the means by which postal services operated during the time of war, in particular between belligerent nations. Essentially, it now appears to me that Mrs Roberts did nothing else other than make use of the services legally open to her (and anyone else) after the outbreak of war.

The British Government felt it right and proper that families and friends could continue to correspond during periods of war. However, in order to avoid accusations of government collaboration, rather than use the GPO, the company of Thomas Cook Limited was used. Cooks were already providing a similar service to the Canadian government.[5] So, in January 1940 a rudimentary service commenced, based in what was then, neutral Holland. Obviously the events of May 1940 made Holland far from neutral and so from June 1940[6] the service moved to the still very neutral Lisbon, which at that time was becoming known as 'the gateway to Europe' for that very reason.

Thomas Cook subsequently used the PO Box number 506 to pass literally millions of letters between the UK and friends and family in Germany and occupied Europe. Eventually inhabitants of the Channel Island and Prisoners of War would become the most common users. Thomas

Cook even placed advertisements in *'The Times'*, to promote the service.[7]

However, along with the service came a strict series of rules. Whilst not illegal to correspond with person's abroad, all such letters would be subject to the scrutiny of the censor. I can now list the specific rules pertaining to the service:

1) Communications must be clearly written (without erasures) and should not exceed two sides of a normal sheet of notepaper. Only one letter may be placed in one envelope.
2) Letters and envelopes must omit the sender's address. They must refer only to matters of personal interest.
   a. No reference may be made of any town (other than Lisbon), village, locality, ship or journey. No indication may be made that the writer is not in Portugal.
   b. Mention of a letter received from or written to enemy or enemy occupied territory is not permitted.
3) Each letter must be placed in an open unstamped envelope, fully inscribed to the addressee, who should be asked to address any reply to your full name, care of Post Office Box, 506, LISBON, Portugal. Poste Restante addresses are not permitted.
4) The open envelope containing the letter should be placed in an outer stamped envelope and sent to THOS COOK & SON LTD, Berkley Street, Piccadilly, London W1 together with a memorandum plainly written in BLOCK LETTERS containing the name and full address of the sender.

5) The communication to THOS COOK & SON LTD must enclose a postal order value 2s which fee will cover the postage of one envelope containing one communication to the neutral country, also of a reply (if any) from the neutral country to Messrs Cook's Head Office in London. An additional fee is payable for airmail.[8]

I believe this document exactly explains the following in our story:

- Mrs Roberts wished to communicate with her old friends the Haushofers.
- She could only write in a personal manner.
- She follows the instructions, pays her 2 shillings and the letter is sent. She probably posts the outer envelope in Cambridge, addressed to Thos Cook, London.
- She cannot give an address (on the actual letter), other than the return address in Lisbon. This explains the impression given that she was actually in Lisbon, an impression that her German friends apparently believed.
- We should not perhaps be too surprised at their ignorance; the service had only just started in Lisbon. (June 1940)
- It may well be that the 'long delay' was simply occasioned by the fact that Mrs Roberts didn't pay the extra money for airmail. (She was of Scottish blood after all!)

I now do not believe that the above sequence of events necessarily infers intelligence involvement in any way. The reason that the letters were to be left open was so that the censor could be involved before despatch. It was therefore almost an inevitability that any 'dodgy letters' would be found out and (at the least) returned to the sender.

The exact same thing happened to the Haushofer letter of 23rd September. An Auslands agent posted the reply back to PO Box 506, Lisbon, but the letter was censored by the British censor and retained. Realistically, it never stood a chance, but I do not think that the Haushofers understood the system. They thought Mrs Roberts was in Lisbon, simply *because of the rules of the system.* See above – rule 2.

We do know that when the censor forwarded the letter to RAF intelligence they were then keen to try and get the Duke of Hamilton to attend a meeting with Haushofer in the spring of 1941. We also know that the Duke of Hamilton was very careful in how he was seen to be assisting in this line of approach.[9]

We also suspect that Mary Roberts sent a further letter as there is an envelope in the Bundesarchiv dated 6th May 1941.[10]

However, I now do not believe that the Roberts letter was anything other friendly greetings, simply because they could not be; the censor would have stopped it. If Mrs Roberts was really taking part in an intelligence inspired, international intrigue would she really rely on the Thomas Cook service? It is also quite right to say that we don't know for sure, because the originating letter has yet to surface. It doesn't feature on the Alexandria, Virginia microfilms, but it may possibly reside in the Haushofer private archive in Germany. What has to be the case is that it cannot be deemed to be contentious, or the censor would have stopped it, before it left the UK, or Thomas Cook would not have sent it as it contravened Rule 2. I can imagine a rubber stamp, specially made, for the purpose.....

Moreover, given the suppression of documentation concerning the Hess affair I am surprised that the series of letters first entered the public domain in 1949. If they really were the third party evidence of intelligence stings I doubt they would have been released that early.

So, I am afraid that I have now changed my mind.

In *Hess: The British Conspiracy* I made the case that the letter was the stimulus for a forged exchange, masterminded by the British Intelligence Community. I went on to explain the linkage between Mrs Roberts and the Intelligence community through her nephew, Walter Stewart Roberts (who was a leading member of SO1)[11] and her son, Patrick,[12] who, until his death in 1937 was a very well connected, high flying, Foreign Office official.

I am now sure that whilst the German response was certainly the intended opening round of an attempted German, non-governmental peace approach, it never stood a chance. Mr Cook, his clerks and the censor saw to that.

Moreover, I fail to see how one can instigate and organise a coup d'état by post! Particularly in wartime.

Eventually, on 22nd November 1940, there is a letter in the PRO from MI5 to the Foreign Office, asking if the letter from Albrecht could be forwarded to the Duke of Hamilton.[13] This appears to follow a censors report dated 6th November 1940. Copies of the report were sent to MI5, the Foreign Office and the Inter Services Research Bureau.

I therefore believe that the first part of the Haushofer/Hess plan had failed. The written letter plan had not worked, largely because of a German misunderstanding of British wartime postal conventions. A not wholly inexcusable flaw. However, it also had the effect of alerting the British Intelligence services to the fact that the Haushofers were trying to arrange a meeting between the Duke of Hamilton and Albrecht. That was perhaps the most important implication to emerge.

Even if the 'intelligence community' had instigated the initial letter from Mrs Roberts and had managed to 'by pass' the censor, the Haushofer reply had certainly alerted British Intelligence that the bait had been taken.

So, I believe that the second approach, the plan B, was now to 'kick in'. Cue the 'neutral intermediary' that was mooted in the Haushofer letter[14] in Chapter 14. Cue also the British Secret Service, now fully alerted as to what was potentially going on and between whom.

Can I now remind you of part of the contents of the Hess letter to Haushofer, dated 8th September 1940?

'Possibly a neutral acquaintance, who had some business to attend to over there anyway, might look him up and make some communication to him, using you or Albrecht as reference.'

This seems pretty clear to me. Someone known to Albrecht and Karl Haushofer would be instructed to 'look up' the Duke of Hamilton when in Britain. (Ironically this was just the role that Hess sought for himself in May 1941!).

This is exactly what I now believe happened except British Intelligence were metaphorically standing alongside the Duke of Hamilton, looking over his shoulder, waiting precisely for when this second approach was to be made. Moreover, the Duke of Hamilton knew jolly well that British Intelligence were aware of the Haushofer approach when he was given the copy letter. So his 'card was pretty well marked' I would say. (If it needed marking, that is.)

However, I now suspect that Hamilton was already 'signed up for' and engaged in a 'sting' way before RAF Intelligence, or TAR Hamilton and the XX Committee, or MI5 got round to really addressing the issue. This is why Hamilton was perturbed in the extreme when RAF Intelligence did get round to interviewing him in early 1941[15]. They had 'missed the bus'. British Intelligence was already on the case, but a completely different department. The potential for a 'hash up' had also just increased, particularly if two operations were simultaneously mounted. So, we know, I think that the RAF Intelligence department was not involved as the May flight took place before they could get involved. Indeed there is even a RAF Intelligence letter dated 13th May 1941 making it clear that they didn't know about the Hess flight.[16]

However, you will remember that the September 23rd Haushofer letter to Mrs Roberts had been copied to three Intelligence departments; MI5, the Foreign Office and the Inter Services Research Bureau.

The latter was simply a cover name for the Special Operations Executive, probably nowadays better known as its acronym SOE. The receipt of this copy letter in their hands, I had thought, confirmed the operation by this branch of British Intelligence that eventually led to the May 1941 flight. SOE was, to an extent, a purely wartime political creation, so as to keep the Labour Party happy. Ever since the 1920's the Labour Party, not without good reason, had been suspicious of the Intelligence Services largely on account that they were staffed almost exclusively by right wing fanatics (as they saw it). Given the fact that the wartime coalition was just that, a mixture of the left and right, SOE was a trade off against a Labour Party demand for more control of the established services.

So it was that in June 1940, Hugh Dalton, the bright but volatile Minister of Economic Warfare was given overall political control of SOE, which took as its basis the old 'Section D' organisation.[17]

SOE was then split into 2 parts; SO1 (for words) and SO2 (for deeds). As was recounted in *Hess: The British Conspiracy,* SO1 was based in and around Woburn Abbey, Bedfordshire. SO1 relied upon an assortment of ex-journalists such as Sefton Delmer and ex 'City Types' such as Leonard Ingrams to come up with a highly unconventional, but nonetheless successful Black Propaganda Department. In *Hess: The British Conspiracy*, I speculated that it was SO1 that was responsible for luring Hess to England. I based this viewpoint largely on account that its financial director was none other than Walter Stewart Roberts, the nephew of Mary Violet Roberts, whose role has been described above. It all seemed rather nepotic, particularly when I discovered that two beneficiaries under Mary's will were Sir Anthony Bevir[18] and Sir Edward Playfair.

Moreover, I do not know why but Walter Stewart Roberts saw fit to change his name to Walter Stewart-Roberts by deed poll. When his Aunt died in 1958 her passing seemingly was not recorded anywhere and I am tempted to wonder if both these events are related?

Anyway, I now think that whilst SO1 certainly had the intellectual capacity and ability to come up with such a scheme, I suspect that Claude Dansey and MI6 had beaten them to it and had already started to do the work. It is also recorded that Dansey, being an 'old school' SIS man, detested SOE, seeing them essentially as amateurs (which of course they were). Consequently, I would think it unlikely that he would have welcomed collaboration with this newly formed organisation and I will now hopefully demonstrate that we now know for sure that Dansey got involved.

---

[1] *There had been two military planning conferences at the Berghof, 29th/31st July 1940 where the proposed invasion had been discussed amongst Hitler and his Generals.*

[2] *The Blitz is usually reckoned to have lasted from 7th September 1940 to 10th May 1941.*

[3] *See letter - Hess to Haushofer, previous chapter.*

[4] *As did Peter Allen (Martin's father) in the Crown and the Swastika - Hale 1983.*

[5] *Commenced 25th November 1939 - Charles Entwhistle to author. 13th October 1939.*

[6] *ibid*

[7] *ibid*

[8] *The British Postal Museum, London*

[9] *See Picknett, Prince and Prior - Double Standards - Little Brown - 2001.*

[10] *Rainer Schmidt - Botengang Eines Toren – Econ - Dussledorf 1997.*

[11] *SO1 was formed in July 1940 as part of the Special Operations Executive (SOE). Whilst its more famous colleague SO2 dealt with behind enemy lines sabotage, SO1 dealt with political propaganda, drawing on the expertise of the likes of Sefton Delmer and Ellic Howe. Based at Woburn Abbey, Bedfordshire, Walter Roberts was recruited as its 'Finance Officer', alongside many other 'City Types'. In Hess:The British Conspiracy, I drew the not stupid conclusion that the whole Hess correspondence was a product of this new department, using the knowledge that Walter's Aunt Mary was known to be a friend of the Haushofers.*

[12] *In a similar way, I made mention of the fact that many of Patrick Robert's Foreign Office contemporaries, such as Mallett and O'Malley, were now in high ranking positions within the department. Furthermore Patrick Roberts and his cousin Walter Stewart Roberts, were contemporaries of Stewart Menzies, (wartime head of MI6), whilst at Eton.*

[13] *PRO, FO 1093/11.*

[14] *C002188-89.*

[15] *Stammers of RAF Intelligence wrote to Hamilton on 26th February 1941.*

[16] *Robertson to Air Vice Marshal Medhurst. PRO KV 235.*

[17] *'D' for Destruction*

[18] *Bevir was Churchill's private secretary. Playfair was a Financial expert and subsequent Permanent Under secretary at the War Office.*

A SECOND INTERREGNUM

A second respite is now perhaps required to reflect on what has been learned to date.

Rudolf Hess and his master realise the importance of neutralising Britain before embarking on their eastward program in spring 1941.

The Luftwaffe has failed miserably to bring Britain to the negotiating table.

The German Foreign Office has also fared badly. Governmental Peace offer after Governmental Peace offer has been spurned on the basis that the British just do not trust Hitler not to subsequently go back on his word.
.
Rudolf Hess, (fast becoming desperate) has therefore decided to go 'non governmental' in his attempt at a negotiated peace. He knows there are waverers in Britain and Churchill has no other policy. Churchill too is battling to stay in power. The war is certainly not going well from his, or a British perspective.

A letter has been sent via an old contact of Albrecht Haushofer's to the Duke of Hamilton. If that fails, Hess wants to try again using a 'neutral intermediary'.

Unfortunately for Rudolf Hess, the letter sent to the 'old contact' has been intercepted by the British Censor and has been passed to the Intelligence Services.................

16

CARL JACOB BURCKHARDT

1891 – 1974

THE INDEPENDENT NEUTRAL INTERMEDIARY?

Carl Burckhardt was a Swiss academic and historian, who came to International attention in 1937 when he became the last (as events turned out) League of Nations High Commissioner for the Free City of Danzig.

Previously he had spent periods both as a University Professor and a Swiss Diplomat, but it was in the second role as Diplomat that he plays his part in this particular series of events. It seems to me that given his considerable experience in European power politics of the late 1930's he was the obvious choice for Hess's wish for an 'independent neutral intermediary' as stipulated in his letter to Albrecht Haushofer in early September 1940.[1]

Moreover, his subsequent actions and letters would only confirm this viewpoint.

   1) High Commissioner for the Free City of Danzig 1937-1939.

Given the scale of the task, this role was almost mission impossible. The Free City of Danzig was a creation of the much-maligned Treaty of Versailles in 1919 and throughout the 1930's Hitler's Germany had deliberately placed the wholly artificial creation under severe political pressure.

Carl J Burckhardt the Swiss Academic who appeared quite content to act as an intermediary between the Nazi hierarchy and British representatives – 1940-1941.

This pressure merely fermented the fact that 90-95% of the population were of German descent; in a City that post 1919 was geographically 'slap bang' in the middle of newly reconstituted Poland.

Burckhardt took over the poisoned chalice in 1937; the previous incumbent, Irishman Sean Lester, had resigned in 1935 on account of the German shenanigans.

In 1939, Germany invaded and the City was duly incorporated into the Reich. However, the role that Burckhardt had played in the two years of his tenure seem to have been universally acknowledged. Significantly he had also become well known to the Foreign Offices of the leading European players. According to *'Meine Danziger Mission'*[2], on his enforced retirement, glowing testimonials were received from, amongst others, Viscount Halifax, Baron Weizsacker and the British Ambassador to Switzerland, David Kelly.

Equally significant, a fortnight before the invasion of Poland, Burckhardt was summoned to Berchtesgaden to meet with Adolf Hitler. A transcript of the conversation is given below:

Danzig league chief's report to Britain - Aug 16, 1939
Viz. "We landed in Salzburg, stopped briefly to eat, and then took a car to the Obersalzberg. Perched on the great height of the 'Berghof', up the spiralling roadway, past the so-called 'Tea House,' sat the 'Eagle's Nest' of the leader of all the Germans."

"Here is a confirmed report that I made in Basel, Switzerland on August 13, 1939 to the representatives of Lord Halifax and Minister Georges Bonnet - Roger Makins and Minister Pierre Arnal - about the visit and conversation that I had with the Dictator."

Beginning of the Conversation
Hitler: "I hope you had a comfortable flight. My Condor aircraft is not as fast as the Douglas, but it is more solid and useful as a military aircraft. It holds up better against gunfire. You have had a stressful week. I know that you have done your best to find a peaceful solution (Hitler's friendly expression changed here into a menacing mask) but

that all of your work has been ruined by the Poles. I have suggested to [Albert] Forster that he work through the representatives of the League of Nations (Völkerbund). I do not prefer this approach, but I must be extra sure that the League of Nations is handled correctly as concerns the Saar and Danzig Questions (i.e., Hitler was referring to plebiscites here). I stress that Forster has proceeded according to my instructions because I know that this organization is objective. Despite economic repression and threats, Forster has not acted excessively. The Poles, however, who are still members of the League of Nations, I believe, have not made any effort. Last Friday (the day the Polish ultimatum arrived); I would have been satisfied with a telephone call from them. The Poles knew that talks were possible. They did not have to send a note (i.e., formal document)."

Burckhardt*: "Then the negotiations have broken down over some details."*

Hitler (looking annoyed): *"This is unfortunate at such a serious moment. Two days before matter came to a head; Chodacki received instructions from Beck to take steps to bring matters under control. He made a grave telephone call. During which, [Arthur] Greiser has told me, that certain measures were to be taken against [German] border officials; Beck broadcast all of this to the press. (Hitler then became furious) The press said that I had lost the war of nerves, that threats were the correct way to deal with me, that we had given way, because the Poles had stood firm; that I had been only bluffing the year before, and that Polish courage, which the Czechs didn't possess, had called my bluff. I have seen idiotic statements in the French press that I have lost my nerve, but that the Poles have retained theirs (Hitler became so bitter that for a few moments he was unable to speak)."*

Burckhardt: *"You give these journalists too much credit, if you take their comments so seriously. A Reich Chancellor should stand above such trifles."*

Hitler: *"I cannot do that. Because of my origin as someone who rose from the working class, because of the way I rose [to power] and because of my character, I cannot see these things in another light. These statesmen must understand this and reckon with it, if they wish to avoid a catastrophe. It is not true that the British government has no influence over the press. The press is silent when the government wishes it. (Hitler's voice rose to a crescendo) The State Secretary will summon the Polish ambassador and say to him 'the hour has come.' That is the answer to ultimatums and to the lost war of nerves. If the slightest incident occurs, I will smash the Poles so completely that not a single trace of Poland will be found afterwards. Like a lightning*

bolt I will strike with the full power of my mechanized army, the power of which the Poles have no idea. Mark my words."
Burckhardt: *"I understand but I also know that this will lead to a general conflict."*
Hitler: *"Then that is how it shall be. If I must lead Germany into war then I would rather do it today than tomorrow. I will not lead it the way Wilhelm II did; he let pangs of conscience keep him from throwing in his armed forces completely. I will fight to the very last. (Hitler paused) I once said to Lloyd George: 'If you were a private in the last war and I was a Minister, you (i.e., England), would be in a different position today than you are.' Italy (here I had the impression of some doubts on Hitler's part), will fight on my side, no matter what happens. (Here Hitler hesitated) Japan too. Thanks to my fortifications, I can hold in the west with 74 divisions. The rest will be thrown against Poland, which will be liquidated in three weeks. Switzerland has nothing to fear. I will respect their neutrality. How can they (i.e., the English) attack me? Via the air? People try to impress me with numbers and demonstrations of armaments, particularly aerial armaments. (Hitler laughed hysterically) I laugh because I am the specialist in armaments, not the others. Their air force! England has 135,000 men, France 75,000. I have 600,000 in peacetime and 1,000,000 in wartime. My flak is the best in the world, as I demonstrated in Spain. The Russians, and we know them better than do most other people; hundreds of our officers have trained in Russia, have no offensive strength and will not haul the chestnuts of others out of the fire. A nation does not murder its officers if it plans to wage a war. We defeated the Russians in Spain. The Japanese have also defeated them. (Hitler states scornfully) One cannot give us goose pimples by talking about the Russians. (Hitler now states calmly) All of this talk of war is stupidity and it makes people crazy."*
"What then is the question? **Only that we need grain and timber. For the grain I need space in the east; for the timber I need a colony, only one [colony]. We can survive.** *Our harvests in 1938 and in this year were excellent. We can survive, in spite of the triumphant cries of others that we will starve. We have achieved these harvests thanks to the persistence of our people and above all due to the use of chemical fertilizers. However, one day the soil will have had enough ... What then? I cannot stand by and let my people starve. Am I not better off then in putting two million men on the battlefield, than in losing them to starvation? Perhaps there are still among the apostles of humanity (i.e., those who seek peace at any cost), those who remember 1919. I do not want to repeat that. I will not repeat that. Free trade, open borders, that is all practical, we had*

these things. However when everything depends upon those masters of the seas (i.e., the English), when we can be brought low by a blockade, then it is my duty to create a situation whereby by my people can live off of their own fat. That is the only question, the rest is insanity."

"I do not harbour any romantic aims. I have no wish to rule. **Above all I want nothing from the West; nothing today and nothing tomorrow.** *I desire nothing from the thickly settled regions of the world ... All of the notions that are ascribed to me by other people are inventions.* **However, I <u>must have a free hand in the east</u>. To repeat: it is a question of grain and timber, which I can find only outside of Europe."**

Burckhardt: *"I came here because of Danzig. I am not inclined to discuss other matters. A new war will usher in the end of civilization. That is a great responsibility [to bear] for the future. It is better to live in honour than to take such a responsibility upon oneself. The stronger one is, the longer he can be patient. The more honour a man has, the more attacks he can fend off. Someone once said to me that Germany's strength lies in being patient when it comes to the Polish and Danzig Questions."*

Hitler (in a serious tone): *"That is very important. (Turning to Forster) We must mention this to Ribbentrop."*

Burckhardt: *"I am fully convinced that this problem can be solved via negotiations and that the Western Powers are prepared to talk."*

Hitler (in a serious tone): "Why then do they incite the Poles to boast about their ultimatums and to send ultimatums to us!"

Burckhardt (speaking pointedly): *"This is not worth discussing. London and Paris exercise a moderating influence in Warsaw. The Danzig Question is very simple. It is a matter of a complex of international laws that can no longer be violated through one-sided pressure, through force, or through the threat of force."*

Hitler (slamming his fist on the table): "Talks! But on what basis? Do you remember the disarmament talks? I made a generous offer to the Poles. In March I wanted, after I removed the threat of war with Czechoslovakia from my southeast flank, to put out two burning issues: Memel and Danzig. Every time I took a step, and this is borne out by history, I found England and France in my path. What then can I do?"

Burckhardt: *"Prior to March 15th your argument was about the [German] people. It corresponded to certain natural laws that standing international agreements stood in defiance of. There were people who sympathized with these arguments."*

Carl Jacob Burckhardt 1891-1974

Hitler: "*Yes, March 15th has an adverse impact. This viewpoint is not unknown to me. I have heard it before. However, an acute danger must be eliminated through a moderate solution; this would have been better so foreigners think. (Speaking calmly) Four unfortunate accidents occurred concerning Czechoslovakia. Germans were responsible for two of these. The intellectuals were against my solution. The workers and farmers are at peace with it, as it always is when solutions are simple. They cannot imagine much war materiel we discovered in Czechoslovakia. It was a real surprise. We could hardly believe our eyes, and everything was in perfect order! Their inventories amazed our soldiers. The Czechs are and always have been excellent administrators, which is very different from the Poles. The general staff plans of the Czechs were the endeavours of school children, precise, modest, and narrow-minded. This is very different from the general staff plans of the Poles, which we possess, and which far exceed the visions of Alexander and Napoleon. Their technical and organizational state, however, is deplorable. Our soldiers are firmly committed [to war] in view of Polish impudence. Last year my generals were cautious and I had to take that into account. This year I must hold them back. Following my Reichstag address the generals gathered around me and said with great relief: 'thank God the Poles did not accept [my offer concerning the extra-territorial highway to Danzig]'. That was no real solution. For me, however, it is true when I say it was a solution, namely, my contribution to the case for peace. Later on I attempted to address our agricultural needs through a conference. We truly could have worked with the Poles on this subject. By allowing an extraterritorial highway no stone would have fallen from the Polish crown. The extraterritorial highway and Polish roads could have been bridged or connected by tunnels. They did not need to hinder one another. Our separated lands naturally would like to have connections to the Reich. This is essential to me.*"
Burckhardt: "*Has this solution finally been set aside then?*"
Hitler (perking up): "*Unfortunately it was finally set aside by the Poles. Once they had taken this position, they could not go back. This is a shame.*"
(There was a long pause. Hitler then stood up and offered to take me on a tour of the property)
Hitler (walking on the road outside of the building): "*How happy I am when I am here. I have had enough trouble. I need my rest.*"
Burckhardt (stating suggestively): "*You are expressing the sentiments of the entire world. You more than anyone has the chance to give the world the peace and quiet it needs.*"

Hitler: "*No, it is not so. (Hitler dismissed Foerster and stood there nervously while speaking softly) Because I recognize that England and France are inciting Poland to war, in which case I would rather have war today than tomorrow; to lead it this year rather than next year. Surely, however, one should attempt to find a way out? If the Poles leave Danzig at peace, if they do not attempt to hoodwink me with falsified maps, then I can wait. However a condition is that I must stop the suffering of our minority in Poland. No one believes me but I have ordered that sensational cases (e.g., castrations, etc.) not be mentioned in the press. They enrage public opinion very much. However, I cannot hold back the truth for much longer. The limits of patience have been reached.*"

"*I am able to bring forward victims, for example in the South Tyrol. Yet no one gives me any recognition for this, instead they shriek: '[that is] unjust and inhumane!' I can bring forward political victims too, but everything has its limit.*"

"*I did not always know it, but I know now, that England and France belong inseparably with one another. That is the nature of things. I do not intrigue against this situation, which is quite different from those other who intrigue against my friendship with Italy. I fought in the trenches for four years against England and France and I recognize the courage of both of these peoples. Yet there is something about the Anglo-Saxons (and the Americans) that separates them deeply from us [Germans]. What is it?*"

Burckhardt: "*Perhaps it is their fidelity when faced with obligations?*"

Hitler: "*One can interpret that in different ways. We recognize our deeds for what they are. They are hypocrites. I can cite examples.*"

Burckhardt: "*Paix - Pax - Pacts, these words all have the same root, as do the words peace (Friede) and joy (Freude). With the Germans it is always a case of the sense [of a word].*"

Hitler: "**We are an ethnic nation (Volksstaat), the English an Empire. We are an [organic] body, England is an association.**"

Burckhardt: "*But the Czechs and Slovaks are an association.*"

Hitler (speaking calmly): "*The Protectorate is a necessity for the moment. The Slovaks can do what they want. I will not put any pressure on them. They can remain as they are or, if they so desire, they can join themselves with the Hungarians. I will not stand in the way. However, the Hungarians are incapable of ruling over them or of organizing them. I return once again to the same question: grain and timber. If someone wants to speak about these then I will listen. But it is an entirely different matter if they insult me and drown me out with laughter, as they did in May this last year. [This is a very important point. Hitler is referring the May 1938 threat of war by Britain and France relating to the Czech crisis.] I am not bluffing. If even the slightest incident occurs in Danzig or anything happens to our minorities, I will strike hard."*

Burckhardt: *"Forster told me that I should ask you a question - should I allow my children to remain in Danzig?"*

Hitler: "Anything can happen in Danzig any day now, but only if the Poles will it to be so. I believe that your children would be better off in Switzerland."

"I have enjoyed seeing you. You come from a world that is alien to me. However, I have fought for a peaceful solution. I have great sympathy for another man, Lord Halifax. Many people have spoken badly of him to me, but my favourable first impression remains. I believe that he is a man who sees things in a very measured way and who also wants a peaceful solution. I hope to see him again someday."

Burckhardt continued:

"At the moment [I was leaving], before Hitler turned to go back into the Main Room, he had said to me: 'I would like, before it is too late, to speak to an Englishman who can speak German.' I responded, 'Sir Neville Henderson speaks fluent German, from what I hear.' However, Hitler shook his head, 'That does not make sense,' he said, 'he is a diplomat who does not have a keen mind, I would like to speak with a man like Lord Halifax. But he can no longer come in person. How are things with Marshal Ironside? [3] *I hear good things about him. Will you tell this to the English?'"*

Burckhardt added afterward that this final comment of Hitler's was later reprinted by the English in a report following Burckhardt's meeting with Roger Makins[4] *and Pierre Arnal*[5] *in Basel, Switzerland on August 13, 1939. However, this comment was left out of the French version of his report. Burckhardt claims that this occurred for the following reason;*

"(We, the English, the French, and myself,) had a standing and firm agreement that no one was supposed to know of the meeting I had with the two diplomats at my home in Basel. To my great astonishment, however, Minister Arnal was called to the telephone while I was in the middle of my report. Alarmed, I asked, 'what is the meaning of this? It was a precondition of our meeting that no one was to know of it!' Arnal reassured me, 'the only one who knows is our ambassador in Bern. Only he can call me here," and Arnal left the room. During his absence I expressed to Mr Makins Hitler's wish to meet with Marshal Ironside."

"Yet as soon as Arnal returned, what he told me made my transmission of Hitler's wish for a final contact with the English moot. 'The ambassador,' Arnal explained, 'shared with me the news that the entire event of your visit to the Obersalzberg will be published in Paris Soir; and that the report will be so sensational it includes certain untrue elements, among which is the claim that Hitler handed you a letter to Neville Chamberlain in which he asks the Prime Minister to join the Germans in a pact against Russia."

"This news brought to nothing the hopes that I had for my conversation at the Obersalzberg. ... The writer of this ludicrous article was a young journalist. ... As I later learned, on the morning of 11 August he had attempted to enter my office. A secretary had received him and told him that I had gone on a hunting trip in Austria. ... He then went around the city [of Danzig] and met with a number of people, asked questions, and learned that the airstrip had been closed since noon. He then went directly to the airstrip and spoke there with a Polish official who told him that the High Commissioner, escorted by the Gauleiter [of Danzig - Forster], has climbed into the private plane of the Reich Chancellor (Hitler) and flown away. The remaining parts of the report were a combination of this news and the fantasies of the young reporter."

Lastly, Burckhardt reported:

"Yet another thing was missing from the reports of Makins and Arnal, perhaps the most remarkable comment made to me by the Chancellor. Hitler had said to me on that August 11th: Everything I undertake is directed against Russia. If the West is too stupid and too blind to comprehend this I will be forced to reach an understanding with the Russians, turn and strike the West, and then after their defeat turn back against the Soviet Union with my collected strength. I need the Ukraine and with that no one can starve us out as they did in the last war."

"Following the meeting [with Makins and Arnal] I was so defeated by the indiscretion [that had been shown], that I had not reported this final and surprising comment of the Chancellor; it had seemed so completely improbable [that Hitler had said this] as to be part of an hallucination."

This report I believe to be important for a variety of reasons. Firstly it shows the relationship between Hitler and Burckhardt; Burckhardt certainly does not appear to be 'star struck'. Secondly, it appears to me that the conversation was certainly intended for British consumption and thirdly, the Foreign policy objectives appear to be very much a lesson from the Haushofer/Mackinder School of geopolitics.

Hitler was not to be disappointed. As soon as Burckhardt got back to Basle he made his report and forwarded it to Viscount Halifax, Foreign Secretary in the Chamberlain government. The report made the Daily Telegraph and was reprinted on the 60th anniversary of its original publication in August 1939.

A REPORT FROM CARL J. BURCKHARDT, HIGH COMMISSIONER OF THE LEAGUE OF NATIONS, ON HIS MEETING WITH ADOLF HITLER ON AUGUST 11, 1939

Viscount Halifax, the Foreign Secretary, received a message yesterday from Prof. Burckhardt, League High Commissioner in Danzig, recording the tenour of the conversation he had with Herr Hitler at Berchtesgaden on Friday.

This information, as I predicted yesterday, is being treated by the Foreign Office as strictly confidential, seeing that the interview was sought by Herr Hitler, through a personal invitation to Prof. Burckhardt with a request that the matter should be treated in this way.

There is, however, full authority for stating that neither through Prof. Burckhardt, nor any other source, has the British Government received any proposals for a settlement of the Danzig question.

I can also reiterate that the League High Commissioner did not deliver any message from the British Government.

Indeed, it seems unlikely that he had any opportunity to do so, for it is learned that his interview with Herr Hitler lasted only half an hour. The bulk of this was occupied by the German Chancellor in expressing his views on the Danzig situation and asking questions on the circumstances in which local incidents have arisen. Had the interview taken the form of an exchange of views, Professor Burckhardt would have been in a position to give Herr Hitler a precise re-statement of the British viewpoint.

That viewpoint is that any attempt to change the present status of Danzig by force, or the threat of force, which Poland felt compelled to resist, would immediately call into play the British and French guarantees of armed support.

BRITISH ATTITUDE TO CHANGE

At the same time, he could have added, Britain would naturally welcome any peaceful solution of the Danzig problem acceptable to all parties concerned, but particularly to Poland, of whom further concessions are being demanded by Germany.

Such a statement would, in effect, have been no more than a restatement of Britain's attitude as already publicly stated by the Prime Minister and Foreign Secretary.

Professor Burckhardt was in a position to know that there has been no change in this attitude. But it seems improbable that he was invited to express any opinion on such matters. These circumstances account for the fact that no special importance was attached yesterday to the incident. The visit is regarded as no more than an item in the general development of events, a development which is expected to proceed in a variety of forms, both militarily and diplomatically, during the next few weeks.

It now appears to me that in inviting Burckhardt to OberSalzberg, Hitler had yet again opened the 'governmental' peace proposals to the West, even before the Polish invasion had been launched. The essential messages were all relayed to Burckhardt, the need to go east for resources, the wish for co existence etc etc etc. These were to become the themes of the mantra that now formed the basis of the 'peace feeler' season that was about to commence following the Polish invasion.

The next we hear of Burckhardt is in July 1940, nearly a year later when this time he is seen to be approaching the British Cabinet. (See CAB 65 papers – PRO.)

On Wednesday 10th July 1940 The War Cabinet met at 10 Downing Street, London. Present were Messrs Churchill, Chamberlain, Attlee, Halifax and Greenwood. Also in attendance were Lord Simon, General Dill, John

Anderson, Duff Cooper, Viscount Caldecote and AV Alexander.

After dealing with matters concerning Evacuation, Home defence, and The Far East, Minute Number 5 dealt with *'Germany: plans and intentions.'* It reads:

'A telegram had been received from our Minister in Switzerland (No.365) giving an account of a conversation which a traveller, recently returned from a visit to Berlin.'

The War Cabinet agreed with the Foreign Secretary's view that no reply should be sent to this telegram.

A pretty bland statement one might think, until one actually reads the copy telegram, which was attached to the minutes. I now reproduce this, as sent, and would say that I haven't seen it in any previous work on the subject. Burckhardt was now the acting Head of the International Red Cross, based in Geneva, Switzerland.

Decypher. Mr. Kelly, (Berne).
8th July 1940.
D. - 1-35 a.m. 9th July, 1940,
Ra 7,25 a.m. 9th July, 1940.
No.. 365.
IMPORTANT.

Secret and Confidential.
M Paravicini asked me today to meet Dr Carl Burckhardt, Acting President of the Red Cross,, who has just returned, from a visit to Berlin on mission regarding Red Cross relief for refugees in France. Baron Weiszacker had sent an aeroplane for him and he stayed three days.

2. After begging me to treat his communication with the utmost discretion Dr Burckhardt said he was given opportunity for long individual conversations with (Gauleiters, one General and Weiszacker himself. All four told the same story.

3. Hitler had returned to his old idea and hesitated - , before attacking England because he still clung to the hope of working arrangement with the British Empire as hinted at in his recent interview in Belgium with the American journalist Carl von Wiegand. He wanted a European Federation and felt this would be "difficult without British co-operation. There were some "local demands" of Italy which he was bound to support but in general he wanted "a white peace like Sadowa" (two of the talkers used this formula). The General said that while they were confident of their ability to defeat England they realised that it might involve -much greater sacrifices than had the defeat of the French army, most of whom had put up a very poor show and fought half-heartedly.

4. Each of the four had insisted that he was expressing his personal opinion but one of them had asked Doctor Burckhardt whether there was any chance of his having Red Cross business in England when he might see if there was any hope of a "reasonable arrangement."[6] Doctor Burckhardt said he could not do so but would talk to an English friend in Switzerland.[7]

5. The Doctor assured me that (a) his Red Cross mission was very important and not a cover for these conversations and (b) German Government really were hesitating with the preparations for an attack on England and they were willing to call it off if they could do so without the loss of face.

6. He said that he felt sure that this was not due to weakness hut to a faint hope of avoiding further sacrifices involved although he also said that he had watched Hitler's triumphal entry into Berlin and felt that there was no spontaneous enthusiasm.

7. I told Dr Burckhardt (as I already had on the previous occasion), that I thought that our distrust of Hitler, apart from anything else, was a fatal obstacle to any peace. He said that he fully appreciated this but had thought it his duty to Switzerland to inform me of his conversations. He had hesitated about telling me "because it would be most disastrous for him personally if any of this obtained any sort of publicity."[8] Whatever we might think he begged that his report should be treated as absolutely secret.

8. It is very important for our own position here that his wish should be respected as he is most influential here[9] and if he were made to look foolish, my own position and reputation for discretion would be compromised. The situation is difficult enough.

9. Burckhardt mentioned casually that he would have to return to Berlin shortly about the refugee problem.

10. Presumably we shall have no thought of compromising on any such lines but if it is important for us to gain time[10] I venture to suggest that it might be better to leave me Without instructions rather than to return a flat negative. If then Dr Burckhardt should again approach me before returning to Berlin it will show us that - he was really being soundedwhile the Germans will be left guessing as to whether His Majesty's Government are taking their talk seriously or not. So long as secrecy is maintained complete silence on our part can. in no way weaken our war effort while it may weaken that of the enemy by causing hesitation.

I believe that this is significant. Firstly, in that the telegram was discussed at all by the War Cabinet and secondly that no reply was sent, according to minute 5.

What was not minuted was if the telegram was then forwarded to any other departments for discussion, action or debate. A British policy is also becoming established; the need to buy time. By not giving Burckhardt a reply the War Cabinet were buying time by allowing him to say quite honestly that he did not know the British response.

The other theme that is starting to appear is that Britain cannot make peace whilst Hitler is in charge. 'We' do not trust him but 'we' do trust the Americans.

So, I hope the above telegrams and reports give some idea as to the standing of Carl Burckhardt in July/August 1940 when the Hess/Haushofer non-governmental peace mission begins. Extremely well connected with both sides of the conflict, but in a strictly guarded and protected non-governmental way. The non-political status of the Red Cross demanded that it should be so. The 'mission statement' of the International Red Cross is:

"The International Committee of the Red Cross (ICRC) is an impartial, neutral and independent organization whose exclusively humanitarian mission is to protect the lives and dignity of victims of armed conflict and other situations of violence and to provide them with assistance."

Clearly Burckhardt could do nothing that would impinge the above principles. To do so could compromise the organisation terminally, a not unrealistic prospect given that the League of Nations had also recently bitten the dust. Burckhardt was playing with fire, a fact he clearly recognised.

When Richard and I travelled to Geneva in 2007 the Burckhardt archivist made it plain to us that CJB had extensively sifted the archives post 1945 so as to preserve his neutrality. The future of the Red Cross was possibly at stake.

We have already described the Thomas Cook mail service that Mrs Roberts made use of in the autumn of 1940. Perhaps unbeknown to her, she actually had a choice; the Red Cross had also initiated its own service, but only allowed a maximum of 25 words at a time. The Philatelic Society described it thus:

"Following the declaration of War in September 1939 the International Committee of the Red Cross obtained specific agreement from the British, French and German Governments for short messages to be exchanged between members of the same family living in belligerent countries as **un-interned** civilians. Such messages were only to be exchanged via the offices of the International Red Cross Committee in Geneva.

The British Chief Postal Censor approved the new scheme which was introduced in London from 11th December 1939 and extended to provincial centres within a year. A Red Cross Message Bureau was opened in most cities and main towns usually in offices of the Citizens Advice Bureau.[11] Messages of 10 words at a cost of 6d, including a reply on the reverse side, were accepted and this was later extended to 25 words at a cost of 1/-. All messages had to be sent via a Bureau and censorship was strict. At first restricted to relatives and fiancées, this limited communication was soon extended to include friends.

Message forms from the United Kingdom were routed from the Red Cross Bureau to the ICRC in Geneva using various routes as the war situation required. Those destined for the Channel Islands were then sent on to Paris via Germany and then on to the German military headquarters in Jersey. Those for the Bailiwick of Guernsey were forwarded to German military headquarters in St. Peter Port. Conversely messages and replies to the United Kingdom from the Channel Islands followed a similar route back. Overall messages are known to have taken up to nine months to complete their round journey although the average journey was around 4 to 5 months. It is difficult to understand in this age of immediate communication today how terribly restrictive this only means of contact was with a short monthly postal message and a reply that was received so much later......".[12]

Carl Burckhardt therefore had direct access to a mail service should he need to communicate in that way. He was still a trusted intermediary of the Germans and an important messenger to the British. However, he also had other, far more direct routes through third parties.

---

[1] See previous chapter.

[2] Meine Danziger Mission - CJ Burckhardt - Callwey - 1980.

[3] Edmund Ironside (1880 – 1959) would appear a somewhat odd choice for Hitler to make. In November 1938 he was appointed to the role of Governor of Gibraltar. In September 1939 he became Chief of the Imperial General Staff.

[4] Roger Makins in August 1939 was an up and coming English diplomat who eventually became Ambassador to the United States in 1953.

[5] French diplomat 1892-1971

[6] A duplicate in intent of that expressed in the Hess/Haushofer letter of September 1940. The use of a neutral intermediary.

[7] As to who this might be will be discussed later.

[8] Presumably so as to safeguard the integrity of the Red Cross.

[9] A clear statement of his standing at this time.

[10] A clear British policy at this time. "Jaw Jaw being better than War War"

[11] The Citizen Advice Bureau opened it first 200 offices on 4th September 1939.

[12] The Royal Philatelic Society.

17

CARL BURCKHARDT'S UNLIKELY WARTIME VISITORS

'Switzerland in wartime was, as always, the country where deals were done, where the belligerents from both sides could meet, talk and frequently double cross each other.'

Colonel 'Z' - The Secret Life of a Master of Spies[1]

We have already seen and recorded Carl Burckhardt's activities in the autumn of 1939. In August he was summoned by Hitler, directly reporting back to the British. In September 1939 he visited Britain, after which he returned to Geneva to take up his Professorship at the Graduate Institute of International Studies.

I would now like to reflect upon two, somewhat unlikely visitors that made their way to Geneva during 1940/1941. As well as his Professorship, Burckhardt maintained close associations with the International Red Cross, also based in Switzerland. Indeed from reading 'Dunants Dream' it appears that he and Lucie Odier masterminded the organisation and structure of the Relief Committee.

1. Professor Tancred Borenius

The Diaries of Ulrich von Hassell[2] were published as early as 1948[3], in an attempt to demonstrate to the recently victorious peoples of the Western Alliance that not all Germans were pro-Nazi and pro-Hitler. The diaries were seen as part of the post war healing process, a process made all the more pertinent given the threat starting to emanate from beyond the Iron Curtain. Von Hassell, (1888-1944) was a former German Ambassador who was executed following the failed July 1944 attempt on Hitler's life. His diaries from 1938 to the date of his death, record the various approaches that were made to Nazi Germany through various countries and personages in an attempt to forge a peace. As such, his January 1941 entry records the fact that Carl Burckhardt had 'looked me up in Geneva' to tell him that 'very recently' Tancred Borenius, had come to him to explain, 'apparently on behalf of English officials, that a reasonable peace could still be concluded'.

The use of the word 'apparently' always intrigues me. I think it usually means 'giving the appearance of ....but'. Borenius was either on behalf of English officials or not. The very use of the word I believe means that the author had doubts as to its application.

I now believe that this visit was the next stimulus for the Hess flight, not the 'Roberts letter' as the Germans would have anticipated that any 'ghosted reply' would have been caught by the censor. A direct approach was both necessary and vital. It was really the *only* way that a non-governmental peace approach could be efficiently communicated in time of war, orchestrated by the Intelligence services or not.

Carl Tancred Borenius was born in Wiborg, in what was then Eastern Finland, in 1885. I reproduce a CV:

Tancred Borenius – the Finnish Art Historian and part-time envoy.

Date born: 1885.
Place born: Viipuri (a.k.a. Wiborg), Finland, modern Vyborg, Russia.
Date died: 1948.
Place died: Coombe Bissett, near Salisbury, Wiltshire, United Kingdom.

Italian renaissance scholar, dealer, and art magazine editor. Borenius was the son of Carl Borenius, a member of the Finnish Diet. Borenius was educated at the Swedish Lyceum and before Helsinki University (Helsingfors), then Berlin and Rome. In Hesinki, he studied under Johan Jakob Tikkanen (qv). After receiving his PhD in Helsingfors in 1909, he moved to London where he published a version of his dissertation, Painters of Vincenza (1909). The same year he married Anne-Marie Rüneberg, granddaughter of the Finnish poet JL Rüneberg. Roger Fry (qv) became a close friend, providing him entré into the art circles of London. An updated 1912 edition of *The History of Painting in North Italy* by Joseph Archer Crowe (qv) and Giovanni Battista Cavalcaselle (qv) bore notes by Borenius. In 1914 he was appointed lecturer at University College, London, in the position vacated by Fry. When Finland achieved independence, he acted as secretary of the diplomatic mission (1918) and later as representative of Finland in London (1919). From 1922-47 he was Durning-Lawrence Professor at the College. It was during this period that he published his major books. Although initially an historian of Italian art, Borenius also became an expert of the art of his adopted country. His methodology employed significant connoisseurship. He helped found *Apollo* in 1925, to which he often contributed. Borenius' opinion on art was highly valued in England; he was advisor to the Earl of Harewood's art collection and, in 1924, Sotheby's auction house. Together with EW Tristram (qv) he published *English Medieval Painting* in 1929. In 1932 he became active in archaeology by launching the dig at Clarendon Palace (Salisbury). Borenius played an influential role in two scholarly art journals. After admission to the Burlington Fine Arts Club, he contributed many articles to the *Burlington Magazine*, acting as its editor between 1940-45. By then Borenius was no longer considered reliable on attributions at Sotheby's (and considered himself too grand to do the work of cataloguing), and was replaced in 1945 by Hans Gronau (qv). Among his book editing duties, in addition to the *History of Painting in Italy*, he assisted with the volume *On Art and Connoisseurship* (1942) by Walter Friedlaender (qv). He died after a long illness. His students included Enriqueta Harris [Frankfort] (qv). Home Country: Finland/United Kingdom.[4]

Clearly and obviously, Borenius was in communication terms, non-governmental. He relied on direct contact and as such was also out of direct governmental control, or the illusion of direct governmental control. He could not be censored and because of his Finnish passport could presumably travel unhindered through then occupied Europe. He was the ideal messenger boy to the 'neutral intermediary' (Burckhardt) that Hess was suggesting in his letter to the Haushofers of September 1940. I had to find out more about Borenius and go 'beyond' the standard biography. One surely has to ask the obvious question as why, and indeed how, a 56-year-old Finnish Art expert is travelling through enemy occupied Europe in 1941 in order to visit Carl Burckhardt?

I was and continue to be very lucky in this part of research. Whilst researching the 1999 book, I had trawled through the Salisbury telephone book and had spoken to Tancred Borenius's son, Lars Ulrich, known as Peter.[5]

His father's wartime trip had caused some (post event) amusement in the Borenius household on two accounts; firstly that he had been asked to deliver a 'book' to Burckhardt and secondly that he had been given a poison pill the size of a golf ball. The family thought that Borenius would choke on the pill way before the supposed poison would take its effect. Borenius had apparently passed through Geneva on his way to Italy. He also said that he had been given the book by Claude Dansey, prior to his departure.

I must confess that I had not really grasped the significance of the last sentence as at the time I was in the process of getting carried away on the Mrs Roberts/SO1/Polish bandwagon.

Claude Dansey was the Deputy Head of MI6, who were in the process of rebuilding their credibility following the loss of their 'passport office' system of intelligence at the outbreak of World War 2.[6]

Ten years later, after finding my original notes, I spoke to Tancred's granddaughter, Aurelia, concerning her grandfather. She too was very kind and added to my knowledge of her intriguing ancestor.

The CV reproduced above does not really do justice to Tancred Borenius. His granddaughter makes the point that he was extremely well connected, a brilliant raconteur, but wholly impracticable; he could not drive for instance. Osbert Lancaster, in a Daily Mail cartoon, characteristically portrayed him as a rather plump eccentric.

It also appears to me that he thoroughly enjoyed mixing with, cultivating and advising the upper classes. The CV makes the point that he became art advisor to the Harewood Family, (Viscount Lascelles, 6th Earl of Harewood had of course married Princess Mary, the only sister to Princes David, Albert, Henry, John and George in 1922), but this certainly does not appear to be his only commission to the rich and famous of 1930's England.

He acted for the Methuen Family[7] of Corsham Court in north Wiltshire and the National Portrait Gallery hold photographs of Borenius with Phillip and Ottoline Morrell,[8] prominent members of the 'Bloomsbury Set'. He catalogued the porcelain collection of Frederick Leverton

Harris[9] and occasionally acted as dealer, buying and selling works of art for the rich and formerly rich. On 8th December 1927 *The Times* noted that Borenius had acquired a picture for £350.

We have already seen how Borenius advised Viscount Lascelles, though it is perhaps fair to say that as the 1930's reached their climax, the 'quality' of Borenius's appointments book also increased. Borenius had been cultivating Royal connections; in 1922 he sent the Duke and Duchess of York a copy of his latest book, *'Travels in Italy'* as a wedding present.

In 1936 Prince George and Princess Marina visited Wiltshire, stopping at Wilton House over the weekend of 11th/12th July. On the Saturday it was recorded that the couple met Tancred Borenius in Salisbury Close.

A fortnight later he was presented to the King, this time in a Diplomatic capacity. Aurelia Borenius told me that as he got older he not unnaturally rediscovered his political energy, largely on account of what was happening in Eastern Europe. (In 1939 Borenius's sister had to flee the family home in Wiborg so as to escape the invading Russians.)

In February 1937 he attended a reception at Hyde Park Hotel to commemorate the centenary of Alexander Pushkin's death. Samuel Hoare was in the Chair.

On 7th December 1937 The Duke of Kent was the principal guest at the Anglo Finnish Society. Tancred replied to the Duke's toast. In 1940 he was recorded as a member of the Executive Committee. On 23rd September 1941 he addressed the Royal Institute for International Affairs at Chatham House on the subject of 'The Eastern Frontier of Finland and the East Carelian situation'.[10] It will be remembered that Albrecht Haushofer had also addressed the institute in 1937.

Coombe Bissett Churchyard – the last resting place of Tancred Borenius and his wife Anne-Marie.

In May 1939 he attended a reception at the Swedish legation. Baron Knut Bonde was also recorded as an attendee.

A year later I suspect he briefly returned to the art world. On 19th May 1940, nine days after the German invasion of the Low Countries, there was a major Art Sale in London. The Duke of Kent bought *'The Altieri Claudes'*, two classical Italian paintings painted by Claude Lorraine in the late 17th century. The Duke paid £3990 and £840 for the two paintings that were previously sold for £6090 and £1785 in 1884. I suspect the proximity of the German Werhmacht to London may have had a depressing effect on the 1940 Fine Art prices.[11]

I do not know for sure that Borenius was involved in the purchase, but given that the two men certainly knew each other by this time and the pictures were full square in Borenius' sphere of expertise, it is certainly not inconceivable that he was involved. In 1947, when the Duke's executors sold the pictures on a healthy profit was achieved.

Tancred Borenius's sister had married into a Polish family and given his dislike of all things Russian, Borenius became Hon.Secretary General to the Polish Relief fund. The headquarters was in London at 10, Grosvenor Place, SW1 and on 1st May 1940 the British College of Nursing magazine recorded Tancred Borenius bidding farewell to a group of Canadian Poles embarking on a foreign mission. This organisation was clearly substantial. The British government had contributed £100,000 in clothing and other forms of relief. It was through this organisation that Borenius came to meet and know General Sikorski. It must also say something about Borenius that the Hon.Secretary General of the Polish Relief fund wasn't even a Pole.

However, as Von Hassell records, when Burckhardt met with Borenius in Geneva, Borenius went through and recited the usual peace demands; restoration of Holland and Belgium, some kind of Poland etc, etc. Then came the inevitable stumbling block, *"...one was highly reluctant to make peace with Hitler. The main reason, one simply can't believe a word he says"*

Von Hassell continued by saying that the English Consul General had also told Burckhardt the same thing.

The last point to consider is how Borenius got to Geneva and so we return to the issue of wartime communication and British Intelligence. I have already stated how Peter Borenius had told me that before embarking to Geneva his father had been briefed by Claude Dansey and given a book to deliver,[12] together with the impractical cyanide pill. What I had not really 'thought through' were the implications of what I had just been told. Harris being dim again. 10 years later, at least I realised I needed to do some work.

Firstly, why was he given a suicide pill? Surely, if he really was visiting as an Art Historian, the need to consider killing yourself would not be pertinent? I can only conclude that he was in possession of information that would render the use of the pill necessary were he to be captured?

Secondly, I would love to know how he physically got to Switzerland? If my supposition is correct and he was travelling as an independent traveller, then the only route available to him would be England/Lisbon/Spain/Vichy France/Switzerland. Stockholm was too dangerous. Fast Air flights in and out only started in late 1941 and the subsequent travel through Germany would be asking for trouble. I really can't see Claude Dansey arranging to drop Tancred from a Lysander or some such and even if he did, this straight away implies a governmental sponsored approach, which is exactly NOT what being inferred. Governmental Peace feelers had fallen on sterile ground.

No, I now believe that the British MI6/MI9 had arranged for passage for Tancred, through the only route available to him. We also do not know if he were accompanied?

I now think it pertinent to learn a little more about Claude Dansey, the man who briefed Borenius in early 1941.

Claude Dansey – the MI6 deputy general during the war years. Why did he see fit to brief Borenius, the art librarian prior to his 1941 trip to Geneva?

Claude Dansey (1876-1947), was the epitome of a British Secret Service agent. Devious, untrustworthy,

"Dansey was an utter shit....." according to Hugh Trevor Roper.[13] Dansey had endured a strange childhood under a dominant father, many siblings and was supposedly buggered when aged 16 by one of Oscar Wilde's lovers. However, buggered shit or not, he rose to become the Deputy Head of SIS or MI6. At the end of the second world war he was literally showered with honours from around the world and Anthony Read and David Fisher very much make the case that whilst Deputy to Stewart Menzies, it was Dansey who was the real 'power behind the throne'. An Intelligence Officer since 1900, he was certainly astute enough to realise that the traditional European 'Passport Office' system made MI6 very vunerable to the effects of invasion, which of course is precisely what happened in 1940.

Consequently, throughout the 1930's he had effectively established an alternative system, the 'Z' system. The 'Z' system relied on individual intelligence gathering, often using established businesses as a 'front'. Nigel West in 'MI6'[14] deals with this method of working and details some 'front' companies.

- Menoline Limited
- H.Sichel and Sons – wine merchants
- Lamnin Tours - holidays

And,
- Sir Geoffrey Duveen and Company.

It was this last company that aroused my interest as Nigel West/Rupert Allason described the company as *'International Fine Art Dealers'*. Precisely the same as Tancred. Geoffrey Duveen was actually a practising barrister and nephew to Lord Duveen, having recently left the art-dealing firm. Geoffrey Duveen's office was literally adjacent to that of Claude Dansey on the Eighth floor of the north-west wing of Bush House, together with the other 'front companies' that Dansey and MI6 were hiding behind.

The art dealing company had made an awful lot of money by selling European Art to wealthy Americans in the latter part of the 19th century[15] and the first half of the 20th Century. The archives of the firm are well catalogued and are housed at the Getty Research Institute, Los Angeles, California. They are also available on the internet and I should not have been too surprised to find that Microfilm 466 (208) is a copy of Box 353, which in turn holds the correspondence between Borenius and the Company.

It is pretty clear that Borenius was well known to the Duveens and vice versa. For instance, on 9th July 1938 they both attended an Exhibition of 20th Century German art at the Burlington Galleries. On 3rd May 1938 they had attended the opening night of *Die Zauberflote* at Covent Garden. The Times recorded that Borenius had 'completed the Royal party'. Borenius was more of an academic than Duveen the 'trader' and together with Bernard Berenson was used to 'authenticate' or 'attribute', with sometimes varying degrees of success. Typically Borenius would catalogue works that Duveen would then buy and sell on.[16]

So, I hope that I can clearly demonstrate a definite linkage between Borenius and a Company with stated links to MI6. Dealing with the rich and famous, would seem to make it a sensible choice.

We should also not forget that Carl Jacob Burckhardt was the grandson of the Jacob Burckhardt (1818-1893) the famous historian of art and culture and indeed Burckhardt himself initially studied art history at university. It does appear that Art certainly was 'prima facie', a common thread that bound the attendees at the early 1941 Swiss meeting.

However, I suspect that Dansey whilst living in Switzerland in 1934-1936 was little interested in Art. In 1934/35 it appears that Dansey had been thrown out of the Intelligence Services on account of some financial irregularity, but this now seems to be no more than a cover whilst Dansey was in the process of building the parallel intelligence system, well away from the constraints of the traditional 'passport control'.

Switzerland was an ideal choice for a base and Dansey worked quickly. Soon there were offices in Basle, Geneva, Zurich, Lausanne and Lugano. This time the information gathering would be based on people and businesses, not governmental control systems. Many of the notable intelligence successes eventually came via the Swiss offices, such as the Lucy Ring and the contact with Canaris.

Indeed as Read and Fisher state, *"Dansey's most important station - particularly in the early part of the war- remained Switzerland."*

At the outbreak of the war Dansey returned to London. Partly to chaperone Menzies, partly to pick up the pieces after the Venlo affair finally blew the pre war network apart. I can find no evidence to suggest that Dansey wasn't in Britain in January 1941 so as to be able to brief Tancred.

So, this is the **first visitor; Tancred Borenius.** In my view a bizarre, yet wholly understandable choice for messenger. However, who was he really delivering messages for?

Moreover, had Claude Edward Marjoribanks Dansey and his organisation already made contact with Carl Burckhardt? Indeed, given the interception of the Haushofer letter, was Albrecht Haushofer also on His Majesty King George VI's payroll? I wholly realise that this question has not been raised before and is indeed pure speculation, but Chatham House worked closely with MI6,[17] Haushofer was a frequent visitor to Britain throughout the 1930's and his true views of the Fuhrer and Nazidom would be known to a number of high ranking Britons. Switzerland in 1940/41 was jam-packed with SIS agents and at the end of the war Karl Haushofer seemed to almost disown his own son. Was that because he knew or suspected that he had acted disreputably? Would it really be too surprising if in 500 years time, when the PRO reluctantly release some WW2 MI6 files we learned that Borenius, Burckhardt and Haushofer were actually British agents? I don't think so.

Indeed *The Times* article of 13th February 2010 makes the valid point that whilst much has quite rightly been made of the use of 'Ultra' intelligence, the role of 'Humint' has been downplayed and remains understated.

Albrecht Haushofer
Much is known about Albrecht Haushofer, my second visitor, and yet little is known about him, concerning the key events of the Hess affair.

Both works[18] by James Douglas-Hamilton centre on him and his role in the affair. Quite properly too. I have already recorded Haushofer's pre-war meetings with the Marquis of Clydesdale, as he was then known.

I would now like to centre on his role as the 1940/41 messenger/middleman/roving reporter; in part a German equivalent to Tancred Borenius, in part an advisor to the German Deputy Leader. There are similarities between the two men; Borenius, I believe, was probably quite unknowingly delivering a 'spoof' set of proposals to Burckhardt in 1941. Haushofer in turn was happy to receive and deliver them to Hess, but knew enough to suspect that ultimately they would never work. The interesting question is whether he allowed, or even encouraged Hess to continue, knowing that his mission was never going to succeed.

However, what we do know is that Albrecht Haushofer had been very busy in the spring of 1941. We have already seen how he was instrumental in the exchange of correspondence in September 1940, instigated by Rudolf Hess.

From 2nd to 5th February 1941 Albrecht had visited Stockholm. (It will be remembered that at this time the Duke of Hamilton was at Lesbury, Northumberland from 25th January to 4th February 1941). It will also be remembered that Tancred Borenius had been 'recently' despatched to Geneva, which I presume was also at the end of the month of January 1941. It is too easy to speculate what was possibly happening here so I will allow the reader to consider the possibilities. I have yet to discover how Borenius travelled to Switzerland, but I presume it must have been via Lisbon, Spain and Vichy France?

On 21st to 24th February he was with Hess. On 10th March he met Von Hassell in Berlin, presumably to talk of overthrow.

From 12th to 15th April he was back with Hess in Berlin. Once again on 26th, this time with his Father too.

Two days later on 28th April 1941 he met Carl Burckhardt in Geneva. There is also a degree of speculation as to whether he had met Samuel Hoare in Spain (and Geneva) in April 1941, but Haushofer's protégé Stahmer[19] certainly had. Lord Halifax was also in attendance if Stahmer is to be believed.[20] It is also interesting to note that these meetings, if that is what actually happened, were arranged through the Swedish legation in Madrid, according to Wolf Hess.[21] Is that perhaps why Haushofer went to Stockholm in January 1941?

Whether Haushofer (and indeed) Hess had met with Hoare and Halifax in Spain we will have to wait until at least 2017 as the relevant files are currently embargoed. In any event, Haushofer's almost manic travels (in the middle of a war) surely indicate almost manic activity. Doing what and on whose behalf? We know from letters to and from his parents that whilst at one level he considered the flight a 'fools errand'[22] he was pleased with the 28th April[23] meeting. Whether this was because he thought he could convince Hess to fly – for whatever motive or reason we may not ever know. What appears to me to be an absolutely foolish notion is that Hess acted alone in making the flight to Britain.

I also hope that the reader is now convinced of the role of Carl Burckhardt. Very much the 'neutral intermediary' first proposed by the Hess letter of September 1940.

---

[1] *Hodder and Stoughton - 1984*

[2] *Former German Ambassador to Rome.*

[3] *Hamish Hamilton - 1948*

[4] *Sources: Sutton, Denys. Dictionary of Art 4: 302-3; Encyclopaedia Britannica Online; Vakkari, Johanna. "Alcuni contemporanei finlandesi di Lionello Venturi: Osvald Siren, Tancred Borenius, Onni Okkonen." Storia dell'Arte 101 (2002): 108-17; (obituaries:) Douglas, R. Langton, and Evans, Joan, et al. "Dr Tancred Borenius." Burlington Magazine 40 (1948): 327-8; "Professor Tancred Borenius." The Times (London) September 4, 1948; p. 6; [Sotheby's appraisal:] "Carmen Gronau." Times (London), March 11, 1999. Bibliography: and Tristram, E. W. English Medieval Painting. New York: Harcourt, Brace, 1929; English Painting in the XVIIIth Century. Paris: Hyperion Press, 1938; The Picture Gallery of Andrea Vendramin. London: Medici Society, 1923; revised with Douglas, Langton, and Strong, S. Arthur: Crowe, J. A., and Cavalcaselle, Giovanni Battista. A History of Painting in Italy, Umbria, Florence and Siena, from the Second to the Sixteenth Century. London: J. Murray, 1903-14; edited: Friedländer, Max J. On Art and Connoisseurship. London, B. Cassirer, 1942.[4]*

[5] *Died 27th July 2006.*

[6] *The passport office system was wiped out when Europe was overrun by the Nazis. However, its operational usefulness was suspect prior to May 1940.*

[7] *The Publishers.*

[8] *Ottoline Morrell was a prominent member of the Bloomsbury Group. Phillip Morrell was a Liberal politician. As a result of this association Borenius met artists such as Roger Fry, Augustus John, Bertrand Russell, Clive Bell and Henry Lamb. Ottoline Morrell was also cousin to Elizabeth Bowes Lyon.*

[9] *Frederick Leverton Harris was a Member of Parliament and benefactor to the Fitzwilliam Museum.*

[10] *RIIA 8/758.*

[11] *Coincidentally, the pictures were sold by RB Brassey, who formerly used to live at Cottesbrooke Hall, Northamptonshire, and the village in which I reside.*

[12] *I was told that the 'book' was actually a codebook and Borenius was greeted with the words, 'Thank God' when it was safely delivered.*

[13] *Anthony Cave Brown - 'C' - Collier Books - 1987.*

[14] *Nigel West - MI6 - Weidenfeld and Nicholson – 1983.*

[15] *"Europe has a great deal of Art and America has a great deal of Money."*

[16] *The Annunciation and Expulsion from Paradise by Giavanni de Paolo (1435) being such an example. It is now in the National Gallery of Art, Washington.*

[17] *Haushofer it will be remembered had addressed the Royal Institute.*

[18] *Motive for a Mission and The Truth about Rudolf Hess.*

[19] *Heinrich Georg Stahmer was a former pupil of Haushofer's appointed as Secretary to the German Embassy in Madrid.*

[20] *The Stahmer revelation is quite plausible concerning Samuel Hoare; he was based in Spain after all. Lord Halifax is a different matter altogether. He travelled to the US on board the newly commissioned King George V in January 1941. We know he returned to the UK in August / September 1941 and had attended a War Cabinet on 25th August 1941. (CAB 65/19/22). I find it difficult to conceive that the UK Ambassador was 'flitting' back to Portugal mid appointment. It would of course be logistically possible via the PANAM clippers, but dangerous in the extreme?*

[21] *W.R.Hess - My Father Rudolf Hess - WH Allen – 1986.*

[22] *Letter to his parents - 19th September 1940.*

[23] *Letter to his parents, ".....not wholly unsuccessful diplomatic mission."*

194

18

DOUGLAS DOUGLAS-HAMILTON

14TH DUKE OF HAMILTON

Whilst researching the Hess affair I have met many interesting people; Wolf Hess, Bill Kean, Andrea Schroder-Haushofer, some descendants of the main players and Stephen Prior.

Stephen Prior was one of the four authors of *'Double Standards.'*[1] Stephen and I had met on two occasions for supper, once at the Farmers Club in London, the other in Northampton. He was perfectly charming and during our conversations claimed to have worked for British Intelligence. I remember finding this particularly intimidating at the time, as he had asked to see me. He told me that he also ran a hotel somewhere near to Roslyn Chapel in Lowland Scotland. His interest in the Hess affair had apparently arisen by reason of his purchase of Rudolf Hess's Iron Cross, at an auction. Hess had previously given the cross to a soldier named McBride, on the night of 10th May 1941. Prior appeared to be similar to Richard and I in that he certainly did not believe the 'official story'. Good chap, I thought.

His book, *'Double Standards'* when published in 2001 drew on an extensive amount of basic research, the majority of which I could only admire. In particular he had been granted access to the Hamilton Archives in

Edinburgh, which, to my knowledge was the first time this source had been used and quoted, outside of the Hamilton family.

I was very saddened therefore, to learn that Stephen had died from an aggressive form of cancer in 2003.

However. When working on this book I have naturally gone over much of the same ground as Stephen and whilst apologising in advance for any disparagement, I now think that some of the work is terribly flawed. In particular that part of *'Double Standards'* pertaining to Dungavel House, I simply do not believe at all. I also do not believe the conclusion that Hess died with the Duke of Kent in Scotland in 1943.

When I met Stephen he had invited me to visit him at 'his hotel' and after 'beginning to have doubts' shall we say, about Stephen I did a little research of my own. It appears that Stephen was the manager of the Templar Lodge Hotel at Gullane, East Lothian. After his death in 2003 the hotel closed and is now in 2009 semi derelict and awaiting redevelopment. Whilst under Stephen's control the hotel seemed to base its marketing strategy on attracting various groups of minority interests, the majority of which were linked to UFO research, the paranormal and The Knights Templar.

One visitor commented, "I had at that time contact with a music scene in Gullane at the Templar Lodge Hotel and the character who ran it claimed to be an ex head of MI5's department of parapsychology. There were reasons to doubt that, though, but he did seem, according to a guy who had been working for the UK's version of the NSA, to be operating a strange unit of people in some of the rooms that had computers and staff time dedicated to researching end days material on as much global material as they could find. If the Angels would come to be with Nigel in front of a delegation that could be staged by this security service parapsychologist called Stephen Prior at the Templar Lodge Hotel in Gullane near Edinburgh, then maybe something special and interstellar could take place. We prepared and sent one hundred and eighty letters to Church leaders of all denominations all over the World............"

The Independent reported that Stephen had also arranged for a Japanese Film crew to film the nearby hills from the roof of his hotel for possible UFO sightings.

I suspect, but do not know for sure, that this is how Stephen met two of his co-authors, Messrs Picknett and Price, who appear to be well known writers in the fields of the 'paranormal, esoteric and secret societies.'[2] Robert Brydon, his third collaborator is a more conventional military historian, though even his TV script credit is for 'The Occult Reich'.[3]

Consequently, I fear that their heady mix of detailed fact and supposition has been mixed, distilled and blended with some even wilder theorising to produce a wholly flawed conclusion albeit based on some really good basic research. I would like to draw on this basic research, which I think very well done, but please do not confuse this endorsement with any further recommendation. At best their conclusions are semi-plausible nonsense.

Much of the life story of Douglas Douglas-Hamilton is well known and published, but as we have already seen there is much more still to be learned, as the chapter on Prestwick airfield has hopefully already demonstrated.

In particular, I now believe that Douglas-Hamilton was virtually an agent of the Foreign Office, firstly pre-war, as an overt intermediary and then, once the Foreign Office initiatives had run out of steam he still continued, this time playing a role; the role of potential revolutionary, albeit with the script being ably written and supplied by British Intelligence. He really was an ideal candidate for the role.

Douglas Douglas-Hamilton owned at least four planes registered in his own name in the 1930's as follows:

G - ABPD AW133 - De Havilland Gypsy Moth - August 1931
G - ACPK X9382 - De Havilland Leopard Moth - April 1934
G - ADVC BB812 - De Havilland Tiger Moth - October 1935
G - AELF VTA32 - Percival Pro Vega Gull - July 1936

In addition, Scottish Aviation Limited registered 17 Tiger Moths in December 1935 and there are also listings of similar planes registered in his three brother's names throughout the 1930's. All were the type eminently suitable for the Dungavel type of airstrip, though the Percival, with its 200hp engine was capable of taking 4 persons over 600 miles at 150 miles per hour. These figures are really still quite respectable today. It appears to me that Douglas-Hamilton used his planes in much the same way as we would use larger type of motorcars today. Extensive European transport was undertaken as a matter of course.

Clearly aviation played a large part in Douglas-Hamilton's life. He was made (the youngest) Commanding Officer of 602 (City of Glasgow) Squadron in 1927, was Chief Pilot to the Houston Mount Everest expedition of 1933 and shortly after helped establish Scottish Aviation Limited with his close friend, and best man David McIntyre.

I think these details are reasonably well known and documented. I would now like to record his activities as effectively a Foreign Affairs Agent, which, by doing so I hope to illustrate exactly why he was targeted by Rudolf Hess. This role effectively combined the aviation interests with that of a serving MP. Douglas-Hamilton had been MP for East Renfrewshire since 1930. Clearly he was a very busy man.

As has been discussed previously, the aftermath of the Everest Flight ensured that both Douglas-Hamilton and David McIntyre became famous throughout the United

Kingdom and Europe. Both men travelled extensively throughout Europe subsequent to the Everest flight.

The Tatler, for example, records Douglas Hamilton as being in Klosters in early 1936, Davos and Kleine Scheidegg in 1939.

Dougal MacIntyre, in the work concerning his father, also records a 1934 skiing trip to Basle by his father and Douglas-Hamilton in what appears to be a DeHavilland Puss Moth.

However, James Douglas-Hamilton gives the most detailed listing of his late father's trips.

1936 witnessed the Berlin Olympics and the Hess/Douglas-Hamilton 'did they/didn't they meet' banquet, hosted by Ribbentrop. Douglas-Hamilton also was present at a later banquet hosted by Adolf Hitler in honour of Sir Robert Vansittart. According to his brother David, it was here that Douglas-Hamilton met Albrecht Haushofer for the first time.

During August 1936, with Goring's express permission, Douglas- Hamilton was given a tour of the major Luftwaffe airfields and again in October 1936.

In January 1937 Douglas-Hamilton was again in Austria, skiing and met with Albrecht Haushofer on 23rd of that month. Albrecht introduced Douglas-Hamilton to his mother and father.

In March 1937 Albrecht visited London and the two men met again. On 29th April 1937 Albrecht gave his address to Chatham House on the subject of 'Raw Materials and Colonies: A German view'.

In June 1937 Albrecht returned to London yet again. The two men met again.

In November 1937, Douglas-Hamilton married Lady Elizabeth Percy, the daughter of the Duke of Northumberland. Albrecht Haushofer was invited, but declined. I must say that I do find it a little odd that Douglas-Hamilton invites a German Diplomat who he could not have known for much more than a year to his wedding? I should also record that David McIntyre was Douglas-Hamilton's best man.

In April 1938, Haushofer returned yet again, this time spending time at Dungavel House, prior to moving to London in May 1938.

I do not know precisely the relationship between the two men. In any event I am not sure it is relevant to the story to hand. What is absolutely clear however is that Douglas-Hamilton was certainly a very close acquaintance of the leading German expert on British Foreign Policy. James Douglas-Hamilton also reports on how his father was quick to report his findings. Matters aviation to the RAF, matters Diplomatic to the Foreign Office.

Letters and correspondence continued to come from Haushofer, one in July 1939 was forwarded by Douglas-Hamilton to Halifax, Butler, Chamberlain and Churchill.

Douglas-Hamilton was essentially acting as a direct conduit to the British Government from that part of the German government operating through and relying upon the Haushofer family. This role was recognised by Douglas-Hamilton's attendance at a Foreign Office meeting in London on 9th June 1939.

Amongst those present at the meeting were:

Lord Halifax - Foreign Secretary
General von Reichenau - a leading 'Hitlerite' General
Prince Adolf zu Mecklenberg - member of the International Olympic committee
Sir Robert Vansittart - anti appeasement politician
Kenneth Lindsay MP - for Kilmarnock
Sir Louis Grieg - close friend of King George V1
Douglas Douglas-Hamilton

The fact that Douglas-Hamilton was invited to attend what essentially was a European summit is actually quite extraordinary, were it not for the role that he was playing at that time; Duke, Governmental Diplomat, Conduit for peace feelers and, not least of all, a front line Airman.

The truth is that after 3rd September 1939 nothing changed, except the means of communication. Direct communication, person to person, became more difficult for the reasons previously detailed and different alternatives had to be utilised. It only took a month...........

On **6th October 1939** the following letter appeared in *The Times*.

Sir,

Many, like yourself, have had the opportunity of hearing a great deal of what the men and women of my generation are thinking. There is no doubt, in any quarter, irrespective of any party, that this country had no choice but to accept the challenge of Hitler's aggression against one country in Europe after another. If Hitler is right when he claims that the whole of the German nation is with him in his cruelties and treacheries, both within Germany and without, then this war must be fought to the bitter end. It may well last for many years, but the people of the British Empire will not falter in their determination to see it through.

But I believe that the moment the menace of aggression and bad faith has been removed, war against Germany becomes wrong and meaningless. This generation is conscious that injustices were done to the German people in the era after the last war. There must be no repetition of that. To seek anything but a just and comprehensive peace to lay at rest the fears and discords in Europe would be a betrayal of our fallen.

I look forward to a day when a trusted Germany will again come into her own and believe that there is such a Germany, which would be loath to inflict wrongs on other nations such as she would not like to suffer herself. That day may be far off, but when it comes, then hostilities could and should cease, and all efforts be concentrated on righting the wrongs in Europe by free negotiations between the disputing parties, all parties binding themselves to submit their disputes to an impartial equity tribunal in case they cannot reach agreement.

We do not grudge Germany lebensraum, provided that lebensraum is not made the grave of other nations. We should be ready to search for and find a colonial settlement, just to all peoples concerned, as soon as there exist effective guarantees that no race will be exposed to being treated as Hitler treated the Jews on 9 November last year. We shall, I trust, live to see the day when such a healing peace is negotiated between honourable men and the bitter memories of twenty-five years of unhappy tension between Germany and the western democracies are wiped away in their responsible co-operation for building a better Europe.

Yours truly
Clydesdale

Interestingly, this letter was originally going to be a group letter, from all MPs serving in the armed forces. However, Chamberlain decreed that it should come solely from Hamilton, lest it be construed as showing a lack of support for the armed forces. It was co written by Kurt Hahn, the post war founder of Gordonstoun School and subsequent guardian of Karl Haushofer's grandson.

With respect to the eventual outcome of the Hess affair, this letter effectively marks the end of Douglas Douglas-Hamilton's active involvement with *governmental* peace initiatives. Thereafter, he was still fully involved, but in a *non-governmental role,* or to be even more precise, a *quasi non-governmental role.*

It appears to me that this letter, which purports to come from Hamilton but is written for him, is effectively a letter to Albrecht Haushofer, not the Editor of *The Times.* We know that the letter received publicity in Germany at the time and seems to me to be an attempt to blame Hitler for the war that was about to be unleashed on Germany. Very much the themes that were to be developed and expanded upon in the next year to eighteen months.

Please be under no illusion, the 14th Duke of Hamilton and his brothers, were wholly involved, up to their necks and beyond, in pre-war attempts to foster relations with Germany. Stephen Prior believes that he was a member of the Anglo German Fellowship, having found a receipt for his subscription. This comes as no great surprise, whether he was in fact a member or not. That having been said, I am wholly convinced of his patriotism. Wholly convinced.

Prior to the War he was led by his conscience. Once declared, I suspect he was then being led by the same persons who had gained control of the Haushofer letter to Mrs Violet Roberts, dated 23rd September 1940. I should also make the rather obvious point that the government knew all about Hamilton's pre war activities - he openly told them himself. Hardly the action of a revolutionary. The government also knew that he had been contacted through Mrs Roberts in September 1940. The censor had done his job well.

Once the war had commenced Hamilton's priorities changed. He was an active member of His Majesty's armed forces and was appointed Commanding Officer of RAF Turnhouse, a position to which he had been appointed at the onset of the Battle of Britain in summer 1940. In May 1940 the then Duke of Hamilton was also appointed as Lord Steward after Churchill had taken the honour away from the 8th Duke of Buccleuch on account of his blatant 'peace mongering'. Whilst the position is largely ceremonial, with the actual role being performed by the Master of the Household, the Lord Steward also has certain rights and duties in connection with the Royal Sign Manual, the autographed signature of the Monarch. Given that Hamilton was already in the RAF, serving in France at the time, I am a little surprised that he was given this honour? Furthermore, how was his letter to *The Times* of 6th October 1939 interpreted? As we have already seen there were plenty alternative Dukes and Earls in Scotland at the time. A perusal of the list of holders shows no discernable family preferences; all the major names have been present over the years.

The summer of 1940 was spent fighting the Germans and then, as we have seen, in September 1940, nearly a year after his letter to The Times, Albrecht Haushofer tries to make contact with Hamilton. The attempt fails, with the letter being intercepted by the censor, realistically in mid/late October 1940. It had to come from Lisbon, Portugal and pass through the British censor.

The letter from Albrecht Haushofer to Mrs Roberts was dated 23rd September 1940. The censor, we know, had the letter no later than 6th November 1940. By 22nd November 1940 MI5 write to the Foreign Office asking if they can send the Duke a copy? On 7th December a reply comes back; yes, the letter can be forwarded.

On 12th November 1940 Hamilton had taken 10 days leave from RAF Turnhouse. Apparently the 1940 Hamilton diary no longer may be found, so we cannot be sure as to his destination.

On 20th January 1941 Hamilton met The Duke of Kent for lunch and again on 23rd January 1941 the two men met at ....Prestwick.

On 26th January 1941 a further 10 days leaves were taken. Stephen Prior has discovered that according to the Hamilton archives the leave was taken at Lesbury, Northumberland, and the ancestral home of the Duchess of Hamilton's family, the Percy's.

In March 1941 a further period of leave from RAF Turnhouse was taken, but this was apparently to do with the approach by RAF Intelligence to Hamilton, requesting that he might attend a meeting in Lisbon with, presumably, Haushofer. The last recorded 'sighting' of Hamilton was on 28th April 1941 when The Times recorded Hamilton greeting a contingent of Empire Airman at a 'British Port'. The Port is not recorded, but the airman was subsequently taken to a depot near London, so presumably was in the south of England.

At this time, James Douglas-Hamilton also reveals that his father was taking advice from Lord Eustace Percy as to how to avoid being used and presumably abused, by RAF intelligence.

I find the choice of confidant interesting. Lord Eustace Percy was a cerebral member of the Northumbrian family and a recently retired MP. In 1935-36 he had been a member of the Baldwin cabinet as Minister without Portfolio. From 1911-1919 he served in the Diplomatic service. As such, he would be well experienced in governmental wartime machinations and well experienced to advise his Scottish relative in his hour of need.

I suspect however, that by this time there was already another intelligence operation underway. One that did not really require any active involvement from Hamilton, but did ultimately rely upon his passive acquiescence. It appears to me that he was far too busy to be organising a wartime coup d'état, even if he wished to.

---

[1] *Picknett, Prince and Prior – Double Standards – Little Brown – London 2001.*
[2] *Ibid.*
[3] *Ibid.*

THE FINAL INTERREGNUM

THE BIG
STUMBLING BLOCK

We have already seen how the governmental peace feelers in 1939 and 1940 ultimately failed to go anywhere, simply because the British did not trust Hitler.

Neville Chamberlain, coming from the world of commerce and business, just felt cheated after Czechoslovakia but did at least effectively then draw 'the line in the sand' with the 1939 Anglo French Treaty of Protection for Poland. The failure of the earlier Anglo French and Russian initiative (because Poland and Romania would not allow Russian troops on their soil) followed by the subsequent Molotov/Ribbentrop pact of 1939 merely reinforced the British view of Hitlerian deviousness. As Sir Robert Vansittart wrote in 1940, *"The future of civilisation is at stake. It is a question of we or they now, and either the German Reich or this country has to go under, and not only under, but right under.......We have had much more than enough of Dahlerus, Goedeler, Weissauer and company."*[1]

Realistically, once war had been declared in September 1939, any British/German peace was only likely to be concluded if Hitler was no longer the German leader. This was the big stumbling block facing Hess. He was Hitler's most loyal follower.

Organised German resistance against Hitler was also in its pre-formative stages, making his internal removal unlikely. The sad fact remains that in 1939/40 most Germans were full square behind their leader, particularly whilst he was being militarily successful. Minorities were certainly being persecuted, but the majority found it convenient to turn a blind eye. Even the Prussian Generals kept their counsel on account of the restoration of their Eastern territories. Hitler certainly had enemies, but there was no real co-ordinated resistance on a scale to be meaningful. Realistically, in 1939/40 the lone assassin was probably the most likely to succeed, such as Georg Elser, the carpenter from Wurttemberg, who hid the bomb in the Munich Burgerbraukellar on 8th November, 1939.[2]

That having been said, the British were also becoming more secure for three reasons: Firstly, the Battle of Britain amply demonstrated that a German invasion of Britain would be militarily difficult. Secondly, the United States of America were gradually becoming more involved and thirdly, and potentially the most important by far, a group of boffins in wooden huts in Bletchley, England had got wind of the fact that a German invasion of Russia was very much on the cards. If only the U boat threat could be countered perhaps there really was light at the end of the tunnel?

Therefore, if Britain didn't make peace perhaps it wasn't the end of the world? Germany and Russia might even fight each other to a standstill, neutralising each other in the process. A high risk strategy for Britain indeed, particularly as the Wehrmacht was undefeated and the 'heartland' was at stake, but, nevertheless, a realistic and viable political option.

However, at least Britain now had some knowledge on which to base the decision. Ultra decrypts had been using Luftwaffe communications since 1940. There may well even be British staff college reports weighing up the likelihood of German success and concluding that a failure to make peace may well be the best military outcome for Britain, the prospect of millions of future deaths not withstanding.

Therefore, in early 1941 the Germans certainly wanted/needed a peace settlement more than the British. The issue was becoming desperate. Even more terrifyingly for the Germans, the British knew that to be the case.

---

[1] FO371/24408.

[2] It failed on account of Hitler leaving early. The bomb exploded, killing 8 people.

19

COMPLETING THE CIRCLE

'When of a gossiping circle it was asked, "What are they doing?" The answer was "Swapping lies.'

Richard Brinsley Sheridan (1751-1816)

This book, you may recall, started with the basic premise that to affect a revolution in Great Britain, (without an outright military victory), one needs the acquiescence of the Monarch. Whether to prorogue parliament, or to directly appoint another Prime Minister certainly requires the active consent of the Monarch. That having been said, had Germany successfully invaded Britain in 1940 the conqueror could of course, impose whatever constitution was deemed appropriate. Therefore, what follows, presupposes that a peace settlement was to be negotiated and not imposed.

So far, I hope that I have demonstrated the following to your satisfaction.
- To effect a change of government Hess would have to be in a position to either meet with or be in a position to influence the King.
- For whatever reason Hess was targeting Prestwick airfield.

- Germany was under growing pressure to neutralise Britain prior to unleashing Barbarossa. 15th May 1941 was the appointed date.
- There were a whole host of individuals within Britain who would be quite willing to negotiate with Germany for a whole host of different reasons.
- There had been all sorts of approaches from the Germans, ever since September 1939. The major stumbling block had been the British Government's necessity to remove Hitler as German leader. The British could see his 'game plan' and didn't like it one bit.

Rudolf Hess and Adolf Hitler desperately wanted the West to be neutralised before heading east. The Luftwaffe had failed twice; firstly by losing the Battle of Britain and secondly by just failing to bomb Britain to the negotiating table. The German Foreign Office had failed to the extent that they had even made matters worse. The German nation so far, was still reasonably solid behind its victorious leader, but now the stakes were about to get higher. Much, much higher and as far as I can see, without a safety net should Russia prove harder to crack than envisaged. The Germans eventually embarked on Barbarossa without an effective alternative.

However, Rudolf Hess had initiated the Haushofer/Hamilton letters back in September 1940 and I suspect that this had led in turn to Tancred Borenius somewhat bizarrely trekking off to Geneva in January 1941 on the say so of Claude Dansey and MI6. The book that he was carrying was, again I suspect, an Intelligence plant, following their discovery in November 1940 that Haushofer was trying to contact Hamilton. There may well have been forged letters too, but I am struggling to see how they would have plausibly got past the censor and yet continued to be seen as a non-governmental reply.

I am also fascinated by Borenius and the fact that he was close to the Lascelles family and The Duke of Kent. Is this the reason that he went to Geneva? We also have yet to discover if he brought anything back with him from Geneva? If Borenius was appearing to represent Kent/Lascelles, then much actually makes sense. These people, along with Hamilton, certainly had direct access to the King and Hamilton even had some form of power over the King's signature, should the need arise.

It also explains Haushofer's interest in Sam Hoare. If the King were to prorogue Parliament, then a pliable replacement would have to be put in place. According to Hoare himself, *"My staff and I made it clear beyond a doubt that the British Government would have nothing to do with any peace negotiations..."* [1] Quite so.

What is not perhaps so clear is whether Hoare gave the impression that *he* would have nothing to do with peace negotiations? Surely, if Hess were acting on the supposition that he was about to ignite a coup, he would have to have some as idea as to who might be installed in Churchill's place? That, I believe is the role that Hoare was assigned and played with skill. Hoare had been an intelligent agent in Russia in 1919, so was already used to the 'game'.

I should also mention that there is a line of thought that Hoare was working as a *synarchist* alongside Montagu Norman, the Governor of the Bank of England, in an attempt to impose a 'Pan European' super state, ruled over and governed by bankers, industry and not governments. Subscribers to this view point to the Hoare Laval treaty as an example of Italian appeasement, the installation of Hitler as Chancellor of Germany, the formation of the

Bank of International Settlement in 1930 and the loss of the Czech gold reserves to Nazi Germany in 1939.

Max Aitken, Lord Beaverbrook, is also cited as being part of this 'coup attempt' and it has been suggested that his resignation as Minister of Aircraft Production on 1st May 1941 was as a prelude to some form of action in this regard. In *Hess: The British Conspiracy* I also made note of the fact that Burckhardt had been visited by a member of the London 'City' circles in March 1941 (yet another meeting for Burckhardt) and certainly the diary of Montagu Norman during the spring of 1941 makes interesting reading; meetings with the Red Cross and Campbell Stuart, former head of the PWE.

Whatever they were doing, clearly Hoare, Hess, Hamilton and Burckhardt were very busy doing *something* in the spring of 1941. If nothing else, their diaries and itineraries demonstrate too much activity to then simply dismiss the Hess flight as the solo initiative of a crazy man. I now think that these meetings, both sides of the English Channel, were held to finalise the various details of what was essentially a coup attempt appearing to emanate from the very highest levels. I cannot however produce MI6 archives to prove my theory. Simply because they have yet to be released.

The only problem for Hess was that he was being duped. Very plausibly duped, but duped nonetheless. Hoare was a patriot (possibly not brave enough to be anything but)[2] as was Hamilton. As was Kent.

The location of the Duke of Kent on 10th May 1941 has also been the subject of some speculation. According to *'Double Standards'* and Stephen Prior, he was Dungavel airstrip. I find this very hard to believe because:

- Hess was not going to Dungavel because he could not land there.

- I don't think Stephen actually has any evidence to support his theory.
- The Countess of Sutherland has written to me, telling me that he was at Dunrobin Castle!

However, I am afraid that I am not wholly convinced by any of the above claims.

The Duke and Duchess of Kent. A family photograph taken in late 1939. Did the Duke play a part in facilitating the Hess flight?

In September 2008 I placed an advertisement in the *Daily Telegraph*, enquiring if any reader knew the whereabouts of the Duke of Kent on 10th May 1941. I think it fair to say that I was and continue to be frustrated with the Royal Archives/Duke of Kent archivist's obfuscation and so tried to get independent evidence.

Dunrobin Castle: The home of the Duke of Sutherland. Was the Duke of Kent here on 10th May 1941?

Helen, my long suffering secretary, was somewhat taken aback when she fielded a very prompt call from Elizabeth, Countess Sutherland informing her that the Duke of Kent spent the weekend of 9th-11th May 1941 at her home, Dunrobin Castle, 40 miles or so north of Inverness. Apparently, during the war she had been working at Raigmore Hospital in Inverness, but came home occasionally. I asked the Countess to put down in writing what she had told me and this she was kind enough to do. Her letter was postmarked 3rd September 2008. It reads,

"Thank you for your letter (JTGH - I had written previously, to thank her for her trouble) Dunrobin was a hospital in both World Wars. A very small part of it was kept for the family – only my Uncle and Aunt who had no children & me (their niece). I was working in Raigmore Hospital, Inverness but came home occasionally for a few days. I happened to be there when the Duke arrived for the night.

The visitor's book has a hand written notice saying,

War period 1939-1944 Book not kept.

(King George VI and the Duke of Kent stayed at Dunrobin during this period.)

After he was killed he was brought back to Dunrobin and his coffin was kept in the front hall until the King arrived to accompany him back south. I remember how amusing he was - very easy to talk to, - nice to everyone."

I was absolutely delighted to receive this letter and it confirmed some things that we already knew, the fact that the Duke of Kent's body was taken to the castle after the aircraft crash in 1943. The fact that the castle was used as a hospital. However, I looked at Raigmore Hospital in Inverness and was a bit surprised to learn that it did not open until September 1941.[3] Moreover, the Countess said that she was there *'when the Duke arrived for the night'*, rather than *'the weekend?'*

The real problem here is that the official records are yet again lacking. Yet again – said with feeling. The Duke of Kent had been engaged in important work, visiting wartime airfields throughout the length and breath of Britain. He had been created an Air Commodore in April 1940, with the role of Staff Officer in the RAF Training Command.

National Archive File Air 33/7 gives voluminous detail of the many visits carried out by the Duke in the above capacity, but does not of course cover the period we are interested in. There are 42 files covering the Duke of Kent during 1941-42, but not one covers the weekend on 9th-11th May 1941.

I think we know where the Duke was on the Friday, 9th May and I think we know where he was on the Monday, 12th May. It seems to have passed into legend that on the Friday the Duke was at RAF Sumburgh and on the Monday RAF Wick. Sumburgh is on the Shetland Islands and a notoriously difficult airstrip on which to land. For this authority we have to rely on Norman Glass, Caithness and the War 1939-1945.[4]

I felt I needed to check further and so duly despatched my daughter Emily to Kew to look at the Operational Record Books (ORB's) of the Two Stations. Surely they would record the fact that the King's brother had been to stay? But no, nothing. There was no record of any visit.[5]

So, I am afraid I think we have a real problem. The ORB's make no mention of any visit, the Countess of Sutherland, with all due respect, may have made a mistake and anyway, I don't really understand why he would choose to stay at Dunrobin. He obviously flew into the airbases so as to carry out his visits and surely, if he was going anywhere, he would have flown back to Pitliver House, Fife, where he and his wife Marina and children had moved to at the outbreak of the war? There were plenty of airbases, both RAF and Royal Naval Air Stations close to home, that would facilitate the Duke an easy 'weekend at home with the wife and kids'.

The Duke used a DeHavilland Flamingo to perform his duties and this plane had a range of 1345 miles at a speed of around 200mph. In other words, he could quite easily have flown to anywhere in Scotland with ease. Moreover, there is no airfield near Dunrobin (that would take a relatively large plane such as a Flamingo) so presumably the Duke would have flown on the Friday to RAF Wick and then driven down the coast the 50 miles to the Castle? It just all seems a bit unlikely to me, but may of course be absolutely correct.

So, I tried another approach.

When the Duke died in 1942, unfortunately his immediate staff also died with him. They were:
- *John Arthur Lowther - private secretary*
- *Michael Strutt - equerry*
- *John Hales – valet*

I tried to ascertain where each of the three men was on 10th May 1941. I failed. John Lowther's papers are in Suffolk Record Office.[6] No luck.

Michael Strutt's family didn't reply to my request and John Hale's family in Norfolk were kindness personified, but again no luck.

So, I must confess that I have real doubts as to where the Duke was on Saturday 10th May 1941. I do doubt Dunrobin, but I feel even that location more likely than Dungavel, for that makes no sense at all.

What I was able to discover however, was that the Duke of Kent *did* have friends in and around Prestwick (15 miles away from Dungavel). When planning The Duke of Kent's 1941 trip to Canada,[7] the question arose as to where he might stay the night before flying out from Prestwick. A note states that there would be no problem in that regard as the Duke has 'a friend with a house no further than 1 mile from the end of the runway'. Intrigued, I contacted the staff at Carnegie Library at Ayr who again were very helpful.

I enquired of Sheena Taylor, the librarian, which houses in the area might be possible venues for the Duke of Kent. She gave me the following names:

-   Orangefield House has already been mentioned in the context that it was a Georgian House converted in the 1930's to an aerodrome control tower, by the expedient of tacking a glass conning tower onto the roof. It was finally requisitioned in June 1941.
-   Eldo House was adjacent to Orangefield House and was occupied by Geordie Douglas Hamilton.
-   Adamton House. WL Carlow occupied Adamton House, prior to its being used by the USAAF as an officer's mess.

And then:

-   Lochgreen House.

Lochgreen House. I find this house very interesting. Richard and I visited Lochgreen House in 2009 and discovered that it is a very attractive mansion on the Monktonhill Road, between Prestwick and Troon, just about a mile from the airfield. It is now in 2009 a five star hotel. However, I had already ascertained from Sheena that the owner of the house in 1941 was Sir Fergus Morton, a High Court judge. She also mentioned in passing that the tenant was Loel Guinness and yet again my heart started missing a beat. Loel Guinness was a famously wealthy member of the banking side of the Irish Brewers and Bankers, and I knew from previous research, a close friend of the Duke and Duchess of Kent. When Loel Guinness was married for the second time in November 1936, the Duke and Duchess of Kent gave him a pair of china birds and Tancred Borenius chipped in and gave his usual present of a book; presumably his latest?[8] Loel Guinness was also an aviator, entering the 1930 King's Cup Air Race in a Blackburn Bluebird IV. A fellow competitor was Lord Malcolm Douglas-Hamilton, also in a Blackburn Bluebird IV. He was also a regular attendee at Cowes, owning a large Ocean going yacht, Atlantis.[9]

The reason he was in Prestwick however was, as we have already discovered, that he was a serving Officer in the RAF and in May 1941 was in charge of the newly commissioned Fighter base at RAF Ayr. Hector Maclean, his station controller describes him thus, *"In early 1941 Hector was posted as a Controller to RAF Station Ayr, a new fighter base in the course of being constructed at Heathfield near Ayr. The Station Commander, who was also the Sector Commander, was Wing Commander Loel Guinness, an Auxiliary Officer who had Commanded 601 County of London Squadron. It was said that when he came to Heathfield - shortly before Hector arrived - that things had ground to a halt. When Loel contacted the contractors he was told the Air Ministry were dragging their feet and the contractors had not been paid. Loel Guinness asked how much was owed, wrote a cheque and buildings began appearing almost like magic!"[10]*

Lochgreen House, Monkton. The wartime home of Loel Guinness. Was the Duke of Kent staying here on 10th May 1941?

Consequently, this all seems very odd to me. Very odd. On 10th May 1941 we have the Duke of Hamilton in charge of a large Scottish Air sector including RAF Ayr, which in turn is under the immediate control of Loel Guinness. Loel Guinness is a close friend of the Duke of Kent whose precise location on 10th May 1941 is uncertain. Tancred Borenius is a close friend of Loel Guinness and the Duke of Kent and Tancred Borenius has trotted off to Geneva in January 1941 to see Carl Burckhardt.

The only part of Scotland not under the Duke of Hamilton's direct control (the east coast) was under the control of JO Andrews, a recently appointed (February 1941) German specialist and close friend of all concerned. Throw in the Duke's brothers, both RAF intelligence Officers, David McIntyre, the senior staff of RAF Prestwick/Aye, and the fact that all of the above are congregated in Lowland Scotland, on or around an airbase actually owned by the Duke and Hamilton and his family and I think we are entitled to wonder just what is going on?

I now know far better than to claim that the above proves a conspiracy, but, I do feel entitled to now say, 'blimey what a coincidence!' I shall leave it at that and let you the reader decide.

It appears to me that the Duke of Hamilton and Duke of Kent having spent much of 1939 and 1940 trying to avert war then allowed their names to be used in an MI6 inspired ruse which, if nothing else, bought the British war effort more time. MI6 learn that Hamilton is being targeted through the mail censor and launch an operation allowing the Germans to believe that Hamilton (and the Duke of Kent?) will facilitate a meeting between Hess and the King, with a view to a change of government. As far as the Germans are concerned, that course of action will also get over the stumbling block of the Churchill government not negotiating with Hitler; firstly the Churchill government would be replaced and secondly the replacement would be negotiating with Rudolf Hess – not Hitler.

Consequently, Tancred Borenius, being one of the few necessarily qualified messengers (Not British, based in Britain, knows the participators) is packed off to Geneva to tell/relay Burckhardt the plan/ruse. Burckhardt tells Haushofer/Hess. Haushofer checks out Hoare to make sure it is viable and that there is a potential British Quisling/Petain.

The Poles are brought into the plan to add to its credibility and so Sikorski has to fly back to Scotland.

It may well be that there are other bit part messengers who gave the necessary appearance of being non governmental, Baron Knut Bonde comes to mind in this respect,[11] but really, once Hess knows where to go, relatively little information needs to be relayed to the British – realistically just a date and time of arrival.

Ernest Bevin was supposed to know that Hess was coming via the Messerschmitt factory in Augsburg, but given that the Luftwaffe Enigma machine had been compromised in 1940, Bevin's story could be just a cover to protect the 'golden goose'. It may or may not be true. However, it appears to me that Hess's arrival was really no more than an unwanted by product of the British attempt to buy as much time as possible until her enemies started to fight each other. That was the important result, not Hess's captivity. The German invasion of Russia gave Britain hope, not the capture of Hess. His capture was a potential embarrassment that could cause huge damage if handled badly.

[1] *Ambassador on Special Mission - Sir.Samuel Hoare - Collins –1946.*
[2] *See David Eccles.*
[3] *www.Ambail.org.uk "September 1941 when the first ward was opened to the public."*
[4] *North of Scotland Newspapers 1994.*
[5] *Air 28/784 (Sumburgh) and Air 28/1570 (Wick).*
[6] *Thank you. 7th Earl of Lonsdale.*
[7] *Canada hosted much RAF training during the war.*
[8] *The Times, November 23rd 1936.*
[9] *He also owned the 'Calypso' made famous in the 1950's and 60's by Jacques Cousteau.*
[10] *www.thefew.info*
[11] *See Double Standards*

20

THE AFTERMATH
AND
SOME UNEXPECTED
CONSEQUENCES

Some unexpected consequences now need consideration.

The Scottish Crown Jewels are the oldest Crown jewels in Great Britain. Consisting of the Crown (1540), the Sceptre (1494) and the Sword (1507). They were first used as a set in the 1543 Coronation of Mary 1st of Scotland. They are priceless and have been kept in Edinburgh Castle since the early 1700's.

Known as the 'Honours of Scotland', in 1939 they were taken from the Crown Room, put into a chest, which in turn was covered by sandbags in the cellar beneath their usual resting place. The perceived danger was enemy bombs. It is not at all clear what the perceived danger was deemed to be, when on 12th May 1941, (the Monday after Hess had crashed on the previous Saturday night), the jewels were literally taken from the already secure chest in the Crown room cellar and re-hidden.

This time, they were taken to the 1386 St David's Tower and buried beneath the latrine closet in the basement. The sword was concealed in the adjacent wall. According to Mr Hutton the reason for the move was 'to prevent the Honours falling into enemy hands'.[1]

The location remained a secret throughout the war and just four letters were sent from the castle revealing the location. The letters went to:

- HM King George VI,
- The Secretary of State for Scotland - Thomas Johnston,
- The Governor General Of Canada - Alexander Cambridge, Ist Earl of Athlone,
- The King and Lords Remembrancer - John Alexander Inglis,

Thomas Johnston was a staunch Labour Party MP and amongst the duties of the Remembrancer has responsibility for the Crown jewels and Treasure Trove. However. The question must be why? Which enemy hands were the jewels in danger of falling into? Who gave the order?

The **explanation** I suspect was simply the reaction of MI5. The 1992 release of Hess papers showed that they didn't have a clue as to what was going on (because they weren't in on the ruse) and so they reacted by hiding the symbol of monarchy in Scotland.

The second unexpected consequence concerns the **Marquis of Tavistock,** the Reverend Dennis Rokeby and one Allan Page.

After the 1994 publication of my pamphlet I was approached by Allan Page who lived in Kettering, some 10 miles from my home. He was brought up in Kettering and was befriended by the local priest, Dennis Rokeby.

Rokeby was born in Germany with the name Rausch and like the Royal family, in 1917 anglicised his name. Friendly with Vera Brittain during the 1930's at the start of the war he moved to Stranraer in west Scotland. His passion was photographing railway stations and his collection is maintained to this day in Swindon.[2]

Within his Parish was Cairnsmore, the Scottish retreat of the Marquis of Tavistock, some 2-3 miles outside Stranraer.

Allan Page was a conscientious objector and after a spell at work in a London sewage works made his way to Stranraer to spend time with Rokeby.[3] Rokeby soon befriended the Marquis and would spend time with him at Cairnsmore. Allan Page would go with him. As such he was at Cairnsmore on 10th/11th May 1941, the weekend that Hess made his flight.

Somewhat surprisingly, according to Allan Page, plain-clothes detectives descended on Cairnsmore and placed the Marquis and his houseguests under house arrest. Allan told me that as a young man he was persuaded to smuggle a letter out of the house during the time of their incarceration and often wondered as to its contents.

In *Hess: The British Conspiracy*, full details were given of the Marquis of Tavistock's activities in the period leading up to and after the outbreak of war. In particular his trip to Dublin in March 1940 to meet the German legation was analysed with a view to its legality. There is no doubt that the Marquis was the ultimate pacifist and continued to be so throughout the course of the war. It is probably correct to say that persons of less stature would have been arrested under the 18b regulations.

So why was he effectively arrested on 10th May 1941? What had he done, or perhaps given the impression of having done?

In much the same way as the Scottish Jewels above, I suspect the **explanation** was an MI5 reaction to the Hess affair. If in doubt – control. The above reactions also indicate to me that this particular branch of the secret service were not in on the ruse. The Duke of Buccleuch was treated in a similar way.

A third unexpected consequence was the treatment of Rudolf Hess following capture.

I have already likened the capture of Rudolf Hess to an episode of Dad's army and superficially that was very much the case. Taken by pitchfork to the farm worker's cottage, offered tea and then whisked off by the local Home Guard to their Scout Hut HQ in Giffnock. Interrogated by Roman Battaglia and eventually taken to Maryhill barracks.

I had assumed that the 'amateur hour' description was symptomatic with the fact that Hess was not expected where he ended up. I have already stated my belief that Hess had landed at Eaglesham simply because he was out of fuel and lost. Whilst that was the case I am sure, I now believe that there was far more going on that evening than has previously been acknowledged.

Firstly, file WO/3288A details a letter from a Colonel Duke bemoaning the fact that correct procedure was not followed. Hess (according to Colonel Duke) should have been taken to the nearest military unit, which was No2. Holding Battalion, RASC at Barrhead, 7 miles from Eaglesham.[4] I presume he wasn't, on account of the undoubted enthusiasm of the local Home Guard Unit.

However, Stephen Prior, in *'Double Standards'* also details the undisputed fact that Hess gave his Iron Cross to Sergeant McBride'[5] and quite correctly questions why?

File WO3288A details that Sergeant McBride and Sergeant Morris[6] were also 'given' a Box of Bengal Matches, a flash lamp and Hess's autograph. No mention is made of the Iron Cross. We know for sure that the

McBride family retained the Iron Cross, because it was this artefact that Stephen Prior much later bought at Auction.

Why would Hess give away one of his proudest possessions to a junior member of the Scottish Home guard? It may of course be the case that it was stolen, but was it given to reward McBride for some service rendered? Either case is reasonably bizarre, but there is absolutely no doubt the gift was made.

When Richard and I last travelled to Renfrewshire in early 2009 we met with Mr and Mrs. Dougal McIntyre, the son and daughter in law of David McIntyre, the 'Pioneer of Prestwick'. There is little doubt in my mind that had Dougal's father not have died at a relatively young age in an aircraft accident, he would have been feted in later life as a true Scottish pioneer. We have already seen how it was his drive and vision that developed Prestwick airfield.

I now reproduce the minutes of our meeting, which I believe to be fair:

Memorandum
Scottish weekend – 1st to 3rd May 2009
Attendees: Wilbourn R (RW), Harris J (JTGH)

1. *We left Cottesbrooke on the Friday night at c.8.00pm and spent the night at Travelodge, Dumfries, arriving there at around 12.30pm.*
2. *The following morning we arose, ate our pre packed breakfast and set out to Prestwick. We travelled via Stranraer, saw the old seaplane base at Cairnryan and stopped at the site of the old Turnberry landing strip.*
3. *We arrived at Prestwick and lunched at the North Beach Hotel.*
4. *En route to McIntyres we called in at Lochgreen house, which now a hotel. This was where, it is alleged, Loel Guinness was the tenant in 1941 whilst CO- Prestwick. They knew nothing, though Mrs McIntyre said that the McIntyres*

had the house after the war. During the war she thought that Lord Lovatt had the house and the upstairs was a marine dormitory.

5. *We then travelled to meet Dougal McIntyre, (DM) at Prestwick. He is the son of the late David McIntyre and JTGH had become aware of him through his book 'Prestwick Pioneer'.*

6. *DM was unaware of our true interest and so, as previously discussed, JTGH and RW detailed how they had arrived at the meeting, it essentially being the culmination of 20 years research into the Hess affair.*

7. *Upon hearing the Hess connection, Mrs McIntyre, who seemed quite outgoing, announced that her father in law had been taken to meet Hess on arrival in Scotland. Her husband tried to contradict her, but failed and she added that her mother in law had laid in bed with a weapon of sorts underneath, lest she be kidnapped.*

8. *Dougal tried to downplay this, but this faux pas, if that is what it was, added to the sense of unease that continued throughout the meeting.*

9. *JTGH went through a series of questions thereafter and DM was very helpful, but these were very procedural in nature. Afterwards both RW and JTGH felt that Mrs M had let the cat out of the bag.*

10. *The McIntyres and Hamiltons were still friends, and despite a self-professed ignorance of the Hess affair, DM then went on to say that he had trawled through the Hamilton archives at Lennnoxlove, and had also produced the Hamilton book on Hess to show us.*

11. *RW and JTGH were both of the opinion that DM was being very defensive in his answers, but, to be fair, was very helpful when answering unimportant questions.*

12. *He was also the Scottish radio controlled aircraft champion!*

13. *RW and JTGH then left and travelled to West Kilbride to visit the site of ROC site G3. This spotted Hess when he hit the Clyde estuary and was still essentially intact. It held a panoramic view of the Clyde.*

14. *RW and JTGH then travelled to Bishopton to try and gain access to the Royal Ordance base that had been decommissioned. We failed. It was now in the ownership of BAE Systems. The gate men gave us photocopies of information pertaining to Dargavel House, which is contained within.*

15. *We then went back to Prestwick and called in at Rosemount House (such as was left of the original). This was the Command Base of Prestwick (and Ayr) during the war and overlooked the base.*

16. *The owner said that his family had acquired the house in 1947 after the war. They had demolished part, but the gossip was that when Hess had arrived, the first call was to Rosemount. (The CO was Loel Guinness, friend of Duke of Kent).*

17. *We also circumnavigated the Prestwick airfield, locating the Chipmunks.*

18. *We left and spent the rest of the night checking the prevailing light conditions at 10.30 DST (Dusky) and 11.09 DST (Dark). We retired.*

19. *We arose and breakfasted. RW had been on WiFi earlier and stated that he believed the mistake arose over Broadlaw. So we set the sat nav and set out for the Tinto hills.*

20. *After some deliberation and debate we found Broadlaw and were surprised how similar it was to its neighbours of similar height. Seemingly there was little to distinguish it, a fact that may have led Hess to go too far to the north?*

21. *We travelled home after a Lockerbie pub lunch.*

I think this information to be pretty important. Firstly, that David McIntyre was taken to identify Hess (Certainly not mentioned anywhere), Secondly that his wife subsequently was in fear for her life and thirdly that the 'first call' was to Rosemount House, the operational command of RAF Ayr/Prestwick.

I believe that these events are all adequately explained by the fact that Hess was aiming at Prestwick and Prestwick knew he was coming. I also wonder if indeed David McIntyre had previously met with Hess, pre-war and that perhaps explains why he was asked to visit Hess? David McIntyre travelled extensively throughout Europe in the 1930's in just the same way as his friend the Marquis of Clydesdale.

The problem we have is that, once again, we hit the barrier of intelligence records. There are precious few available, but who knows who was at Prestwick and its environs that evening? We know that Loel Guinness was. (At Rosemount House) We know that David McIntyre was. I should love to know where the following were:

- The Duke of Hamilton's three brothers (One lived at Prestwick, one was Head of RAF Fighter Intelligence)
- Fred Winterbotham (Head of RAF Intelligence), pre war confidant of Hess and Rosenberg.
- J O Andrews
- And, of course the Duke of Kent.

I suppose for good measure we should also add the King and Queen to that wish list. They are recorded as being at Windsor that weekend[7] and I have no evidence to the contrary.

Unfortunately, until deemed unimportant, I fear that we will never know. I certainly do not think that any of the above information, however, disproves my theory.

I would now like to briefly look at the **post 10.5.41 history of the major protagonists** in an attempt to see if any conclusions may be drawn from their subsequent treatment. I do so on the basis that it is unlikely, but far from impossible that persons who have been unloyal, or even treacherous would be subsequently feted. I do so however with a slight sense of unease as the British, in particular, are very good at cover-ups. As Richard Deacon states, *"As so often happens, the authorities covered up the would-be traitors and only publicised the imaginary ones"[8]*

So, in no particular order,

Mary Violet Roberts (1864-1958). Mrs Roberts continued to live in Cambridge, England at 10,Wilberforce Road, eventually dying there in 1958. Like her husband 26 years earlier she chose to be cremated[9] and as far as I aware there is no gravestone. Neither were there any announcements in the local papers. Try as I might, I have therefore been unable to locate a picture of her, though Cambridge University Library does hold one of Herbert Ainslie Roberts. As has already been stated amongst the principal beneficiaries of her will were Sir Anthony Bevir, Private Secretary to Winston Churchill and Sir Edward Playfair, Permanent Under Secretary to the Minister of War.

Walter Stewart Roberts. Walter Roberts retired from the Secret services in 1948, complete with CMG and returned to the London Stock Exchange. He died in 1974.

Claude Dansey (1876-1947). Dansey retired from the Secret Services in 1945 and died in Bath, Avon in 1947. In 1945 he was awarded the Legion d'Honneur by France and the Legion of Merit by the US. The British had already knighted him in 1943 and now added a KCMG for good measure.

Prince George, Duke of Kent (1902-1942). Following a successful trip to Canada in the autumn of 1941, the Duke returned to his duties as Airfield Inspector. He was killed in a controversial air accident in August 1942, when the Sunderland flying boat in which he was travelling crashed into a remote Scottish hillside in Caithness. His body was subsequently taken to Dunrobin Castle.

The 14th Duke of Hamilton (1903-1973). The impact of the Hess 'saga' never really left him. A portrait of him that hangs in Lennoxlove even has a 'ghostly shadow' of

231

Rudolf Hess superimposed over part of the image. In the war years he sued to clear his name, Churchill stopped him going to the US, for fear of what he might say, yet after the war he still remained at the head of the Scottish aristocracy, both in name and role. He played the prominent role at the coronation of Queen Elizabeth II in 1953 that was expected of him and was granted the following additional honours:

> Privy Counsellor
>
> Order of the Thistle (1951)
>
> Chancellor of the University of St Andrews (1948)
>
> Lord High Commissioner to the Church of Scotland (Various)
>
> President of the Boys Brigade
>
> President of the Air league
>
> Together with various directorships (British Linen Bank, Scottish Aviation)

> If Hamilton really was a traitor and the government knew, are any of the   above likely? I think not.

Lord Halifax. Despite a 1942 request for a return to Britain, Edward Wood remained as Ambassador in Washington until 1946. He died on his Yorkshire Estate in 1959, aged 78.

Viscount Templewood. Samuel Hoare returned from Spain in 1944 when the threat of Spanish involvement was over. He was created a Viscount and entered the House of Lords. He died, aged 79 in 1959.

Tancred Borenius. Tancred Borenius died in 1947 and is buried in Coombe Bissett churchyard, Wiltshire.

Loel Guinness (1906-1988). After the war Loel Guinness resumed the life of a jet setter, with property literally all around the world. He married 3 times and spent most of his time visiting the various properties. He also acquired the 'Calypso' which later became famous as the research vessel of Jacques Cousteau, the inventor of the aqualung. He died in Houston, Texas.

David McIntyre. After the war McIntyre also resumed his pre war role as a director of Scottish Aviation Limited. He died in a plane crash whilst on a sales trip in North Africa in 1957.

The Douglas-Hamilton brothers. I have already dealt with Douglas.

Geordie Douglas-Hamilton (1906-1994). Head of Intelligence – Fighter Command. Post war served as Lord in waiting to King George VI and Queen Elizabeth II. Much decorated post war.

Malcolm Douglas-Hamilton (1909-1964). Post war emigrated to the United States and was killed in an Air crash in 1964. Awarded OBE in 1943, DFC 1944.

Lord David Douglas-Hamilton (1912-1944) – Shot down whilst on a reconnaissance mission.

Carl Jacob Burckhardt (1891-1974). Burkhardt was never particularly trusted by the British government, largely because of suspicions of pro-German bias whilst at Danzig, 1937-1939. I think it fair to say that post May 1941 this distrust was intensified. In the autumn of 1941 Burckhardt visited London. According to Caroline Woodhead,[10] Anthony Eden had 'considerable misgivings....in view of his political ambitions and possibility that he might put out peace feelers on behalf of the Germans, whether in official or unofficial circles...' I suspect that Eden knew exactly what had happened a few months earlier and was worried as to what Burckhardt might do or say. The British Civil Service duly went spare trying to politically accommodate Burckhardt and he eventually met RA Butler, in between shooting pheasants[11]. He was not interviewed by the Prime Minister or the Foreign Secretary. The visit, once completed was met with a sense of 'relief and satisfaction'. One could say that by Autumn 1941 Britain had got what it wanted and no longer needed to fete Burckhardt.

At the end of the war other odd things happened. As will be detailed later the Battaglias visited Geneva for their holidays, perhaps to repay their debts? At the same time Burckhardt saw fit to rebuff various attacks from newspapers as to his precise role in the early part of the war. By this time he was President of the International Red Cross Committee and insisted on political neutrality to the extent that he would not condemn the Nazi regime.

I now wonder if this somewhat extraordinary position was a reaction to his activities in 1941 and that various persons within post war Germany were in a position to 'dish the dirt' should the need exist? Again, as has already been related, the Burckhardt archives were extensively weeded post war and spread over a number of depositories. However, the 'Verzeichnis des Schriftlichen Nachlasses' reveals some surprising correspondence. Reference B1/c/73 appears to deal with various allegations from Swiss and Foreign press as to Burckhardt's activities in 1941. Firstly, they do not appear to be the allegations of a solitary voice, 6 Swiss papers and 4 foreign newspapers carried the story. Given what we have already learned perhaps we should not be too surprised.

Carrying on in the same vein, Burckhardt saw fit to write a number of letters concerning an attack by the socialist newspaper 'Berner Tagwacht' entitled 'Fall (Downfall of) Haushofer – Carl J.Burckhardt'. Presumably by way of defence Burckhardt saw fit to write to The Duke of Hamilton, Lord Templewood and Duff Cooper. All three politely replied together with a number of European diplomats. It seems to me that much was at stake. Burckhardt's reputation, whilst obviously important to him was, I suggest, very much secondary to the continuation of the perception of Red Cross neutrality. Without that perception, the Red Cross would cease being an effective agency. (As it was Russia had effectively banned the Red Cross during WW2).

Consequently, during the post world war soul searching and 'score settling' the continuation of the institutions such as the Red Cross would assume great import, particularly as the winter of 1946 saw much of central Europe short of food and in the throws of near third world conditions. To 'out' the President of such an Institute would not therefore be sensible. In 1948 Burckhardt was succeeded by Paul Ruegger. It may be relevant to record that Burckhardt's presidency was amongst the shortest of any holder (the second recipient held the post for 46 years), but of course this may be purely coincidental. After Burckhardt's retirement in 1948, the world of academia beckoned and he spent the rest of his life as an historian. Carl Jacob Burckhardt died in 1974.

Wladyslaw Sikorski. (1881-1943). Sikorski continued as Head of the Polish Government in exile until his death in July 1943. The Liberator bomber in which he was flying crashed on take off from Gibraltar. Much controversy remains as to whether the crash was an accident or something more sinister. However, on 11th May 1941 Sikorski landed at Prestwick and then spent the day in Glasgow, before flying off to Findo Gask in Perthshire, where he had established an HQ. I have little doubt that before his departure to Perthshire, Roman Battaglia had given him a thorough briefing of the previous nights events. There is no proof of this as far as I am able to establish, but I would stake my mortgage on this supposition, if nothing else. As has already been stated, I do not know the extent, (if any) of Polish involvement in the Hess affair. We have the evidence of Sikorski's anxious wish to return to Britain whilst in America and Canada in spring 1941. We have the debate as to 1) why he chose to fly and 2) why he chose to fly to Prestwick, but above all I suspect we have the fact that Poland was THE reason why Britain and her Empire declared war on Nazi Germany in September 1939. If a clever MI6 ruse was really being mooted, surely this fact could not be ignored.

Rudolf Hess (1894-1987). And so we move onto the main player himself. I think there are all sorts of questions that need to be addressed; where did he *precisely* go post capture, what was the truth concerning his World War 1 wound and was he murdered or did he really manage suicide, aged 92? However, the common theme, throughout the 46 years following the flight that Hess survived was silence. Absolute silence. From May 1941 to August 1987 Rudolf Hess was silent. No public pronouncements, no statements, no press releases. Admittedly some no doubt authorised release of letter excerpts[12] – but with one exception. The exception was the Nuremberg war trials, which I have no doubt at all, posed a major challenge to the British authorities.

I believe that the British Secret Service had lured, or rather tempted, Hess into Scotland, Churchill had imprisoned him for the next 5 years and then, on fear of his life, had charged him with the four charges of:

conspiracy to wage aggressive war,

waging aggressive war,
war crimes,
and crimes against humanity.

Nuremberg 1946: A still photograph of the Trial showing the major criminals in the dock. Was Hess's appearance stage-managed to conceal the true details of the 1941 flight?

The eventual outcome was that Hess was charged with two counts and acquitted on the latter two counts.

However, one would might expect that the circumstances surrounding the 1941 flight to play a pivotal part of the trial. The lead up to the flight, the rationale, the reasons, the detail, surely Hess would explain all. Tell all, then we would understand precisely how Hess was really a martyr to peace.

As it transpired Hess at Nuremberg was a shambles. On 30th November 1945 Hess admitted that he had 'simulated loss of memory'. In 1946 Hess was noted to have smuggled in *'Three Men in a Boat' by Jerome K.Jerome*. The final statement of 31st August 1946 was wholly unapologetic, but made no mention as to the lead up to events prior to 1941. Quite extraordinary.

Various theories have been put forward as to why this may be the case. I think that if I thought I was about to be killed I may well think justified in telling the truth as to why I saw fit to fly to the enemy at the start of the war. What had I really to lose?

The attention that was shown to Hess by the 'brainwashing scientist' Donald Ewan Cameron bears scrutiny. In his final statement at Nuremberg, Hess makes mention of the Soviet show trials and those with 'glassy and like eyes in a dream'.

Is this a reference to the fact that Hess had been 'interfered' with, so that he might lose short-term memory? The role that Cameron played post-war in brainwashing certainly transcends the scope of this work, but its possible application to Hess in 1946 Germany certainly bears further scrutiny.

Anyway, what is for sure is that the 1941 flight certainly was not explained. Through the use of smoke and mirrors and Hess's questionable sanity, the whole issue was conveniently sidestepped. Once Hess was in Spandau that was it. No further utterances came forth. Third party recollections eventually surfaced (Tony le Tissier, the

Hess family), but no first person statements. How jolly convenient. Hess died in 1987.

Albrecht Haushofer (1903-1945). Haushofer was shot outside Moabit prison in Berlin in late April 1945. Eventually the regime that Haushofer was simultaneously working for and trying to undermine turned against him. Apparently Himmler had kept him alive whilst he had aspirations of a peace treaty with the Western Allies. So, the question arises as why precisely he was shot, or indeed imprisoned?

Immediately after the Hess flight Haushofer was summoned by Hitler to the Berchtesgaden to account for his actions. He was then sent to Berlin for further interrogation. Eventually he was released in July 1941.
Given that Hitler 'looked after' the Hess family after the failure of the flight, one can only surmise that his actions as regards Haushofer are those of someone who wondered if Haushofer had, in some way betrayed his master, whether by 'overegging' the chances of success, or even lying to him? Hence the written test to compare and contrast with what he had been previously told. Eventually, after the July 1944 bomb plot Haushofer went into hiding, thus condemning him to death on his eventual capture.

Karl and Martha Haushofer. Prepare for more conspiracy. Karl and Martha Haushofer were found dead at their Bavarian property, in 1946, shortly after interrogation by two British Agents. They had apparently committed suicide. I would just ask you to question that fact. That's all. By their premature demise, all the German players who were aware, or likely to be aware of the finer details of the Hess flight were either dead or in Spandau prison. Burckhardt's silence was also assured so as to preserve the Red Cross as a viable organisation.

What if the elder Haushofer had started giving interviews about how his eldest son was instrumental in broking a 1941 peace? Not good with 20 million dead as a result of the Nazi invasion of Russia? End of conspiracy.

****

So, is it possible to draw any conclusions from the post war histories of the major players? The Germans were either dead or in prison. The Swiss kept their mouths shut because it was in their best interests to do so and seemingly none of the British players were 'done down' in the slightest. If anything they all seem to have prospered for the rest of their lives. As good British Intelligence men do, they also all kept their mouths shut. 'Blabbing' was bad form and many even resented Fred Winterbotham for spilling the beans about Ultra in the 1970's.

I can only conclude that the Hess affair was indeed an Intelligence inspired ruse. I can find no evidence to the contrary. It started as a direct consequence of the interception of the Haushofer-Roberts letter of 23rd September 1940 and ironically, a German misunderstanding of the British Wartime Postal system.

---

[1] *Telephone call to Mr.Hutton, Steward of the Castle, 5th August 2008. From an article by Burnett and Tabraham.*
[2] *National Monuments Centre, Swindon, Wilts.*
[3] *He was injured following a bombing raid.*
[4] *WO 3288A Colonel Duke was far from impressed. "Their laxity (RAF Intelligence) was most unfortunate as the prisoner might have had urgent operational information to divulge."*
[5] *Number: 2310157.*
[6] *Number: 2595648*
[7] *William Shawcross - Queen Elizabeth The Official Biography - Macmillan 2009. "On the evening of Friday 9th May, he (Churchill) wrote to the Queen - she had probably left for Windsor". It appears*

that Shawcross had some doubts too? Why say probably? The Queen replied on Monday 12th May 1941.

[8] British Secret Service - Richard Deacon - Grafton-1991.

[9] At Cambridge Crematorium.

[10] Dunant's Dream - Caroline Woodhead - Harper Collins - 1998.

[11] Ibid - The Foreign Office knew that Burckhardt was a keen shot.

[12] Most notably in Ilse Hess's 1953 Prisoner of Peace.

21

'THE BRITISH ILLUSION OF PEACE'

THE CONCLUSIONS

In attempting to draw conclusions from the 'Hess Affair' I ask seven questions and try to summarise my thought, thinking and reasoning behind Hess believing that a peace was attainable.'

What made Hess fly?
- One thing is for sure. Hess decided to fly on his own volition. It was wholly his initiative and had been from August 1940. No one was forcing him to fly. He had assimilated the various evidence that had been presented to him and had decided that the probability was that by flying he would achieve a peace settlement between the German and British nations.

  In coming to this conclusion I believe he drew on the following data:

  The impact of 'flying missions and achievements' in history. Everest, The Atlantic and even Chamberlain's flights; all had immense impact on the population. Aviation was very much part of the Zeitgeist, as indeed was Fascism.

  The Churchill led government was in trouble. On 7th May 1941 there had been a vote of confidence which, although had been won had sent shockwaves through Churchill and Eden. Chips Channon called it,

"A triumph on paper, but in reality the Government has been shaken and both Anthony and Winston know it".

The fact that a vote was even necessary was a reflection of the mood of Parliament. Beaverbrook had resigned the week before the flight.

- The knowledge that slowly the British were being battered into submission, despite the failure of the Battle of Britain. London was looking like, 'A battered old war horse'.[1] The Atlantic U boats were still in the ascendancy.

- MI6 through Borenius and others were telling Haushofer/Hess that a coup attempt was plausible, emanating from the highest levels and detailing how Churchill could be circumvented. Supporting the plot Hess had pre-war evidence of German sympathies from much of aristocratic Britain. The fact that the apparent approach was 'non governmental' made it more likely to succeed as there was no precondition of the removal of Hitler.

- Hoare, in Spain was saying the same thing, but possibly for different reasons. Again, Burckhardt would no doubt relay back the 'City' intelligence of March 1941 to Haushofer.

- The psychological impact of his arrival, exactly one year after the invasion of the Low Countries and France, together with the worst night of bombing during the blitz.

- The German Intelligence Service in Britain was pretty hopeless and did not provide any useful intelligence of its own. Hess was blind in intelligence terms. Haushofer was his best bet, but could he even be sure of Haushofer?

- However, in reaching his decision to fly, I fear that Hess took too much credence of the following:
  > Information coming from Geneva and indeed via Burckhardt/Haushofer.
  > The desperate need for a settlement before 15th May 1941.
  > The fact that he was being told exactly what he wanted to hear from more than one source.
  > The potential for status should he succeed.
  > The knowledge that his family would be 'looked after' should he fail.

So it was he decided, (not gambled), to fly.
He dared.

Why a solo mission?

I think this easy. By giving the impression of a solo mission, it made the whole thing deniable if it failed. It did not appear to be a government initiative. If Luftwaffe involvement could be demonstrated, such as Hess flying in a formation, or part of a raid, then immediately the mission becomes governmental. If the mission were overtly governmental then Stalin would straight away smell a rat. Why on earth would his new 'best friend' Adolf wish to make a peace with Britain?

Did Hitler know?

Yes, Hitler knew. Perhaps not from the earliest stage of the preparations, but certainly he went with Hitler's blessings. Hitler 'looked after' the Hess family throughout the war and I suspect Hess told his Fuhrer of the final details whilst in Berlin at the start of May 1941. There are various stories revealing Hitler's acting abilities and I suspect that he gave a master class on receipt of the news that Hess had flown. He had to make out that Hess had gone on his own volition to prevent suspicions of an Anglo German peace.

Did the British know?

Yes, Britain knew that Hess was coming as we effectively invited him. If there really was a coup attempt underway I doubt Churchill would have gone to the cinema on hearing the news of Hess's arrival. I suspect however, that probably no more than 10 Britons knew that Hess was coming that night. Amongst them, MI6, Churchill, those at RAF Prestwick HQ, The Duke of Hamilton and JO Andrews.

Were the major British protagonists loyal?

Absolutely. I think? This was definitely an intelligence sting, probably inspired by the German success at Venlo. Furthermore, in extremis, in 1941, I do not believe that the King would have signed anything against Churchill's wishes. (In 1939/40 I am not so sure). Moreover, being based in Berlin and Munich, there was no way that Hess could ultimately gauge the opinion of Hamilton, Kent and the King unless he went and found out. He was relying wholly on 3rd party, uncorroborated evidence. There was only one way to find out....

Why did the British do it?

Primarily to buy time. Nothing else. A 1941 German/Russian war was possibly a 'good outcome' for Britain. Revenge for Venlo may also have featured in moments of weakness. In time America might even join the War. The danger of this strategy was however obvious were Germany to defeat Russia.

Why did the British not exploit the issue?

Simply because Churchill was petrified of losing American support. If the American population at large thought the British were suing for peace, Churchill's only hope would be extinguished. Britain really would be on its own. Imagine too the reaction if Germany started to release incriminating evidence as to British peace feelers? However, I would question if, 68 years later, the same criteria apply? The papers must surely now be able to be released?

Why did the Germans not say that Hess had been tricked?

Simply that to do so would be a sign of weakness. They had just been outwitted. Moreover, in the 1920's there had been a sense in Germany that World War 1 had been lost partly on account of the almost supernatural influence of the British Intelligence Services. To resurrect such feelings would be dangerous. At Nuremberg self-preservation would preclude such allegations, although Goering did taunt Hess to 'tell of his secret'.

Was it Hess that crashed at Eaglesham?

Of course it was! If not, there certainly would not have been the subsequent fuss. A dead doppelganger would have been quickly buried. I have also looked at the photographs of Hess, pre and post war and very simplistically can tell no difference. Hess did not appear to have ear lobes in either set of pictures. As to Spandau I have no idea and no way of telling, whether the real Hess was present. If it was not I would be surprised as I would expect the Hess family to have noticed.

Was Poland involved?

Yes. Poland would have to be involved in any settlement, as Poland was the reason Britain declared war. The Sikorski flight into Prestwick is just too much of a coincidence. This would be part of the ruse, especially given that Prestwick had barely commenced cross-ocean aircraft reception. We are also unsure as to the role, if any, that Polish Intelligence may have played. The Poles saw Intelligence matters almost as a national sport, given their proximity to both Russia and Germany and whilst there was an agreement that Poland would share its intelligence with Britain, its wartime host, the suspicion remained that Britain was only told what Poland thought it should be told. That having been said, Poland did share the Enigma machine Intelligence with Britain.

Poland might also explain the role of the Duke of Kent in the Hess affair. It has been mooted that the Duke of Kent was to be offered the Polish throne as part of any restoration.[2]

Therefore, as well as a possible liaison between Hess and the King was Prince George expecting to play a further more exalted role in Polish history?

****

I hope that you are now convinced that Rudolf Hess was lured to Britain as part of a British Intelligence ruse. I wish I could produce the MI6 documents but without such evidence we shall be unable to prove categorically.

However, Hess was certainly not mad. He simply made a mistake in weighing up the available evidence. However, without doubt 'He dared'.

---

[1] Chips Channon - Diaries- Phoenix - 1996.
[2] Lord Bethall, 1972 interview.

APPENDIX 1

SOME FRIENDS OF CARL BURCKHARDT

The historical image of Carl Jacob Burckhardt is very much that of the stuffy academic and international diplomat. We have already seen how he was a confidant of both the British and German governments, at the highest levels, in the period both prior to and after the declaration of War in September 1939.

The discovery I stumbled across concerning Burckhardt was very much the most unexpected of this period of research. So unexpected that when first discovered I was convinced of a plot the scale of which, even in my conspiratorial mind, was far beyond that originally envisaged or even suspected. The accepted view was certainly brought into doubt.

When Rudolf Hess crashed, the basic sequences of events are broadly agreed. Taken to the Baird farmhouse, offered tea, home guard arrive, taken to the scout hut and then interrogation. Stephen Prior[1] quite properly raises other questions concerning the initial apprehending of Hess and asks why Hess apparently gave his Iron Cross to one of his captors. The basic facts seem to be to be consistent with a typical apprehension of an enemy airman; some confusion, some 'pulling rank' and some adherence to usual process. The whole process has been likened to a classic 'Dad's Army' episode (Don't tell him your name, Pike) and I am content that this very display of British ineptitude is indicative of the fact that Hess was not expected in that particular area that night.

I am also content that the actions of most of those involved were the actions of those who were not expecting to be drawn into the Hess affair.

Except possibly for Roman Battaglia?

Roman and Aniela Battaglia (friends 1 and 2).
Roman Battaglia has been known about for some time. He was the Polish consulate who interrogated Hess for two hours in the Scout Hut in Giffnock.[2] Nothing-new there. Peter Padfield makes the point that he was not even originally requested; his landlord Mr.Fairweather[3] at Newton Mearns was ill in bed[4] so Battaglia attended in his stead.

The discovery I was to make however transformed my view of the 'off duty diplomat' into something quite different. I was about to add two and two together and make twenty-two (a not uncommon accusation).

Roman Roger Adam Maria Guido Battaglia was born in Vienna in 1903, the son of Roger Battaglia, 4th Baron Forst (1873-1950) a reasonably famous diplomat and politician, largely in the days of the Austro Hungarian Empire. The family was ancient, originally coming from Venice. He was well educated, graduating from the University of Cracow in 1927 with a bachelor in law degree. From there he joined the Polish Foreign Ministry and worked as follows:

- 1927-29 – Warsaw
- 1929-32 – Paris
- 1932-35 – Warsaw
- 1935-39 – Danzig

On 4th March 1937 he married Aniela Kleber whilst stationed at Danzig.[5]

The still alert reader will wonder perhaps if Battaglia's postings had coincided with those of Patrick Roberts, Mrs Roberts' diplomatic son, but I do not think so, the timings are different.

Appendix 1 Some Friends of Carl Burckhardt

However, the Danzig posting in 1935-39, most certainly did coincide with another major protagonist in the Hess affair; Carl Jacob Burckhardt.[6] Most of the Hess books detail the visits to Burckhardt in the spring of 1941 by amongst others, Albrecht Haushofer, Tancred Borenius and possibly even Samuel Hoare.

My heart started to beat faster. Within a couple of hours of arrival Hess was being interviewed by an acquaintance of one of the men that had acted as a conduit and facilitator to him making the flight! I had to find out more about Battaglia. This proved difficult in the extreme, which made me excited and suspicious in equal measure. The Sikorski Institute in London held a brief resume of his career as above, but in 1945 it listed him as going to France.[7] Thereafter nothing. I searched the Internet death registers; again nothing. Wondering if there might still be Battaglia's in Vienna I googled 'Battaglia and Vienna' and learned that a Mrs Battaglia worked at the Art Museum in the city.

I emailed the art museum and was somewhat surprised (though probably shouldn't have been) to receive an email from Jakub Forst-Battaglia who is the recently retired Austrian Ambassador to Estonia and husband of the lady at the Museum.

He told me that Roman's father had died in near poverty in the Soviet bloc and that Roman, he thought, had emigrated to Canada.[8] He didn't think there were children. My long suffering personal assistant, Helen Cara, who was going to Canada on holiday to visit relatives, was press ganged into making searches whilst in Toronto. Again to no avail.

Whilst on the Battaglia track I also noticed that a file was being suppressed at the PRO, Kew but after a Freedom of Information application I eventually obtained access.[9] Originally closed until 2049(!) this dealt with an application for British Citizenship in November 1946.

Thinking that this must be significant I rushed down the M40 to Kew. To be honest, the trip was a bit of a disappointment. Whilst repeating much of the biographical information I had gleaned from Jakub Battaglia and the Sikorski Institute, the main purpose of the file was to record the various searches that the Home Office had made prior to approving the application for Citizenship in January 1948. Nowhere was there any mention of 'Hess involvement' and not surprisingly, the words 'conspiracy' or 'cabal' also were not present. MI5 even replied that *'There was nothing recorded against'*.[10] This is a bit rich given that there were (and are) 1941 MI5 files specifically dealing with how on earth Battaglia had got close to Hess in the Giffnock Scout Hut![11]

The police also gave Battaglia a clean bill of health, save for the fact that Mrs.Battaglia had been fined 10 shillings for 'fraud on the railway' in December 1945.

But then the important discoveries started to come in:

Firstly. I discovered that it was likely that Roman Battaglia had died in Toronto, Canada in 1967–68. In 1967 a Roman Battaglia was listed at 76 Quebec Avenue and in 1968 the listing had changed to solely Angela Battaglia. Battaglia had apparently been employed as a travel Agent in the City and had established his own firm, Caniaga travel.[12] It appears therefore, that Battaglia had successfully applied for citizenship in 1946/48 and then subsequently emigrated to Canada.

Secondly. In 1945 the Battaglia's travelled to Geneva in May/June 1945 for a holiday.[13] An odd choice, or an opportunity to meet up again with Carl Burckhardt, who, as Head of the International Red Cross still worked there?

Thirdly. The Burckhardt link gets odder. Richard and I had also travelled to Geneva, some 66 years later, in the summer of 2007 as part of that years Harris/Wilbourn vacation. Whilst there we met the very helpful keeper of part of the Burckhardt archive who warned us that the archive was spread across various locations and that Burckhardt had been 'very careful' of what was allowed to remain and what was weeded.

It was therefore with the expectation of failure that I embarked on a search of his archive, hoping for, but not expecting, the evidence of a link between Burckhardt and Battaglia.

I was therefore amazed to discover a listing at the University of Basle for a 1938 letter between the two parties. After jumping through further hoops to gain approval from the modern day guardian of the Burckhardt papers, I received a scanned copy of the original letter, together with further copies of two later letters, dated 1939 and 1940.[14] This was where life became really bizarre.

The two later letters were actually part of a dialogue from Mrs Battaglia to Burckhardt which were essentially letters requesting money!

Dealing with each letter in turn.

The 1938 letter:

Le 15 Novembre 1938

Cher Monsieur Battaglia,

Conformement à notre conversation téléphonique, je vous transmets avec la letter à Monsieur le Ministre Chodaki, une letter au Ministre des Finances de la Republique Polonaise et une annexe provisoire, dont je vous ferai parvenir l'eventuelle rectification.

En vous remerciant de l'amiabilité que vous apportez à l'expedition de cette affaire, je vous exprime, cher Monsieur Battaglia, l'expression de mes meilleurs sentiments.

Appendix 1 Some Friends of Carl Burckhardt

To: Monsieur le Conseiller de Legation Dr.R.Battaglia
Commissariat General de la Republique de Pologne, Dantzig

So what does this first letter tell us?

I think that it discloses a degree of friendship. The two men speak on the telephone and they jointly deal with an issue between Mr.Chodaki,[15] and the Finance Minister of Poland. Burckhardt signs off with yours faithfully/yours sincerely.

It also gives an indication of the level that the two men were operating at. This was high diplomacy at the epicentre of 1930's world politics. World politics that were rapidly approaching their climax.

The 1939 letter

The 1939 letter is very different in tone. Firstly, it is from Mrs Battaglia to Burckhardt and tells us a lot about how world events had shifted against the Battaglia family in the intervening 12 months.

29-11-1939

Monsieur le Haut Commissaire,

Après une longue hesitation je me suis decidé de m'addresser à Vous, puisque les circonstances tout à fait exceptionnelles, dans lesquelles je me trouve, me permettent de vous priez de bien vouloir m'aider dans la situation très difficile de ma vie au présente ... je n'ai pas besoin de vous décrire Monsieur le Haut Commissaire tout ce que j'ai souffert et m'apporté dès le jour, où j'étais obligée de quitter Dantzig, puisque certainement vous le savez. Maintenant nous sommes en France, où mon Mari s'est engagé comme volontaire à l'armée polonaise qui se forme en Bretagne, et moi, je vie dans une petite ville au bord de l'Atlantique dans des conditions tres modèstes – Puisque en quittant la Pologne, nous n'avons pas pu nos ne rien prendre avec nous, et mon Mari est au camp d'instruction au commencement et comme simple soldat.... et ne gagne rien alors notre situation materielle est très difficile et penible. C'est pour cette raison que je me permets de m'adresser à votre grande volonté Le Haut Commissaire en vous priant bien sincèrement de bien vouloir nous prêter un peu d'argent pour cette période si dure de notre vie. Naturellement la grandeur de cette somme dépende tout à fait de votre bonne volonté. Monsieur Le Haut Commissaire, et vous pouvez être tout à fait sur que dès que notre situation va s'ameliorer, nous ferons tout notre possible pour vous rendre cette somme avec notre plus grand reconnaissance-

Croyez moi aussi Monsieur le Haut Commissaire, que si je m'adresse à vous avec cette grande prière, c'est vraiement notre ...est très difficile, et je suis persuadé que vous allez me comprendre...

En attendant votre aimable reponse et avec toute ma confiance, je vous envoie Monsieur le Haut Commissaire mes salutations les plus distinguées.

Angela de Battaglia
Sables d'Olonne (Vendee)
45 Quai G Clemenceau
France

The 1940 letter

Sablesd' Olome Vendee
15-1-1940
45 Quai Clemenceau

Cher Monsieur Le Haut Commissaire – je vous demande bien pardon, que je suis si en retard avec ma réponse, mais j'ai l'impression, et ça me fait une grande peine que vous n'avez pas assez de confiance en nous-

Si, je me suis adressé à vous Monsieur, c'est que vous étiez à Dantzig, que vous avez bien connu moi et mon mari, aussi son travail et sa valeur personnelle, et j'étais persuadée que vous allez bien comprendre la grande difficulté de notre vie actuelle-

Je comprends très bien que notre situation est tout à fait differente maintenant, mais à present je peux vous assurer Monsieur, qu' encore au courant de cette année j'aurai la possibilité de vous rendre votre aimable service, puisque dans quelques mois je vais commencer à travailler dans notre Ministere des Aff.Etr à Angers ... A cause de celui je peux m'adresser encore une fois à vous monsieur en vous priant de tout mon coeur de bien vouloir me prêter encore 4 milles francs; ils me sont undispensables, puisque je me trouve sans aucune réserve, et je suis obligée de m'acheter une bonne machine à écrire et de m'occuper un peu de ma santé et de mes choses ...

Je vous donne ma parole d'honneur que je vous rendrai cette somme de 6 (six) milles francs, dans 6 mois (je pourrais verser à votre conto mille francs chaque mois) – dès le commencement de mon travail au Ministère –

Vous êtes monsieur le seul homme à qui je peux m'adresser avec cette prière. Je vous serai infinissement reconnaissante et croyez moi Monsieur que j'ai vraiment énormement besoin de l'argent parce que même pour une femme c'est une chose infinissement penible et difficile de prier pour cette raison –

Je vous envoie Monsieur mes respecteuses et sincères salutations

Angela De Battaglia

Once again the letters are wholly consistent with the Home Office file that records Battaglia's postings whilst in Britain.

According to the file the Battaglia's fled to France when Poland was invaded in September 1939. As the 1939 letter reveals the couple went to Angers, near Paris, which had become the temporary base for the Polish government in exile. Mrs Battaglia appears to have resided at Sable d'Olonne, on the coast, some 100 miles from Angers. It was from 45 Quai G Clemenceau that she corresponded with Carl Burckhardt. Her husband had left France in June 1940 for England with the Polish Army. On 1st July 1940 he took up residence at 'Faside', Newton Mearns, Renfrewshire, Scotland (Landlord: Mr.Fairweather) and it was from this address that he travelled to Giffnock Scout hut on the night of May 10th 1941. 'Faside' is a large house on Ayr Road, Newton Mearns, the owners of which became the Barr family of 'Ironbru' fame.[16]

He had by this time been seconded from the Army to the Polish Consulate in Glasgow, being recorded as the Assistant Consul, working from 91 Hill Street, Glasgow.[17] Technically he was the honorary consul as he was still working for the army, but in January 1941 he was discharged from the Army on the grounds of ill health. However, he remained in Glasgow. His role was recorded as liaison between the Polish Government and the Department of Health in Scotland, together with a perhaps more suited role as Assistant Legal Advisor to the Polish Foreign Office, (whatever that means?).

It appears that his main role consisted of dealing with the mass of Polish refugees that were making their way to Britain following the fall of France.[18] Is there perhaps a synergy between this role and that of the Red Cross?

In October 1941, 5 months after the Hess affair he was transferred to London and resided firstly at 49 Hallam Street in Mayfair and then, after 1943, in Acton and Ealing. When making his application for citizenship he was residing at 111 The Avenue, Ealing in a house he co owned with a Mieczyslaw Habibcht. Battaglia was working for the BBC, having left the Polish government because 'he was not in sympathy with political changes in Poland'.[19]

I do not know when he was re-united with his wife. Clearly in November 1939 and January 1940 she was on the Atlantic seaboard of France under threat of impending German occupation. Perhaps the reunion was the purpose of the recorded holiday to France in May 1945. Perhaps they had already been reunited in Scotland or London. I simply do not know. If the holiday was a reunion, then who can blame him, or perhaps its purpose was to repay a debt to Burckhardt? Battaglia had been earning the sum of £580 per annum from the BBC in September 1945,[20] so presumably he could afford to repay if that is why he or they travelled to Geneva.

So is it any wonder that I had got so excited? A leading Polish diplomat, a close friend of Burckhardt and Sikorski[21] is the first person to interview Hess on arrival! I began to wonder if the Hess affair was even a Polish initiative.

Lady Diana Cooper (3rd friend)

As part of the necessary work on Lady Diana Cooper I read her biography by Philip Ziegler.[22] I must say that I found it hard to empathise with her, feeling that whilst the biography painted the picture of a woman who was well blessed with stunning looks, connections, money and wealth,[23] she lived a pretty vacuous and unfulfilled life. However, I doubt she was untypical of the upper classes of Britain during the pre war decades.

Pertinent to the story in hand, Diana Cooper, who was at the time married to Alfred Duff Cooper (1890-1954) embarked on a love affair with Carl Burkhardt during 1938/1939. This is not speculation and at the time Diana was married to the recently resigned First Lord of the Admiralty.[24]

Diana Cooper had travelled with her husband on board the Admiralty's ship, The Enchantress to the Baltic in August 1938. Danzig was a port of call and it was there that she renewed her acquaintance with Burckhardt.[25] The affair appears to have carried on throughout 1939 and Ziegler notes that Burckhardt came to London in October 1939. I think this affair with a married woman, the wife of an eminent British politician perhaps paints a different picture of the stuffy Swiss historian that might other wise be the case?

---

[1] *Double Standards - Little, Brown - 2001*
[2] *James Douglas Hamilton - The Truth about Rudolf Hess -*
Mainstream 1993. Hamilton says, ' Whilst in the custody of the Home
Guard, a member of the Polish Consulate from Glasgow , named
Battaglia, asked the prisoner questions ..... '

[3] *Yet again another coincidence. Mr.Fairweather is Douglas Fairweather, the son of Sir.Wallace Fairweather (1859 - 1939), who was yet another Scottish Aeronautical Pioneer! He was killed in a plane crash in 1944 aged 53.*

[4] *Preface to revised edition of Flight for the Fuhrer - Cassell & Co-2001.*

[5] *Letter to JTGH from Dr.Suchcitz - The Polish Institute and Sikorski Museum. 27th January 2006.*

[6] *Burckhardt actually details his role as High Commissioner in 'Meine Danziger Mission 1937 - 1939'. Verlag Georg D.W.Callwey. Munich 1980. Battaglia is not mentioned.*

[7] *Letter to JTGH from the Sikorski Institute 27th January 2006*

[8] *Letter to JTGH from Jakub Forst Battaglia - 6th July 2007*

[9] *HO 405/5008.*

[10] *28th October 1947*

[11] *KV235 - 17th May 1941 ' How on earth he got to know of Hess's arrival.....I simply cannot conceive'*

[12] *Letter to JTGH from Wasyl Sydorenko - University of Toronto Library - 28th April 2008*

[13] *HO 405/5008*

[14] *University of Basle - Burckhardt archive - System number 000032562*

[15] *Marian Chodaki was the liaison official between the Senate and Government 1936-1939.*

[16] *Telephone call to Newton Mearns library, August 2008*

[17] *Sikorski Institute - A 11.474/2/24.*

[18] *Sikorski Institute - A 42/446*

[19] *HO 405/5008. Hardly surprising as Poland had again lost its independence.*

[20] *Ibid.*

[21] *Jakub Forst Battaglia to JTGH - 6th July 2007.*

[22] *Diana Cooper – Hamish Hamilton - 1981*

[23] *She was born Diana Manners on 29th August 1892. Father uncertain.*

[24] *Duff Cooper had resigned over the Munich Agreement of 1938.*

[25] *Diana Cooper had met Burckhardt previously at Venetia Montagu's house.*

APPENDIX 2: The 'twin track' adopted by Nazi Germany so as to attempt to prevent a 'two front war', 1939-1941.

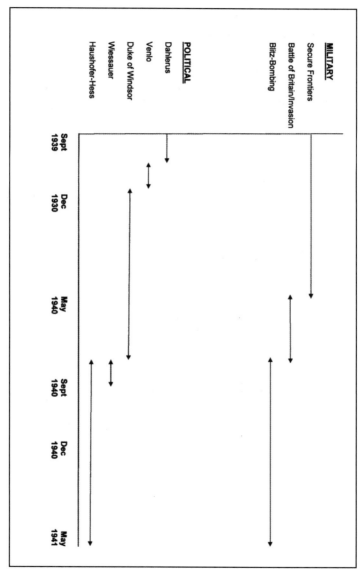

APPENDIX 3

FLOREAT ETONA AND THE BRITISH GOVERNING CLASS

This appendix may well be complete bunkum, in which case I apologise. All I will say is that scattered throughout the Hess affair are individuals who have one common denominator; viz they were the former pupils of Eton College (est 1440).

Given that to date the school has provided the United Kingdom with 19 Prime Ministers, one perhaps should not be too surprised that a large number of former pupils reach senior positions within the government. Furthermore, British society was markedly different in composition prior to the Second World War, with effective power it has been speculated, 'in the hands of fewer than 600 people.'

So, please do not imagine that I am suggesting that the Hess affair was in some way fermented after 'lights out' in an Etonian dormitory, for I am not. I am, however, bringing to the reader's attention what is simply a statement of fact, which, if nothing else may have aided communication between the various departments and persons concerned.

The individuals concerned are listed as follows:

1. Douglas Douglas-Hamilton (1903-1973). 14th Duke of Hamilton.
2. David Bowes-Lyon (1902-1961)
3. Walter Stewart Roberts (1889-1974)
4. Sir Stewart Menzies (1890-1968)
5. Patrick Maxwell Roberts (1895-1937)
6. Victor Cazalet (1896-1943)
7. Peter Fleming (1907-1971)

8. Ian Fleming (1908-1964)
9. Anthony Eden (1897-1977)
10. Hugh Dalton (1887-1962)
11. 8th Duke of Buccleuch (1894-1973)
12. Alec Douglas-Home (1903-1995)
13. Harold Macmillan (1894-1986)[1]

Peter Fleming is listed on two accounts; firstly because he wrote in March 1940, *'The Flying Visit'*[2], which humorously described Adolf Hitler parachuting into Britain in much the same way as his deputy actually re enacted 14 months later.

Secondly, because Peter Fleming's life story goes to illustrate the way in which British society operated at that time. Fleming was a member of the wealthy Scottish banking family and had spent much of the 1920's and 1930's making a living by travelling to exotic locations such as the Mato Grosso, Russia and China and then writing books relating his adventures.

His biographer, Duff Hart-Davis[3] describes in much detail his exotic travels and then, quite unexpectedly and seemingly out of the blue, *"David Bowes Lyon,[4] the brother in law of King George VI, asked him to form a small group which would approach the King 'in a ginger capacity' the main aim being to try to convince the Monarch that the country's defences were utterly inadequate, and that urgent steps must be taken to improve them."*

Consequently, in February 1939 Fleming and Bowes Lyon had an evening audience with King George VI.

This seems quite extraordinary to me. Fleming's father, Valentine had been a soldier,[5] but Peter Fleming's sole experience seems to have been gained by way of his travels.

Seemingly, on that basis Fleming joined Military Intelligence. Quite what regular army personnel would have thought to Fleming's relevant experience, I do not know. Furthermore, I would have the thought the government to be an interested party to any debate as to the country's defences. It does indicate however that the Intelligence community were seemingly quite happy to recruit original thinkers such as Fleming.[6]

Perhaps ironically, perhaps not, Fleming later defined 'strategic deception'[7] as, *"To make your enemy take - or refrain from taking - a particular course of action; and thereby to improve your chances of defeating him. Merely to gull him - to implant in his mind a false picture of the true situation - is only half the battle; it is not enough, even, that he 'should do something about it'. He must do what you want him to do."*

Hmmm……..

Floreat Etona!

---

[1] *Macmillan only attended for one 'half' at Eton on account of pneumonia.*
[2] *The Flying Visit - Johnathan Cape 0 1940.*
[3] *Peter Fleming - A biography by Duff Hart Davis - Johnathan Cape 1974.*
[4] *David Bowes -Lyon, besides being the Queen's brother was also the liaison officer appointed to SO1.*
[5] *Valentine Fleming was killed in 1917 near St.Quentin, France. Winston Churchill contributed to the obituary in The Times.*
[6] *Indeed Walter Stewart Roberts's recruitment to SO1 can be seen in the same terms.*
[7] *Fleming spent much of the war in India as part of British Intelligence and was eventually asked to write the official history of Strategic Deception in the Second World War.*

Bibliography

AIR MINISTRY – *Atlantic Bridge* – HMSO – London 1945

ALLEN, Martin – *The Hitler / Hess Deception* – Harper Collins- London 2003

BAKER, David – *Adolf Galland* – Windrow & Green – London 1996

BAUMBACH, Werner – *Broken Swastika* – Hale – London 1986

BIRD, Eugene – *Rudolf Hess in Spandau* – Sphere – London 1984

BLOOM, Ursula – *The House of Kent* – Robert Hale – London 1969

BOGDANOR, Victor – *The British Constitution in the Twentieth Century* – The British Academy – Oxford 2005

BOYLE, Andrew – *The Climate of Treason* – Hutchinson – London 1979

BREITMAN, Richard – *Official Secrets* – Penguin – London 1998

BREITMAN, Richard – *The Architect of Genocide* – Pimlico – London 2004

BRENDON, Piers – *The Dark Valley* – Cape – London 2000

BRETTINGHAM, Laurie – *Beam Benders* – Midland – Earl Shilton 1997

BRON, Barwa – *Wojsko Polskie* – Interpress – Warsaw 1984

BROOKE, Alan – *The War Diaries* - Weidenfeld & Nicholson – London 2001

BRUCE LOCKHART, R.H – *Memoirs of a British Agent* – Pan – London 2002

BURCKHARDT, Carl J – *Meine Danziger Mission* – Callwey – Munich 1960

CAVE BROWN, Anthony – "*C*" – Macmillan – New York 1987

CHANNON, Henry – *The Diaries of Sir Henry Channon* – Phoenix – London 1996

COLVILLE, John – *The Churchillians* – Weidenfeld&Nicholson – London 1981

COLVIN, Ian – *Chief of Intelligence* – Gollancz – London 1951

COSTELLO, John – *10 Days that Saved the West* – Bantam Press – London 1991

CROSS, Colin – *Life with Lloyd George* – Macmillan - London 1975

CROSS, Robin – *Fallen Eagle* – Caxton – London 2000

DAVIDSON, Basil – *Special Operations Europe* – Readers Union – Newton Abbott 1982

DEACON, Richard – *British Secret Service* – Grafton – London 1991

DELMER, Sefton – *The Black Boomerang* – Secker and Warburg – London 1962

DORPALEN, Andreas – *The World of General Haushofer* – Farrar and Rinehart - New York 1942

DOUGLAS-HAMILTON, James – *Motive for a Mission* – Macmillan – London 1971

DOUGLAS-HAMILTON, James – *The Truth About Rudolf Hess* – Mainstream – Edinburgh 1993

EARL OF BIRKENHEAD – *Halifax* – Hamish Hamilton – London 1965

ENTWHISTLE, Charles – *Undercover Addresses* – Chavril Press – Perth 1992

FALCONER, Johnathan – *RAF Fighter Airfields of World War 2* – Allan – Surrey 1993

FELLOWES, PFM – *First Over Everest* – Bodley Head – London 1935

FLEMING, Peter – *Invasion 1940* – Hart-Davis – London 1957

FLEMING, Peter – *The Flying Visit* – Cape – London 1941

FOOT MRD – *MI9* – Book Club – London 1979

FRAYN TURNER, John – *The Battle of Britain* – BCA – London 1999

GEYDYE, GE – *Fallen Bastions* – Left Book Club – London 1939

GOEBBELS, Joseph – *The Goebbels Diaries* – Hamish Hamilton – London 1948

GRIFFITHS, Richard – *Fellow Travellers of the Right* – Constable- London 1980

HAMILTON, Sir Ian – *The Commander* – Hollis and Carter – London 1957

HAMMOND, Reginald – *Northern Scotland* – Ward Lock – London 1980

HARRIS AND TROW – *Hess: The British Conspiracy* – Andre Deutsch – London 1993

HART- DAVIS, Duff – *Peter Fleming* – Cape – London 1975

HAUSHOFER, Albrecht – *Moabit Sonnets* – Norton – Toronto 1978

HAYWARD, James – *Myths and Legends of the Second World War* – Sutton – 2004

HENDERSON Diana – *The Lion and The Eagle* – Cualann Press – Dunfermline – 2001
HESS, Ilse – *Prisoner of Peace* – Druffel Verlag – Germany – 1954
HESS, Wolf – *My Father Rudolf Hess* – WH Allen – London 1986
HINSLEY AND STRIPP – *Code Breakers* – Oxford University Press – Oxford 1994
HOARE, Samuel – *Ambassador on Special Mission* – Collins – London 1946
HOME, Lord – *The Way the Wind Blows* – Collins – London 1976
HUDSONS HISTORIC HOUSES AND GARDENS – Heritage House - Ketteringham 2009
HUTCHINSON – *British German and Italian Aircraft* – Hutchinson – London 1941
IMPERIAL WAR MUSEUM – *Sonderfahndungsliste GB* – Reprinted London 1989
IRVING, David – *Accident* – William Kimber – London 1967
JENKINS, Roy – *Churchill* – Macmillan – London 2001
JERROLD, Walter – *Lord Roberts of Kandahar* – Partridge & Co – London 1901
JONES, RV – *Most Secret War* – Coronet – London 1978
KASPAR – *Teach Yourself Air Navigation* – EUP – London 1942
KERSHAW, Ian – *Hitler 1889-1936* – Allen Lane – London 1998
KILZER, Louis – *Churchill's Deception* – Simon & Schuster – New York 2004
KIRKPATRICK, Ivone – *The Inner Circle* – Macmillan – London 1959
LAMB, Richard – *Churchill as War Leader* – Bloomsbury- London 1993
LEASOR, James – *Rudolf Hess The Uninvited Envoy* – Allen and Unwin – London 1962
LECKIE, Ross – *Scipio* – Abacus – London 1999
LEE, Celia – *Jean, Lady Hamilton* – Celia Lee 2001
LEE, John – *A Soldiers Life* – Pan – London 2000
LUFTWAFFE – *BF110 g-2 Flugzeug – Handbuch* – Germany 1943
MACKINDER, H.J – *The Rhine* –Chatto & Windus – London 1908
MACMILLAN, Margaret – *Peacemakers* – John Murray – London 2002
MARKS, Leo – *Between Silk and Cyanide* – Harper Collins – London 1998
MASTERMAN, JC – *The Double Cross System* – History Book Club – London 1972
MAZOWER, Mark – *Hitlers Empire* – Penguin – London 2009
MCBLAIN, John – *Rudolf Hess: The British Conspiracy* – Jema – Moulton 1994
McCORMICK Donald – *The Life of Ian Fleming* – Peter Owen – London 1993
McINTYRE, Dougal – *Prestwick's Pioneer* – Woodfield – Bognor Regis 2004
MONDEY, David – *Axis Aircraft of World War 2* – Chancellor – London 1996
MOORHEAD, Caroline – *Dunant's Dream* – Harpers Collins – London 1999
MYERSCOUGH, W – *Air Navigation Simply Explained* – Pitmans – Bath (undated)
NESBIT AND VAN ACKER – *The Flight of Rudolf Hess* – Sutton – Stroud 1999
NOWAK, Jan – *Courier from Warsaw* – Wayne State Press – Detroit 1982
OVERY, Richard – *Bomber Command* – Harper Collins – London 1997
OVERY, Richard – *The Battle* – Penguin – London 2000
OWEN, James – *Nuremberg, Evil on Trial* – Headline – London 2006
PADFIELD, Peter – *Hess The Fuhrers Disciple* – Cassell & Co – London 2001
PEARSON, John – *The Life of Ian Fleming* – Cape – London 1966
PHILBY, Kim – *My Silent War* – Macgibbon & Kee – London 1968
PICKNETT, PRINCE & PRIOR – *Double Standards* – Little Brown – London 2001
PLESHAKOV, Constantine – *Stalin's Folly* – Weidenfeld & Nicholson – London 2005
POGONOWSKI, Iwo – *Poland* – Hippocrene – New York 2000
POLISH MINISTRY OF INFORMATION – *The German New Order* – Hutchinson - London 1942
PRICE Alfred – *The Luftwaffe Data Book* – Greenhill – London 1997
READ AND FISHER – *Colonel Z* – Hodder and Stoughton – London 1984
READ, Anthony – *The Devils Disciples* – Pimlico – London 2004
REES, John – *The Case of Rudolf Hess* – Heineman – London 1947
RHODES-JAMES, Robert – *Victor Cazalet* – Hamish Hamilton – London 1976

ROBERTS, Mrs Ernest Stewart – *Sherbourne, Oxford and Cambridge* – Martin Hopkinson – London 1934

ROSE, Norman – *The Cliveden Set* – Cape – London 2000

RUSSELL, John – *A Silver Plated Spoon* – Cassell – London 1959

SCHMIDT Rainer – *Botengang Eines Toren*? – Econ – Dussledorf 1997

SHACKLADY, Edward – *Consolodated B24 Liberator* – Cerberus – Bristol 2002

SHAWCROSS, William – *Queen Elizabeth* – MacMillan – London 2009

SHENNAN, Andrew – *De Gaulle* – Longman – London 1993

SHIRER, William – *The Rise and Fall of the Third Reich* – Mandarin – London 1991

SHUKMAN, Harold – *Stalin* – Sutton – Stroud 1999

SMITH, Alfred – *Rudolf Hess and Germany's Reluctant War* – Book Guild – Lewes 2001

SPEER, Albert – *Inside the Third Reich* – Phoenix – London 2001

STACHURA, Peter – *Poland in the Twentieth Century* – MacMillan - London 1999

STAFFORD, David – *Flight from Reality* – Pimlico – London 2002

STANLEY LEWIS, W – *Military Map Reading* – Wheaton - Exeter 1941

STETTLER M – Kuratorium CJ Burckhardt – *Des Schriftlichen Nacklasses* – Basle University 1978

TAYLOR, AJP – *The Origins of the Second World War* – Penguin – London 1991

THOMAS, Hugh – *The Murder of Rudolf Hess* – Hodder and Stoughton – London 1979

THOMPSON, Carlos – *The Assasination of Winston Churchill* – Smythe – Gerrards Cross 1969

THOMPSON, J – *The Charterhall Story*- Air Research – Surrey 2004

VASCO.J & CORNWELL.P – *Zerstorer* – JAC Publications – Norwich 1995

VON HASSELL, Ulrich – *The Von Hassell Diaries* – Hamish Hamilton – London 1948

VON LANG, Jochen – *Bormann* – Random House – London 1979

WASZAK, Leon – *Agreement in Principle* – Peter Lang – New York

WEITZ, John – *Hitler's Diplomat* – Weidenfeld and Nicholson – London 1992

WEITZ, John – *Hitlers Banker* – Warner – London 1999

WELSH, Ian – *Prestwick in the 1940's* – Kyle Libraries – Ayr 1992

WEST, Nigel – *MI6* – Weidenfeld & Nicolson – London 1983

WHITING, Audrey – *The Kents* – Hutchinson – London 1985

WINTERBOTHAM, Fred – *Secret and Personal* – William Kimber – London 1969

ZEIGLER, Philip – *Diana Cooper* – Hamish Hamilton – London 1981

ZIEGLER, Philip – *King Edward Vlll* – Collins – London 1990

INDEX

141 Squadron; 94
317 Squadron; 88, 90
602 Squadron; 94, 198
Air Intelligence; 58, 155
Air Navigation; 56-58, 59, 86-100, 102-110
Alexandria, Virginia; 152
Allen, Martin; 9, 123, 124
Altieri Claudes; 185
Anderson, Robert; 97, 99
Andrews, JO; 84, 90-92, 93, 220, 230
Anglo Finnish Society; 183
Anglo French Treaty; 206
Anglo German Association; 40
Anglo German Fellowship; 3
Angus, RL; 80
Ardrossan; 108, 109
Ashbee, Felicity; 88
Astrology; 104-105
Atcherley, RLR; 28
Athens; 126
Atlantic Air Bridge; 68-74
Augsburg Haunstatten; 30
Baillie Scott, Mackay; 123
Barbarossa; 147
Bath, Wiltshire; 122
Battaglia, Roman; 14, 226, 233, 250-258
Bentley Priory; 87, 89
Bevir, Anthony; 156
Bevin, Ernest; 221
Bishopton; 120
Black Law; 106
Bletchley Park; 112
Bonde, Knut; 185, 221
Borenius, Tancred; 178-186, 211, 218, 221, 232, 243
Borenius, Peter; 181, 186

Borenius, Aurelia; 182
Bowes-Lyon, David; 262-263
British Constitution; 18-20, 36-38
British Labour Party; 155
British Railways; 45-47
British War Cabinet; 170-174
Broadlaw; 102, 105, 106, 107
Brown, Capt EM; 30
Bryant, Cecil; 89
Butt Report; 56
Butler, RA; 233
Burckhardt, Carl Jacob; 159-176, 189-190, 192, 221, 233, 249-258
Cadogan, Alex; 21
Caervalerock Castle; 121
Cairnsmore, Wigtownshire; 42
Cambridge Appointments Board; 122
Cazalet, Victor; 73, 262
Chain Home Radar; 95
Chamberlain, Joseph; 123
Chamberlain, Neville; 206
Chatham House; 183, 199
Chavril Press; 149
Cheviot, The; 89, 102
Churchill, Winston; 17, 203, 211, 221, 243
Conyers-Nesbit, Roy; 28, 29, 60, 63, 87, 89, 90
Coombe Bissett, Wilts; 184
Costello, John; 86, 88
Countess of Sutherland; 213, 216
Cuddie, Flying Officer; 61, 94, 98
Dalton, Hugh; 156, 263
Dansey, Claude; 156, 182, 186-191, 210, 230

Danzig, Poland; 159
Dargavel; 119, 120
Deacon, Richard; 105, 230
Deighton, Len; 103
Dollar Law; 106
Douglas-Hamilton, David; 81, 199, 230, 233
Douglas-Hamilton, Douglas; 2, 7, 8, 12, 20, 25, 30, 35, 39, 77-84, 90, 93, 96, 99, 152, 154, 195-205, 220, 230, 231, 262
Douglas-Hamilton, Geordie; 81, 230, 233
Douglas-Hamilton, James; 1, 8, 83, 87, 199, 228
Douglas-Hamilton, Malcolm; 218, 230, 233
Dowding System; 87, 94, 98
Duke, Colonel; 226
Duke of Bedford; 38, 42
Duke of Buccleuch; 38, 43, 203, 263
Duke of Roxburgh; 38
Duke of Sutherland; 38, 41
Dungavel House; 9, 23-35, 39, 55, 58, 63, 107, 108, 198, 200, 212
Dunrobin Castle; 214, 216
Durham Post Office; 60
Duveen and Company; 188
Eaglesham; 8
Eaglesham House/Castle; 97
Earl of Glasgow; 39
Earl of Haddington; 38
Earl of Rosebery; 38, 41
Earl of Stair; 39
Earl of Wemyss; 39
Eden, Anthony; 21, 233, 243, 263
Elser, Georg; 207
Embleton ROC; 89
Eton School; 262
Fleming, Ian; 263

Fleming, Peter; 131, 262
Fleming, Valentine; 263
Flight Map; 7
Floors Castle; 48-49
Floors Farm; 97
Foot, MRD; 3, 12
Forst-Battaglia, Jacob; 252
Freedom of Information; 14
Frost, Martin; 42
Gonville and Caius; 122
Goring, Herman; 199
Graham, Gibson; 20
Grieg, Louis; 200
Guinness, Loel; 83, 84, 218, 233
Habibcht, Mieczyslaw; 258
Hahn, Kurt; 202
Hales, John; 217
Hamilton, General Sir Ian; 38-40, 50
Hamilton, 2nd Duke; 121
Hamilton, TAR; 155
Harris, Emily; 216
Harris, Robert; 115
Harris, FL; 183
Hart-Davis, Duff; 263
Hartschimmelhof; 126
Haushofer, Albrecht; 2, 8, 35, 124, 125, 132-144, 153, 191-193, 199, 202, 239
Haushofer, Heinz; 124, 125
Haushofer, Karl; 8, 39, 123-125, 132-144, 148, 153, 239
Haushofer, Martha; 124, 125, 239
Hess, Rudolf; 7, 8, 12, 14, 16, 19, 21, 30, 63, 94, 131-144, 147, 148, 192, 210, 236, 242
Hess, Wolf; 3, 12, 195
Hitler, Adolf; 112, 113, 147, 161-168, 186, 206, 210, 245
HMS Wagtail; 83

Hoare, Sir Samuel; 183, 192, 211, 212, 221, 232, 243
Hope, Sir Archibald; 84
HRH. Duke of Kent; 9, 14, 27, 93, 183-185, 212-216, 218, 220, 230, 231
HRH King George VI; 20, 209, 220, 263
Hume, Alec Douglas; 38, 41, 263
Ingrams, Leonard; 156
International Red Cross; 174-175, 177, 233
Irving, David; 2, 17, 119
Jahnke, Kurt; 148
Kaiser Wilhelm; 123
Kalundborg; 62, 103
Kean, Bill; 195
Kelso; 48-49
Kilburnside; 31
Koblenz; 124
Lady Diana Cooper; 259
Lady Elizabeth Percy; 199, 204
Lady Isle; 107, 108
Leasor, James; 2
Leigh Mallory, Trafford; 92
Leith, Gordon; 29, 30
Lend Lease; 114
Lennoxlove, Haddington; 27, 49-52, 58
Lesbury; 204
Lester, Sean; 161
Liberator Aircraft; 74
Lighthouse-Coquet; 65
Lighthouse-Longstones; 65, 103
Lighthouse-Troon; 66
Lisbon; 149
Lochgreen House, Monkton; 218
Lord Beaverbrook; 212
Lord Halifax; 200, 231
Lord Palmer; 38
Lord Percy; 205
Lord Semphill; 39
Lord Steward, The; 43
Lownie, Andrew; 3
Lowther, John; 217
Luftwaffe; 114, 207
MacKinder, Halford; 17, 115, 116
McBride, Sergeant; 226
Mclean, David; 109
Maclean, Hector; 84, 92, 219
Macmillan, Harold; 263
Marquess of Bute; 39
Marquess of Linlithgow; 39
Marquess of Tweedale; 39
Marquis of Lothian; 39
Marquis of Tavistock; 224
Maxwell, Patrick; 40, 119, 262
Maxwell, Sarah Maxwell; 119
McBlain, John; 3
McIntyre, David F; 77- 84, 198-199, 220, 227-229, 233
McIntyre, Dougal; 28, 92, 199, 227-229
MeBf110; 29, 30-33
Mein Kampf; 112
Menzies, Stewart; 262
Methuen family; 182
MI5; 14, 153, 155, 204, 224, 225, 253
MI6; 9, 14, 156, 188-191, 220, 247
Molotov/Ribbentrop pact; 113, 206
Morrell, Ottoline; 182
Morris, Sargeant; 226
Morton, Fergus; 218
Norman, Montagu; 211, 212
Nuremberg Trial; 237
Odier, Lucie; 177
Overy, Richard; 130
Padfield, Peter; 3, 9
Page, Allan; 225

Passport Office System; 188
Pintsch, Karl; 66, 108
Pitliver House, Fife; 216
Playfair, Edward; 156
Pocock, Maurice; 48, 61, 88, 89, 93, 96, 98
Poland; 113, 247
Polish Relief Fund; 185
Possil Park; 120
Prevailing light conditions; 64
Princess Marina; 183, 184, 216
Prior, Stephen; 8 , 27, 195, 204, 212, 226
Public Records Office (PRO); 9
Queens Gate, London; 126
Raigmore Hospital, Inverness; 214
RAF Abbotsinch; 53
RAF Acklington; 47, 48, 88
RAF Aldergrove; 71, 98
RAF Castle Kennedy; 53
RAF Charterhall; 48, 49
RAF Drem; 28, 53
RAF Dundonald; 53
RAF East Fortune; 53
RAF Farnborough; 30
RAF Grangemouth; 53
RAF Ouston; 62
RAF Prestwick/Ayr; 4, 8, 66, 68-74, 76-84, 92, 99, 103, 107-108, 219
RAF Renfrew; 53
RAF Strathaven; 54
RAF Sumburgh; 216
RAF Turnberry; 53
RAF Turnhouse; 53, 83, 96, 203, 204,
RAF Usworth; 53, 96
RAF West Freugh; 53
RAF Wick; 216
RAF Wigtown; 53
RAF Winfield; 48, 49

Ramsay, Captain Archibald; 39
Riddle, Huseph; 84
Roberts of Kandahar; 2, 40, 119,
Roberts, Andrew; 3
Roberts, Ernest Stewart; 123
Roberts, Mrs ES; 124
Roberts, Herbert Ainslie; 122, 126
Roberts, Mary; 2, 8, 12, 40, 118-127, 131, 144, 148, 151, 153, 156, 203, 204, 231
Roberts, Patrick; 2, 124, 126, 153, 250
Roberts, Walter; 126, 153, 156, 230, 262
Rosemount House, Monkton; 83, 97
Royal Observer Corps; 60, 89, 95-100
Royal Signals Corps; 97
Salisbury Close; 183
Schroder-Haushofer, Andrea; 195
Sealion; 147
Scottish Aviation Limited; 78, 79, 198
Scottish Crown Jewels; 223, 225
Sikorski, Wladsylaw; 4, 8, 68, 72-74, 82, 185, 221, 235, 258
Simon, Sir John; 21
SO1; 2, 8, 14, 156
SOE; 155, 156
Spandau; 8
Spectator; 3
Spencer, Richard; 3
St Mary's Loch; 105
Stafford, David; 103
Stalin, Josef; 112
Strutt, Michael; 217
Storeys Way, Cambridge; 123
Templar Lodge Hotel; 196

The Times; 202
Thomas Cook Limited; 149-151
Thomas, Hugh; 9
Tinto Hills; 105
Trinity House; 65
Troon; 107
Trow, Mei; 3
Tweedsmuir; 106
Ultra Decrypts; 207
Usher Family; 38, 41
Vansittart, Robert; 200, 206
Viscount Lascelles; 182, 183
Von Hassell, Ulrich; 178, 186, 192
Von Reichenau, General; 200
West Kilbride; 108
Wilbourn, Richard; 2, 10, 11, 76, 92, 105, 227
Winterbotham, Fred; 230
Woburn Abbey; 2, 42
Z System; 188
Zu Mecklenberg, Adolf; 200